AF207921

PLAY IT
AS IT LIES

A Journey through Fatherhood and Golf

Matthew F. Filner

Back Nine Press

Back Nine Press
Chicago, Illinois
www.back9press.com
Twitter and Instagram: @backninepress

9 8 7 6 5 4 3 2 1

First Edition

Library of Congress Cataloging-in-Publication Data:
Filner, Matthew F.

Play It As It Lies: A Journey through Fatherhood and Golf /
By *(Author)*, Matthew F. Filner, Back Nine Press *(USA)*
pages cm

ISBN 978-1-956237-10-8 *(hardback)*
ISBN 978-1-956237-09-2 *(e-book)*

1. Non-Fiction. 2. Golf. 3. Family. 4. Fatherhood.

For Theresa, Aidan, and Elliott

In Memory of Vic Rosenthal
(1955-2023)

Table of Contents

Introduction

One of the foundational rules of golf is Rule 9.1: "Ball Played as It Lies." No matter what happened on its travels from where you last hit it, no matter how many tree branches, or rocks, or divots, or thick stands of fescue, wherever your ball stops, you must play the ball wherever it comes to rest. You may hate the stance, the fact that it's in a divot, the tree branch that impedes your backswing, but no matter, you must play the ball as it lies. There are no foot wedges or winter rules in golf that allow you to move your ball—it's one of golf's oldest and most basic rules. This rule helps us handle adversity, test our patience, and manage our emotions when good luck turns bad. In golf, as in life, it's how you react and respond. This book is about fatherhood and golf, and how much each has helped me understand the other. It's about what it means as a father and a golfer to truly "play it as it lies."

I have two amazing boys—Aidan and Elliott—for whom I have spent much of my adult life trying to be the best father I could be. And I've failed, a lot. I've had a lot of bad swings, so to speak, and my mistakes as a father have put me in some difficult spots. But no matter how bad my previous shot was, in fatherhood as in golf, I've learned that the best way forward is to learn from your mistakes, keep your poise and perspective, and do your best to be a good father. After being a father now for over 18 years, I've come to believe that the best way to be a father is to play it as it lies.

In short, the best way to be a father, and a golfer, is to stay positive and in the moment. It's easy to get stuck in the past. We've all moaned, *how did I miss that putt?!* Or, *how could I have done that?* How many of us follow up that suffering comment, that self-pitying pose, with a well-struck drive? Not many. It's also easy to get caught looking too far ahead into the future. We've all thought to ourselves: *I just need to stay one over for the next six holes to shoot my personal best.* How many of us then slice our very next drive into the trees? Many of us. In golf, getting out of the moment—getting out of our process—is a round-killer. I think the same is true with fatherhood. Remembering fondly the days when my sons actually listened to me caused me to miss their teenage cues. And dreaming about what and who they might be when they grow up obscures the brilliant child in front of me. The only alternative is to stay in the present. This book is about many of those times, highlighting the best moments of fatherhood, my greatest triumphs on the golf course, along with many, many failures.

I've been hunting par most of my life. Up until my oldest son reached 18, great stretches—a back nine here, a 12-hole stretch there—never translated to reaching the goal of an entire round at par. The quest felt Sisyphean. After I came to realize the full meaning of playing it as it lies, the quest became much more achievable.

This commitment has led me to be a pretty good golfer. As of this writing, I maintain a handicap index of 6.4, which puts me roughly (according to the USGA) in the top 15% of all golfers. While I'm clear-eyed that a handicap index is really just an on-your-best-day index and that I'm more than capable of shooting well into 80s (and the 90s, at a particularly challenging course), I do have some really good days. I've had two rounds at par, and a fair number at 2-over and 3-over par, and I've played some very difficult courses in the upper 70s. But the quest to keep my ball in play—to maximize my GIRs and minimize my big scores—is perpetual.

Similarly, while I think I've done many good things as a father—and without question I have been a better father to my children than my father was to me, and than his father was to him—I still seek that elusive par. I don't really know what an average father is, and so I have no idea on this front whether I'm worse, better, or on par as a father. None of us will ever know. But whatever par is, I seek it. Because I know I make mistakes, some majors for sure, that also means I need some really great days. I need to reach my boys in ways they haven't been reached before. I have helped them learn to lay on their tummy, to walk, to tie their shoes, to ride a bike, to shave, to drive, to find the right words to say to their first love, to learn how to handle their first major breakup, and to finish their toughest assignment. This quest is never finished, as long as we all breathe oxygen on this planet. But I know that playing it as it lies is my foundation—there are no mulligans in fatherhood. There is only my best judgment, hoping that my mistakes keep my ball in play and my children safe. And when I have a chance for birdie, or even eagle, that I am not afraid to bury the putt.

Playing the ball as it lies is also about paying close and careful attention to detail. Too often in my life, I've arrived at my ball, looked for a distance plate or yardage poll, pulled the club and struck the shot. The ball would fly too far, or too short, and I would catch a flyer or fail to get the ball through the thick rough. Too often, in short, I didn't sweat the details. And I paid for it on the golf course. As a father, not paying close enough attention to my sons caused a lot of hardship for them, and for me.

Over the years, I've learned that our boys are often only able to give the most subtle signs. My sons are masters of hiding their true feelings and experiences. They don't announce that they are happy or sad, if they are thriving or struggling. They don't process their lives with me (as a side, but important, note: my wife Theresa has mastered the skill of "side talking" and gets them to talk much more than I do). But the signs are there in plain sight, if I'm only paying attention. I have to observe how they are eating; the slump or rise of their shoulders; the speed with which they snap at me; the amount of time they linger in the bathroom. These are all subtle signs, and it took me years to learn to watch for them, to know that they are telling me everything I need to know as a dad, if I'm only paying attention.

But playing it as it lies is not just about fatherhood, it's also about being a father—our thoughts, comments, actions, and reactions. It isn't just about paying attention to my boys, it's about paying attention to myself. It's not just about accepting my boys for who they are, and accepting whatever predicament we are in together, it's also about accepting myself for who I am, and accepting whatever predicament I am in. This book is therefore both about learning to accept others, most importantly my wife and sons, but also about accepting myself both in and out of these roles.

Most of us are young when we become parents. My parents were 24 years old when I was born, helplessly young. I was older—33 years old—when my first son was born, but while those nine years gave me enormous perspective, that age feels remarkably young. As a result, at the same time when we are trying to figure out how to accept our children, we are trying to figure out how to accept ourselves. It took me a long time to accept that I am who I am, with all my quirks and foibles. In a society that airbrushes every imperfection, acceptance is difficult, and I am no exception.

The same is true on the course. As I've learned to slow down and pay attention to my kids and myself, I've also learned to observe much more closely during a round. Of course, we all notice the wind, but I've learned to distinguish different types of wind, the direction, the speed, the relative swirl, even the height. I'm not a professional at it—I don't have a caddie, using the wind to calculate a number to the nearest yard—but I'm much better at paying attention.

I've learned to notice the minute details of the lie. Of course, I always paid attention to a lie in the fairway versus a lie in the rough. But now I look at the blades of grass around my ball. Are there any blades that will come between my ball and the club? Will those blades of grass tend to force the ball left or right? Is it a flyer lie? Now I notice more than whether my feet are above or below the ball; I notice how much my feet sit above or below. I no longer take an absent-minded practice swing whose purpose used to be to "feel" the proper moves. Now, I try to observe where my club is bottoming out, and whether I should adjust my stance fore or aft. I used to assess whether the green was elevated or not, and whether

the pin was cut in the front, middle, or back. Now, I try to pay attention to how far from each side the pin sits and roughly how many
yards the pin sits above or below my ball. If I know the course, I
try to gauge in advance whether it is better to land left or right of
the pin, and where there might be slope behind the pin to funnel
my ball. I'm not particularly sophisticated about it—you won't find
me calling out "73 front, 79 pin"—but I have become a golfer who
tries to take in all the information available to me as I walk to my
ball; in short, I try to pay attention.

I've also been incredibly fortunate to travel to some of the greatest golf courses in the United States. Although I lived in Ireland to
pursue soccer, I never golfed there. And in my year in Japan, golf
was squeezed out, both literally and figuratively. But in the United
States, I've been able to travel and play amazing courses—18 of
them, in fact. I've travelled to San Diego and played both courses
at Torrey Pines. I've hiked the urban jungle and walked Bethpage
Black. I've made the pilgrimage to Bandon Dunes. In my home state
of Minnesota, I've gone "up north" and played three outstanding
courses there: the Classic, the Quarry, and the Wilderness. I've gone
east to my wife's home state of Wisconsin, where I've visited Whistling Straits, Sand Valley, Erin Hills, and the lesser known but still
outstanding Troy Burne. These courses all make an appearance in
the chapters below: where I play golf and meet fathers of all kinds.

Finally, a note about my wife, Theresa. This story is about fatherhood, and golf, but Theresa has been ever-present throughout all of
it. She has encouraged me to pursue this Sisyphean life, knowing that
coming home even-par was highly unlikely. She has been with our
kids all those hours I was gone, at work or at play, and also has been
my muse as we raised our children together. Fatherhood has never
been a solitary endeavor for me, and so it's sometimes ludicrous to
write about what it is like for me to be a father. We're partners and
we have made all the decisions about parenting together. More on
Theresa in the chapter I've titled "The Turn."

Yet at the same time, because I suffered as a son to my father, I
tend to think of fatherhood as a personal endeavor, one in which
I have to overcome the sins of the past. I've pursued a lot of things

outside of fatherhood in my life, whether it was a "piled higher and deeper" degree, or an important role in my community. But nothing is more important than my family, and I do my best to be a "scratch" husband and father to these three people with whom I share my life.

What follows is a memoir of stories organized according to the years of my fatherhood: from our zero year, when our oldest son was first a dream and, almost 10 arduous months later, a reality; to the 18th year, when our son was graduating from high school and our younger son was just beginning his high school journey. In each chapter, I explore my fatherhood-life, first with one child, a few years later with two, and through all the trials and triumphs, all the fears and fun. Some chapters put me at ease, knowing I can handle the place my "ball" has landed. Other chapters put me in the bracken, far from the comfortable confines of the life's narrow fairways. But no matter, I play it as it lies.

I also tell the stories of my explorations of some of the greatest American golf courses. As any astute father will notice, however, the timing isn't right. I didn't play each of these courses during the same year as I was a father. Anyone who has had a newborn in the house knows that a trip to Torrey Pines is likely to result in a divorce, rather than a great story. While my wife has been incredibly supportive of my golf journey, she's not crazy—there are limits. And those limits were most significant when our kids were young, when we were sleep deprived, and with our kids depending on us for just about everything. Those rounds would have to wait. But when I caught up with golf, I learned many lessons on these courses about how to approach parenting and reinforced some other principles of fatherhood I had already adopted and tried to maintain. I hope these lessons come through to you, dear reader.

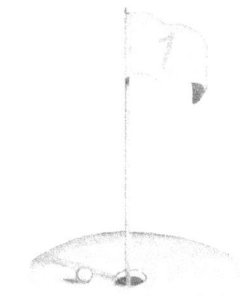

Discovery

(2002-03)

Two weeks," Linda—our midwife—told us. "If we reach two weeks after the due date, we're going to have to start to talk about other options." My wife Theresa was determined to have a natural childbirth. We had read many of the books together: *What to Expect When You're Expecting,* and so on. We knew about the c-section rates and the profit motive for doctors and hospitals to have as many c-sections as possible. We also knew that the recovery from a c-section was months, not days. She didn't want that. She wanted to get through a natural childbirth with a midwife at her side, birthing our first born.

I was all in. I would be the ultimate assistant producer. "Whatever you want, I'll get," I told her. You want a reuben with fries? I'm on it. You want to banish toast from our home? I'll eat soft bread. Daily walks up and down the local hills? My running shoes are on. It was springtime in our medium-sized Michigan city, and I had to prepare my students:

"My wife is due with our first child," I said as my body flushed. I tend to be a confident public speaker, including in classrooms, so I was thrown to be blushing in front of my students. They could tell.

"Expect that one day over the next few weeks, I will simply not show up. There won't be any advance notice, no calls or emails. I won't have time. If I'm lucky, I'll find time to ask our assistant to put a sign on the classroom door. But don't bet on it." Some students smiled at me, feeling excited for me. Other students, I could tell, were annoyed—how dare I interrupt their college-age self-absorption. But I didn't care.

"When I don't show up, just know that we're having a baby, and that I'll be here the next class meeting, assuming that the boy is born healthy and his mom is doing well." I smiled. Most of my students smiled back. I asked if they had any questions. No, their silence showed me. Get on with the class.

So, we walked hills. And ate spicy food. And did whatever we had heard would help get the baby out. And Theresa was ready, oh so ready. Some women, I've heard, love being pregnant. Something about the glow of pregnancy. Theresa, not so much. Between our son kicking her all day and night, to the constant pressure on her bladder, to just feeling so done with pregnancy, she was ready for the birth. And yet, nothing happened. Not on the due date, not on the day after, or the day after that. We followed the same routine, doing whatever we thought might work.

On a Friday at the end of May, 13 days after the due date, we decided to get some falafel at the local international deli and walk to the college campus where I worked. Theresa had been experiencing pretty regular contractions for several hours and they were organized by the time we arrived on a hill overlooking a college softball game. The contractions were seven minutes apart as we ate and watched the college students focused entirely on their game.

"I'm so excited to meet him," she said over and over. She had a nine-month relationship going, and she didn't even know what he looked like. I was trying to feel vicariously connected, but mostly I was just thinking about her. She continued, "What if the two-week delay means something is wrong?" I didn't know what to say.

"I'm sure he's fine," I said, but didn't really believe it. *How the hell would I know why he's two weeks late?* I thought it but would never say it. I had to stay positive.

To this point, the contractions had been uncomfortable for Theresa, but didn't change what we were doing. Not anymore. "I have to stop," she clenched. So, we stopped. It was a beautifully clear afternoon, which soon became a star-filled night. I had to leave for an hour or so to meet with some students, and when I came home around 9:00pm, Theresa had a concerned look on her face, increasingly aware of the reality of the moment. "I think it's happening." I knew she meant it. After a few hours of contractions, I decided to try to get some sleep since I could. Theresa woke me up about an hour later, with contractions consistently five minutes apart—as precise as a Swiss watch.

"It's time."

I awoke as if the fire alarm was sounding. I called our midwife, Linda, and she said to call her back when the contractions were three minutes apart. By 2:00am, the contractions had reached the magic number and I called Linda again. Linda had asked before whether Theresa could respond to my questions during a contraction. Before then, the answer was always "yes." But not anymore—there was too much pain. "Come to the hospital now," Linda ordered.

As we pulled out of the driveway, we noticed even in the dark of night that the white iris in our garden had finally opened up after weeks of threatening. A positive omen if there ever was one. The five-minute drive to the hospital was surreal. No cars on the road—a cool, crisp night, streetlights flashing—and Theresa in tremendous pain every few minutes. She moaned something awful and there was absolutely nothing I could do. I was filled with anxious excitement; she was filled with pain.

Our first born is on his way, I thought.

"It hurts!," she screamed.

We parked and I walked her slowly to the emergency room. She had to stop walking every couple of minutes. The nurse walked us to the Labor and Delivery Room. Theresa had grown silent, but not because of any less pain. Neither of us paid much attention to the walk-through the hospital maze. *How could I have been so stupid?*

When we arrived at Labor and Delivery, they ushered us into a private room. The hospital was largely empty, so Theresa had many nurses giving her attention. The nurses!

"Please sign this," "and this," "and this," they commanded. Were we buying another home? "Just a pinch," a nurse said absentmindedly as she inserted the IV. "This won't hurt at all," another said as she attached the external fetal monitor (EFM).

For the next half hour, we just talked as Theresa withstood regular and painful contractions and we waited for the EFM test to finish. "How is he doing," Theresa asked through scared eyes.

I said, "fine—his heart is running steady." I don't know for sure, but I think Theresa knew that something wasn't right. From where I sat, we were both still tense and excited, looking forward to the next stage when Linda would arrive and would help Theresa through the natural birth that they had assiduously planned. But I think Theresa somehow knew that would never happen.

The nurse came in a few minutes later, with a strained look on her face. "Your baby is experiencing late deceleration," she firmly stated. *What the !@#$%^ does that mean?* "Can you explain what that means?" I said as calmly as I could muster. I looked at Theresa, I had never seen such a look on her face. It was a combination of terror and exhaustion. The nurse, in her most medical voice, told us: "When during a contraction the baby is not getting enough oxygen, the heart rate drops to conserve energy. This is a potentially *fatal* condition if that continues throughout labor."

With those words, everything changed. We were terrified. We didn't even know this kid, and yet ... Theresa and I looked at each other ... nothing had prepared us for this moment. Our son was in danger.

The nurse said to Theresa: "I spoke to your midwife. We are going to try to increase the amniotic fluid and lessen the deceleration by adding fluids to Theresa's IV." I'm not sure either of us heard her. Theresa responded with a scared and resigned "okay," not alert and engaged. Sadly, but inevitably, everyone's focus turned away from

Theresa and toward the EFM—would it work? Twenty minutes of intensely painful contractions later, Linda arrived. I could see Theresa was feeling some relief, but all she said was "Is he going to be okay?"

Linda brought confidence and many decades of experience. But while Theresa may have been relieved to see her, her body was reacting to the IV: she began to shiver uncontrollably. She was freezing, as apparently the fluids were cold. Linda immediately ordered some blankets, but no matter how many blankets the nurse put on her, the shivering wouldn't stop. I could hear Linda order the nurse: "Get her some oxygen, now!" While Linda presented a calm face to us, the tone of her voice was clear: this is not okay. Our son was still experiencing late deceleration, and nothing they were doing was changing anything. Linda came in again: "This condition is very rare in low-risk pregnancies." I have no idea why she told us that—maybe to explain to herself what she had already decided was going to happen. But we were in the dark. Theresa only knew the pain of the contractions, the barrier the oxygen mask created between her and us, and the terror for our son. For the first time, the terror reached me. We only cared that it was happening to our son.

Linda announced, "I'm going to break your amniotic sac to look for meconium. If there is meconium, I'll know that your baby is experiencing fetal distress. We'll have to have an emergency c-section." I was floored. This is no longer wait and see, I'm no longer the assistant producer—they were taking over. She broke the sac and there was so much meconium—it was dark brown. "We're going to do an emergency c-section, now. There is no question." It took my breath away.

Theresa, with so much fear in her eyes, looked at me for reassurance: "I'm so scared. Is he going to be okay?" Linda was working—she smiled, but it was a stressed smile. What could I say? I tried to muster the most confident "yes," but I'm not sure either of us believed it.

We had read so much to prepare ourselves for labor and delivery. We were well-read, as it were. *What to Expect When You're Expecting* was supposed to prepare us. Yet nothing we read had prepared us for this moment. It hit us like a brick wall. Theresa continued to experience intense contractions, and her shivering had only worsened. Now, we were also terrified for our baby. Linda left the room to call the obstetrician and get changed. The nurses returned with scrubs for me, shots for Theresa, and many, many more forms to sign. It was happening so quickly. "We'll be going into the O.R. within 30 minutes," the nurse announced.

A new technology had been recently introduced that allowed parents to save cord blood for possible future use. We had been convinced by some company to purchase the technology, and I had it ready … in the car. The nurses told me that I had about 20 minutes to get it. I looked at Theresa. "Go," she said, through gritted teeth. So I took off, for a middle-of-the-night run through a deserted hospital. But it was for naught. Remember when I mentioned that we hadn't paid much attention to the maze of the hospital when we entered? Well, I got lost. I ran and ran and couldn't find the parking lot. I finally decided to get outside and figure it out from there. I had run to the opposite side of the hospital.

"Shit, shit, shit," I said louder than intended. I ran around the building and eventually found the car. I grabbed the cord blood package, and ran back, only to get lost again. Finally, after turning a five-minute trip into a painfully long 20-minute journey, I arrived back at the room to find Linda holding Theresa's hand as they worked through another contraction.

While Theresa and I were physically together, we were miles apart emotionally. She would have to get through the contractions guided by the expert women in the room. The anesthesiologist came in to explain the spinal procedure. "Okay," was all she could say. She just wanted to get our baby out. Her shivering continued unabated, as the nurses tried (unsuccessfully) to draw Theresa's blood. They brought her into the operating room alone. I was to stay outside until they were ready. I tied and untied my scrubs about a dozen times, trying to stay calm. After what seemed endless, but was probably only about 20 minutes, the nurse came out. "We're ready." The scene was surreal. Theresa was laying on the table, with a screen bisecting her body. Above the screen was only her head; below was her torso. The nurse led me to her head. I didn't know what to do. I tried to comfort her, but I couldn't hold her hand. She was shaking. I could see everything over the screen; she could see, and feel, nothing.

"This is *not* what I wanted," she told me firmly. "Is he okay?" she asked, with more fear than I had ever seen.

There was no calm, no comfort, no serenity in this room. Only bright, cold, and metallic. I was overwhelmed by the moment, as if I were watching a movie. It didn't feel real. I just watched. I watched the obstetrician calmly make the incision and Linda preparing for the birth. At 5:33am, just about two-and-a-half hours after we arrived at the hospital, our son emerged. I saw his ear first, bright purple with greenish-brown meconium all over his body. The nurses brought him to the recovery table behind me. I could turn around; Theresa could only listen. "Is he okay?" she demanded. The shaking continued.

"I can see him." After a few seconds of cleaning him and suctioning his nose and mouth, that child let out a massive scream. His bright purple body looked less than human, but as they cleared him and his clearly working lungs brought oxygen to the rest of his body, he began to turn a bright pink. He hands and feet remained purple for a few more minutes, but he was beautiful. He continued to scream as the nurses weighed and measured him, and finished cleaning him off.

I was anxious. "Can I come over?" The nurse nodded, as I left Theresa's side. I reached out to him. His little purple hand grasped my finger. The nurses swaddled him, and I brought him over to Theresa. She could only look at him since her arms were still strapped down and the obstetrician was still sewing the stitches. But she was in love with Aidan—we both were.

A few minutes later, the nurse pushed Theresa, with Aidan in her arms, into the recovery room. For the next two hours, the nurses checked Theresa's and Aidan's vitals. I held him as he slept. I held my wife's hand, as she took in the trauma of the past few hours, and we marveled at the miracle in front of us. By 8:00am, we were moved into our room, where we would spend the next three days falling head over heels in love with our baby.

There is a rule, at least in the hospital where Aidan was born, that newborns can't leave the hospital until the baby has pooped. Over the course of the three days that we were in the hospital, he hadn't done his business, and we were starting to worry. Don't get me wrong, Aidan had done more than his share of peeing. Morning, day, night, with no warning whatsoever. The boy could pee up a storm. On the second day, as Theresa slept, the nurse came in for her usual baby checks. "Can I join you?," I asked.

"Of course," the nurse smiled, like she must at all the new dads. We went together into the baby room, with Aidan in my arms. "Please put him on this baby table," she gently guided. I had never seen such a table. Perfectly at arms height, this table was more a small crib on wheels, with high railings to make sure the baby doesn't fall out. We were surrounded by about half a dozen other babies, all sleeping. "Please take off his diaper so I can check him," she instructed. I followed orders. Dry as a bone. In the second between me taking off the diaper, and her starting to say, "be sure that you keep the dia—," Aidan let out a massive stream of pee, an impressive geyser at least three feet in the air. I lunged back with the diaper—inexplicably still in my hands—and managed to douse the spigot. *How can such a small body create such pee force?* The nurse assessed the damage: pee all over my son and his baby table, pee on the floor and all the nearby equipment, even pee on some of the nearby babies. She looked at me, smiled as if to say *"you idiot! All you new fathers are alike!"* But instead she said, "It's no problem, it happens all the time." The only saving grace at the moment was that I was so sleep deprived that I didn't have the energy to worry about it. Aidan was already leaving his mark.

Back to *Waiting for Poop*. We really wanted to go home. We knew that the stress of labor had caused our son to release a good portion of meconium before he was born, so he had to refill before he would be ready to go. But it wasn't clear whether he would do it in time, and the hospital made it clear that this wasn't one of those rules to be broken. As we would find out over the course of his childhood, Aidan's digestive system was very sensitive to stress. And while we tried to keep the hospital room as stress-free as possible during the first few days, the powers that be, all with good intentions, conspired to create substantial stress in his life. For example, the heel prick. Twice a day, a cheerful nurse would walk into our room and sing, "time for the heel prick." Because newborns are so plump, finding an easy blood source is no small task. So, they have to prick the heel, and then squeeze the newborns foot to draw enough blood. Every time they did it, our son would scream at the top of his lungs. I asked what they needed to draw blood for. I was told "to test his blood." *Obviously!*

"But why do you need to test his blood?," I queried on the third heel prick.

"Because we need to know whether his various systems are working well."

"What are you looking for when you test his blood?"

"A special hormone that is increased under stress."

"But, don't you cause stress when you prick his heel and he screams?"

"Um, yes."

With that, the heel pricks were finished. The nurses looked at me like I was crazy: it's just a simple heel prick. Maybe it was, maybe it wasn't. I don't know. But I reasoned that there was nothing that they could find that we wouldn't be able to tell simply by being with him, and if we had any concerns, they could do the test then.

The next stressor was the state-mandated hearing test. I'm sure that the initial drive to mandate hearing tests in Michigan was borne out of genuine concern about newborns. Probably, there were too many babies who had hearing problems that were never properly diagnosed in the hospital. So, the state legislature and the governor agreed to mandate hearing tests for all newborns. A specialized nurse came to our room several times to ask, "is now a good time to test his hearing?" We said "no" the first two asks, when our son was either sleeping or feeding (as he did most of his awake time—he was ravenous). The third time, however, we had no good answer, so we agreed. I accompanied Aidan to the hearing room.

The nurse looked at me with a cheerful but stern eye. She had clearly done this too many times to count.

"The rule for a valid hearing test is the newborn has to be awake, and has to remain perfectly still. Do you understand?"

Well, I understood, but after knowing my son for just over two days, it was crystal clear that he could not remain perfectly still. Maybe there are some newborns who remain still when awake. To those of you who have parented such a child, congratulations! For the rest of us, however, an awake and non-moving newborn is a physical impossibility.

"I'm sorry, but my son was just born. I don't think he will remain perfectly still, and I'm not going to hold him down—he'll just scream." I tried to reason with her. It didn't work. After she ignored my apparently lame attempt to impose logic, I simply laughed. *Are you insane? What newborn ever remains still? In fact, this test is absurd—there's no way to keep a newborn still.* It wasn't funny.

"I have to give him this test, and he has to stay still." At first, he wriggled and squirmed as she tried to put on the equipment around

his ears. Every time she thought she got the little headsets on his head, he moved so much that they fell off. She grew increasingly frustrated and rather quickly, so too did our son. He burst out crying, and that, as they say, was the end of that. All the test had proven was that we, the adults, could hear just perfectly, and our son has very strong lungs.

So, stress around every corner … and no poop. It was Monday morning, and our planned departure was just a few hours away. After a sleep-filled day and a wake-filled night, he was ready for his next meal. He was a voracious eater from the start, acting like this was his first and last meal. We joked later that year that there was no reason ever to create a four-ounce bottle, since our son could down eight ounces in a minute. And he was like that this morning. After he was finished and my wife handed him over to me for a good burp (and she recovered from the voracious feeding), he got a very strange look on his face. It was a cross between pain and determination, a look we'd come to understand well. He was, in fact, relieving himself, and in so doing, we were so relieved. And with that—and all other hospital requirements met—we were allowed to leave.

The first few months were almost as intense as the labor and delivery. Theresa was recovering from the surgery, post-partum, and all the vagaries of pregnancy, and Aidan was doing what babies do: sleeping, eating, and pooping, although not in any order or with any rhyme or reason. "I really don't think our child will ever sleep through the night," Theresa wearily exclaimed. I agreed. What did he need in the middle of the night? Comfort? Food? It was a magical time, but also in my sleep-deprived haze, it was maddening. Every night, multiple times per night for months and months, he would wake up screaming like the world was ending. At first, we had him in our bedroom, so the many wakeups were almost always feedings. And he would fall asleep in Theresa's arms. But as he grew, and we decided to put him in the next bedroom, the nighttime wakeups brought me out of bed. Sometimes it was a diaper change, and I got pretty good at changing a diaper in the dark with (seemingly) my eyes closed. Like everything in fatherhood, getting the diaper "right" meant getting it wrong the first couple dozens of times.

Far too many times, the only solution to my diaper foibles was an immediate bath, for both of us! I found new and creative ways to screw up putting on a diaper. And there seemed to be an endless supply of practice time. So much production from such a small body.

Torrey Pines—South (La Jolla, CA)

The rest of the year was full of discoveries, of watching that tiny boy grow. I was thinking about him, his so many "firsts," as I drove north on I-5 from San Diego. I was there to bear witness to my cousin's wedding, the lone representative of my family. And on the day before, when I had only dinner commitments, I decided to give it a shot: my first round at a top-100 course. I arrived at Torrey Pines South with no notice, no tee time, and no preparation whatsoever. I walked into the pro shop, put down my credit card and asked, "Do you have a tee time for a single?" The pro looked at me with a mixture of dismay, empathy, and disgust. *You don't have a tee time? You didn't call ahead? You're not from around here!* I could tell he was gauging what to say, not wanting to offend, but also not wanting to bother. He summoned the discipline and smiled:

"You need to go to the starter's booth. They will tell you if there's a tee time. You can pay there." He mumbled something else under his breath—flattering I'm sure—but I wasn't going to let my ignorance or his arrogance get under my skin.

I walked outside and looked around back, seeing the majestic Pacific Ocean for the first time. I tried to breathe. I approached the starter and said, "Hi, do you have any openings for a single?"

He grimaced and offered, "it's pretty busy. We can't promise anything." He took my name anyway, and I tried not to feel despondent. I knew that being a single helped, however, and with faint hope not knowing when or if my name might be called, I hovered nearby. Fortunately, there's a practice green with a loudspeaker just on the opposite side of the clubhouse. So I ventured there with my putter, watching all the excited golfers arrive, hit a few putts, and head to the 1st tee. I could smell the ocean, and I had quickly glimpsed the water, but I hadn't yet let myself get a good look at the course. I didn't want to spoil the moment if I got to play. I remained stuck in a holding pattern for 45 painful minutes.

When my name was finally called, I was shocked to find out that they were sending me out alone. Apparently, they had a last-minute no-show foursome, and I was the beneficiary. There was no time to feel excited or nervous, or really to take in that I was about to play Torrey Pines South, the famous venue outside San Diego and the site of Tiger Woods' historic US Open battle with Rocco Mediate. Playing from the white tees (now listed as the green tees), I hit a decent drive into a brisk wind to the left side of the fairway on this 420-yard opening hole. I pulled my 170-yard second shot with a 6-iron to the left, leaving me short sided. I was woefully unprepared for the spongy kikuyu grass, and thus came up short on the 15-foot chip. My second chip was good, however, and I putted in the one-footer for an opening bogey.

As I walked to the 2nd tee, a cart came up with a golfer in flip flops. The most chill golfer I had ever met, his manner seemed like he was sipping a piña colada and breathing in the ocean under a cabana. But John's attire belied his golfing acumen: he was ready to play and was looking for a game. Although I was glad for the company, my first swing with a witness was a classic over-the-top, rushed duff that didn't make it out of the rough in front of me. John said something self-deprecating and hit a solid 4-iron down the fairway. Three more poor shots later, I stared at a 20-footer for bogey. Either John didn't notice, or he was so chill that he didn't care, but we walked to the 3rd tee ready to encounter the rest of Torrey together despite my lousy double bogey.

"Where you from?" John asked, more to start a conversation than to find out the actual location.

I uttered, "upper Midwest, Minnesota." He made some joke about Fargo. I didn't want to tell him that's in North Dakota. Instead, I tried to draw him back to golf. "Play here much?"

"Yeah, this is my home course." As if I couldn't tell. Where else in the US would a golfer show up to the 2nd tee in flip flops, hop out as if he was strolling on the beach, and stripe a shot down the fairway? He added, "my son and I love to play here." I don't know if my eyes revealed my momentary shock, but I couldn't believe it. *He's a father? He doesn't look old enough and doesn't look responsible enough.* I'm not sure what I thought a father looked like, or why a man in flip flops who appeared to be in his thirties couldn't be a father, but I couldn't believe it.

I thought of something to ask. "How old are your kids?" I didn't know he had more than one child, but something was quickly dawning on me that this man had some experience with fatherhood.

"I've got two sons, 17 and 14."

The conversation had rid me of my terrible double on the 2nd hole, and I was now intrigued to know more about this father-who-looked-like-a-child. We arrived at the 3rd tee, the majestic, downhill par-three, which is one of the most picturesque holes in golf. In the distance, parasailers rode the wind gusts up and down the coast. They were mesmerizing, and yet I had to focus on the hole that Rocco nearly aced in that historic playoff. Into the wind, I decided to play an extra club down the hill—my 8-iron was solid, leaving me left below the hole about 25 feet. A steady putt up the hill momentarily settled me with a par on this memorable hole. But I wanted to know more about this enigmatic father.

"Does your son like to play?," I asked.

"He does, but we don't play very often."

"Why not?"

"He surfs."

Of course, a surfing golfer, or a golfing surfer. I wasn't shocked that his son loved to surf—he had that look. I was a bit shocked that he was old enough to be a father of teenagers. It turns out that we were very close in age, although his kids were older.

"Do you ever worry? I mean, about him?" I expected John to shrug it off, to tell me that surfing is perfectly safe.

"I worry every time he's in the water. I'm worried sick."

"Then why do you let him do it?" We had arrived at the 4th tee, with the wide expanse of the Pacific to our left. My question hung in the air as we quickly pivoted to the drive. My miss is a slice, not a hook, so this drive wasn't particularly intimidating. I hit a high fade, that rode the wind deep into the right rough, almost to the 5th fairway. I would be playing it as a par five. John, it turns out, does fight a hook, and his drive seemed headed straight for the ocean. He grunted something about "more room than it looks" on the left, and we set off on our own journeys down opposite sides of the fairway. I thought about my question, and wondered if it bothered him. For some reason, my mind drifted to my maternal grandfather, Elmer, the closest thing I had to a loving father-figure, who had signed me up for a golf camp at the University of Maryland, where I took a lesson from future PGA Tour member Fred Funk. I thought about how Elmer would have answered my question. *You can't stop a child from doing something they are determined to do.* I knew Elmer was right because, in 1963, he hadn't stood in my mother's way when she announced that she would be attending the March on Washington, despite his fears for her safety. Elmer knew that each child is their own person, and the best thing a parent can do is to help guide them on their chosen path.

By the time we arrived at the green, each via two shots, we had both forgotten my question. I wanted to find a way to bring it up again, but between poor shots that too often carried us in opposite directions, and the beauty of our surroundings, it didn't happen. We played almost nine holes together, sharing golf stories and encouraging each other. We had a nice rapport, but still, this man in flip flops had something important to teach me about fatherhood. I just knew it.

Somehow, after we got through the gauntlet known as the 12th hole, I loosened up. It's a bit of walk back to the 13th tee, so I asked: "That question I asked you before, about your son and surfing. Why do you let him do it?" When golfers think of Torrey Pines, they may very well think of the par-five 13th. After about 300 yards, the fairway drops down into a deep valley, and then climbs back up immediately to a highly perched green, stepped with numerous bunkers on the way. John looked behind us at the crashing waves.

"I have no choice; it's who he is." I smiled and said nothing. *It's who he is.* There was so much truth in John's words that we both seemed freed up. With the wind at our backs, we both had the best drives of the day. Mine was so good that it elicited a "wow" from John, apparently aiming his view right and surprised to see my ball fly straight. I was surprised, too.

As we walked down the fairway together for the first time, our minds seemed to wander between thinking about our kids and the upcoming shot. We don't get to stop our kids from being who they are … that's not what a father does. Even guiding them is a fool's errand sometimes. *They are who they are.* It's our job to help them be the best version of that self. I had a choice: hit a 3-wood and bring rough or worse on both sides into play; or, hit just about any other club and end up in the same place. If it hit it 100 yards, it would likely catch the downhill slope and roll to the bottom. If I hit it 30 yards further, it would likely drop and stop. Sixty yards further, and it would likely catch the uphill and roll back down. I pulled the club that I was most comfortable with hitting it straight—pitching wedge—and laced it straight down the fairway to the bottom of the valley. *I am who I am.*

The third shot calls for a 100-yard shot straight up the hill. Anything short would either land in a bunker or roll back down the massive hill. Anything long would land in the rough behind the green, creating an impossible chip back down to the pin. I added a club and hit my 50-degree wedge to perfection. Although I overshot the front pin by 12 feet, it was a simple-enough putt back down the hill. No Tiger heroics for me, and I settled for a well-played GIR, and John and I fist pumped with a pair of pars. It felt good, and I couldn't help but smile as we walked toward the 14th tee.

Over the rest of the round, I posted one-over. I was quickly learning that playing at a world-famous course was no different than a round on any other course: you aim for fairways and greens, and *try staying in the moment.* I had learned this golfing mantra over the past few years, when my golf game was littered with bad shots: *Catch and Release.* I had to catch those bad shots, understand what I did, and then release them. I had to let them go. I couldn't be the kind of golfer who would stew over the bad shots, lamenting all the missed opportunities to score. No, I had to let those shots go. I had to be the kind of golfer who would say, "oh well," after every bad shot. I had to wear flip flops. I had to watch my son surf, even as I worried myself sick.

I had seen the 18th hole enough on TV to know that it was a straight tee shot, with bunkers framing both sides of the fairway in the driving zone, and an ominous pond just in front of the green. I faded another drive, but fortunately so far right that I missed the bunker. That left me with a relatively simple hybrid back to the fairway. From 125 yards, I hit an extra club and faced a treacherous downhill, sidehill putt from 35 feet. I didn't make it—shut out of birdies for the entire round—but I did make the tap-in for par. While the front had been filled with miserable play, the back was revelatory as I closed under 40. John and I shook hands, wished each other best of luck parenting, and headed on our way. As I left the parking lot, I could only think that we can only be who we are.

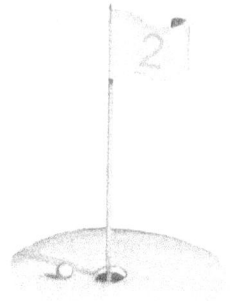

Patience

(2003-04)

Communicating with a child who cannot yet speak is an exercise in mutual frustration. While most kids have learned at least a few words before their first birthday, and some kids are quite verbal, Aidan hadn't spoken words in his entire first year. While he was active and undeniably well-fed, he was quite reticent to put his needs into words. He demanded, a lot. And these demands came with tantrums, almost always involving food. He was happy once he was eating, so we just had to stay on top if his constant need for food. But until he learned words, all of the efforts to quell his tantrums were merely temporary, like changing his diapers. There was always more to come.

Teaching him some sign-language, therefore, was the most significant decision we made. I'm not sure where or how Theresa got the idea, but it was a brilliant one and led to a collective sigh when we were able to communicate with each other. For me, the word that had the most lasting effect was "more." The sign is relatively simple. Just hold your hands clapping distance apart, draw all five fingers together on both hands, and bring the two groups of fingers together repeatedly while saying "more." It was always more with Aidan. More cereal, more milk, more toys, more crayons, more, more, more. Before the sign, it was just screaming and we would have to read his screams. "Do you want more Cheerios? Do you want more milk? Do you want more crackers?" Sometimes, we got it right, but it always left all of us frustrated and upset. Once he learned how to sign "more," we were all so pleased. He was thrilled to be equipped to ask for what he wanted, and we were relieved of the guessing, and the screaming.

So, with some ability to communicate with our son, we were more apt to travel. Usually, travel was nearby, to a local park. Although neither Theresa nor I had forgotten our vocabulary, we tended to talk to each other with the same number of syllables we used with Aidan.

"Diapers." "Snacks." "Wet wipes." "Toys."

We became each other's checklist. And that was the case the day we went just a few blocks away (by car!) to Minneapolis' Triangle Park.

Everything can change in an instant. I wasn't thinking that way as we arrived at Triangle Park. I wasn't thinking of much. I was just so tired. I parked across the street from the park, just in front of a very large dumpster. I unloaded the car: food for a picnic, and toys to keep our son busy for several hours. I had my son and was on gear duty. I put him down to grab the diaper bag. I turned back around as he started to run ... he was headed to the back of the car ... in front of the dumpster ... then across the street. He had that distinctive under-two-year-old run—slower than he would get in the future, but *dramatically faster* than he had been up to this point. As I turned to see him beginning to run toward the street, I also heard the engine. It was a large dump truck, headed our way. The truck driver couldn't see Aidan—he was completely obscured by the dumpster.

It all happened so fast—a new runner headed toward the street, obscured by the dumpster; the truck moving far too fast toward us.

And me, not fully present as I tried to get our gear successfully from the car to the park. The truck flew past us, my son close enough to the enormous tires to hear the rubber meeting the road. I yelled "stop!" Parents looked over from the park. Theresa came rushing over. My voice had come too late. Aidan had no idea that he was just a split second from the truck. The driver never saw that tiny body.

It didn't happen, but I'll never forget that moment. One split second of distraction, one absent-minded second that could have transformed our lives. And it's so easy to get distracted; so many demands on our attention, and this was before cell phones! I was on duty with our son, I was it. I couldn't rely on anyone else to notice when he was in danger. I hadn't noticed the details. When I parked, I didn't think about the dumpster. I didn't think about who would be hidden from other drivers. I didn't think about needing to keep my son in the car while we unloaded. I didn't think about walking to the other side of the dumpster. I didn't notice. Sometimes, it's the details that matter most.

While Aidan spent most of his second year of life near home, sometimes our travel was more distant, like our trip to Washington State. We were excited for my cousin's wedding, but not having travelled by plane with our son since he was very young, we were concerned. Theresa looked at me with a reasonable set of questions: "He moves so much ... what could we possibly do for the four hours on the plane? How could we ever bring enough food? What if he has a tantrum? We will have nowhere to go. Should he have his own seat?" I thought, *shouldn't we just skip the wedding?* I left it unsaid, but we were both thinking it. I cared about my cousin Kathryn very much, and this wedding was a big deal for her. But was it really worth it?

After many machinations, we made a fateful—and fatefully bad—decision that he was small enough that he could sit on our laps. Because he was under two years old, we wouldn't be required to buy a ticket for him. We figured that he would likely sleep for much of the flight, and he would want to be in our arms to sleep, anyway. Why purchase a ticket when we almost certainly weren't going to use a seat?

Well, if you've ever travelled with a highly mobile one-year-old, you know that despite their relatively small stature, they take up a ton of space. And Aidan made his presence known, from the beginning of the flight to the end. We spent most of our time walking up and down the aisle, trying to keep his hands out of his mouth, managing his squirms on our laps, playing whatever games would keep him engaged for a few minutes, and watching him not sleep. Everywhere I looked, other passengers gave me "the look." It was a cross between annoyance and irritation with a sprinkle of empathy. I smiled back. The flight attendant was more direct: "Keep it moving sir … you can't hang out in the aisle." Moving up and down the aisle, pretending we were race cars, was just about the best I could think of. We swore that we would never do *that* again.

Somehow, we made it to northwest Washington for the wedding. Generously being hosted by my aunt and uncle, we made it to their guest room and collapsed on the bed. Or, at least Theresa did. I tried, but within a minute or two, Aidan was starting to wind up—ready to eat, or walk, or play some game with a ball. I took a deep breath and—wanting nothing more than to take a nap—got up and went downstairs to get him a snack. My aunt was in the kitchen.

With a look of exasperation I'm sure, I asked Aunt Martha, "What's your advice? Aidan isn't tired and he would like something fun to do?" She gave me a knowing, empathetic, it's-your-turn-now laugh.

"Why don't we take the dogs for a walk and bring a few toys?"

Great idea. So, we grabbed a soccer ball, a frisbee, and anything else that we thought might be entertaining for a few minutes and set off on a walk toward Lake Washington. I'm not sure if we were walking the dogs, or if Aidan was walking us, but that's how it continued for the next few days. The wedding was to be in a rural community, far from Seattle. While we loved the idea of travelling out of the city, it was much more complicated with a one-year-old. Theresa and I did our usual packing checklist.

"Food? Check." What if we didn't bring enough? "More food? Check." "Water? Check."

"Diapers? Check." What if he made a mess of his diaper? "Extra clothes? Check." "Wet wipes? Check." "Toys? Check."

Theresa and I were learning how to do the emergency checklist, although we knew enough at this point to know that we would *definitely* forget something. It was inevitable. We had gone on a ferry and forgotten diapers. On a long car ride, we realized that we only had one pair of underwear. We had driven to the park in the winter only to realize that we were sans mittens. Our running joke was that by the time our son could get everything together for himself, we would finally figure out everything he needs.

But it was time to go, and we would have to make the best of it. Some weddings are formal, with lots of pomp and circumstance. Not this one. The wedding was outdoors, in a clearing in the middle of the woods. The guests sat in a large half-circle, embracing the couple. Had we not been in these circumstances, it would have been a beautiful wedding. Yet we were in those circumstances, and nothing else mattered.

"I don't feel well," Theresa told me as we sat down for the ceremony. I should have noted the significance of that comment, but I was instead focused on keeping Aidan engaged.

Most weddings don't accommodate for parents' need to keep their child moving, and this was no exception. The only benefit was that I didn't have to worry as much about the swarming Pacific Northwest mosquitoes! Guests couldn't decide which would be more distracting: constantly waiving our hands to swat away the swarm of mosquitoes, or spraying ourselves and creating a cloud of bug repellant. I just keep Aidan moving.

Sometimes, having a young child is a great excuse. While every guest—yes, every guest—was asked to say something about the couple, I used that request as an opportunity to bolt. I took Aidan by the hand and walked back out of the woods to find the serving crew (and their interesting equipment). I had no idea how much fun platters and napkins and tattooed 20-somethings could be for a one-year-old. We introduced him to every tool that servers use. "Would he like to try making spoon music?" one of the brilliant servers suggested. She got a few spoons, and found some plastic buckets and Aidan made the world's worst racket. Hopefully, we were far enough from the wedding that our musical performance didn't interrupt their ceremony. But at the moment, I didn't care. The servers were happy to have some entertainment before their work began. Theresa emerged shortly thereafter, apparently feeling even sicker than before. We wouldn't be staying long at the reception.

The next morning, I woke up with a small hand in my face. I had spent most of the past 22 months being woken up in the middle of the night, so it wasn't strange to be awakened. It was strange, however, to see this little hand outside of a crib. And this little hand had something in it. The something looked like a pencil ... *what is he doing holding a pencil? So close to my eyes? It was a stick of some kind ...* as my eyes adjusted, I realized that it was a stick with an indicator. The kind of indicator that was showing that Theresa was pregnant! Now I was awake. We hugged and kissed, as Aidan knew something good was happening but didn't have a clue what it would be.

I started to piece together the sickness from the wedding. Over the last few days of the trip, we didn't tell Aidan anything about it, because he could only just repeat whatever he heard to everyone else. We were not yet ready to tell the family—we wanted to let the pregnancy advance for a while. Realizing that our lives would be changed enormously in about nine months, we took it slow ... really slow.

Torrey Pines—North (La Jolla, CA)

The year 1957, though often overlooked, was momentous in many ways. Federal troops forcibly integrated the public schools in Little Rock, Arkansas, following the momentous *Brown v. Board of Education*, an early battle in the Civil Rights Movement; the Soviet Union became the first nation to orbit a man around the Earth in its Sputnik spacecraft, launching the space race; Albert Camus, French existentialist, won the Nobel Prize for Literature; Elvis Pressley held three of the top 10 most popular songs; the Best Picture was *The Bridge on the River Kwai*; Omega first released the Speedmaster, what would later become the famous Moonwatch worn by NASA astronauts; and Torrey Pines, designed by then-relatively unknown architect William F. Bell, opened to the public. The North course, due largely to its sibling's length, had always been the little sibling. As such, with the South course getting major tournaments and plenty of press (not to mention, agronomic care), the North course was substantially ignored.

Yet I knew none of this as I made my tee time—easy to get—on the North course with my cousin and two uncles. We were in San Diego visiting my cousin Nathan, who had moved there with his new bride. We decided to play the overlooked and untapped majesty of the North course at Torrey Pines. Although Tom Weiskopf reversed the nines during his redesign in 2016, at the time the North course began with a par five, set—you guessed it—just north of the 1st tee of the South course. We played on what would be a stunning day—72 degrees, sunny, with a light breeze—anywhere. In La Jolla, just north of downtown San Diego, it was a routine day.

Almost a mirror image of the opening tee shot on the South course, the North course opened with a tee shot aimed seemingly straight at the water. With a bit of a downhill for the second and third shots, the view from the tee is the fairway, the rough, a bunker on the right side, a stand of trees, and the ocean. As you stand at the tee, you have to trust that there's a green somewhere ahead.

"Are you going to hit, or what?," my uncle noodled. "We don't have all day."

Actually, we did, but as the best golfer of the foursome, I was expected to get things going. I sent my drive off toward the horizon, with my all-too-common fade into the rough.

After the second shot that put me back in the short stuff, I sized up 175-yard third shot into a green guarded by three bunkers. Carrying the bunker and holding the green wouldn't have been too bad. But with a 6-iron in my hand, I wondered if I could hold the green. Although my shot was struck well, and although it landed on the green, there was no stopping its momentum. I would have to get up and down for an opening par.

Hitting a long shot out of kikuyu is a relatively simple task: steepen the swing and accelerate through the ball. I had executed it without too much trouble several times. Around the green, however, is another story. Full acceleration is nearly impossible while maintaining control. Yet any deceleration in the downswing will guarantee that the sticky blades of kikuyu will grab the club, giving "flub" its onomatopoeic name. I investigated the lie—kikuyu all around the ball, swallowing it like my son attacked his bottles. I would have to be absolutely committed to holding my speed through the ball. I managed to pull it off, chipping solidly to leave myself a two-footer below the hole. I cleaned up the putt and breathed a sigh of relief for my opening par. I would show my uncles how to play.

I was playing with my uncles Kenny and Nelson. They were both fathers—Nelson's son Nathan was golfing with us—and so as a new father I had many questions for them. Uncle Kenny and Aunt Martha had taken me in for three weeks when I was 11, sent by my mother for a needed break from me, no doubt. Uncle Nelson lived about 40 minutes from my college, so I saw him regularly during my college years. They were fathers themselves, and I felt close enough to ask them questions directly and get an honest answer.

"How did you ever find the patience to be a dad?," I asked as we walked off the 1st tee. Young Nathan gave a grunt, maybe because he was too young to have children, or maybe because he didn't think his father showed much patience (I had seen otherwise). But I think Kenny and Nelson took the question seriously.

"What patience?," Kenny blurted out. He laughed at my question, knowing that patience was not his strong suit. When I was with him as an 11-year-old, I experienced firsthand his impatience when I accidentally kicked sand in his face during a beach soccer game. He screamed at me, "you idiot!" He sounded just like my father.

"I'm not patient at all," he laughed. But I had seen how much he loved his kids and had seen him be very patient with them. Maybe he was only remembering the failures, as we are apt to do.

We arrived at the 2nd hole, now played as the 11th, a short par four with a slight dogleg to the right. I wanted to hear Nelson's answer, but I was up on the tee. I hit my 3-wood drive down the fairway, finishing about 110 yards from the green. Eyeing an elevated green surrounded by large and deep greenside bunkers, I would have to be precise with my approach shot. I wasn't. Instead, my wedge faded off to the right, clearing the bunker but leaving a difficult up-and-down. I would need more than the concentration I exhibited on the 1st hole—I would need some precision. Again, I arrived at my ball to find the kikuyu hugging my ball. I didn't demonstrate the same commitment to the chip, leaving it well short of the pin. Two putts later, I was behind the bogey eight-ball already.

I strode to the 3rd hole determined to recover. At the time, the hole measured 150 yards from our tees. The hole calls for a high draw—beginning straight ahead over grass and then flying left over the first of many Pacific Ocean gorges. Any ball over-drawn, or simply short, would be swallowed up among the native plans, which no one seeking to avoid an encounter with an unsuspecting rattler would dare follow. So I took a few practice swings and committed myself to a solid shot. It came out left, and fortunately for me, did not have any draw. In fact, it was headed straight for the hole. I held my breath as Nelson let out Hal Sutton's famous words: "be the right club today!" He didn't have Sutton's Louisiana drawl, and it wouldn't prove to be my 1st hole-in-one, but it was the right club and my ball landed just a few feet from the pin. A short tap in later for birdie, and I was back to level par.

"So, Nelson, how did you remain patient when your kids were very young?," I asked again.

"Well, I tried to have as much fun with them as possible. I tried to keep them really busy. We played all kinds of games, and we tried to laugh, a lot. It wasn't easy. But when I was laughing, I didn't get too mad." *When I was laughing, I didn't get mad.* It was so simple.

I played the 4th through 14th holes in seven-over, with some excellent shots and some wayward swings. Some bad luck, like the plugged lie in the front bunker at the picturesque 6th hole (now, the 15th), undermined a solid-if-uninspired 11-hole stretch. I would have to play the final holes in even par to break 80. Fortuitously, the final four of the back nine (now the front) are some of the easiest holes on the eastern-most side of the course. While my drive on the par-four 15th was still right, it wasn't too far off the fairway, and I was left with only a 7-iron. I flushed it and managed to hold it left enough to avoid the greenside bunker on the right. While my putt from 35 feet was overly cautious, I was able to make the three-foot putt for par.

My eyes opened wide as I caught sight of the 274-yard par-four 16 (now 7th) hole. Because I would not be able to drive the green, despite the urging of my uncles and cousin to try, I chose a 3-wood and piped it straight down the fairway. Only a wedge in, and my 10-footer presented me with the best chance for birdie since the 3rd hole. Again, I didn't give my putt enough pace to hold the line and I missed the birdie putt on the low side. Disappointed but not defeated, I walked off the green ruing my missed opportunity.

The par-three 17th (now 8th) hole plays downhill from 167 yards. Convinced that I had the distance to get the ball on the green with one fewer club, I pulled my 8-iron and hit a beauty, long and straight at the middle of the green. While the front pin position rendered the 40-foot putt more of a compromise than a directive, I was able to get it within 16 inches and tapped in for a third par in a row. One more, and this time, it was a par-five finisher.

At 475 yards, what had been the 18th hole was the most accessible on the course. I knew that a good drive would set me up for a long iron to the green, and even a putt for eagle. At worst, I figured, I would be putting for birdie. And with that distracted mindset, I peeled off another slice. I hadn't even noticed the small stand of pines on the right, but I saw them now, as my ball seemed magnetically pulled to join them. Although I wasn't quite stymied, I had only a low punch between two of them to advance my ball down the fairway. From wedge distance, I was able to draw my ball in from the right side of the green and left myself a 20-foot downhill putt. While I didn't make it, my fourth par in a row meant that I had, in fact, broken 80. It was one of my best rounds of golf of my life, and I was smiling ear to ear. When I was laughing, I couldn't get mad.

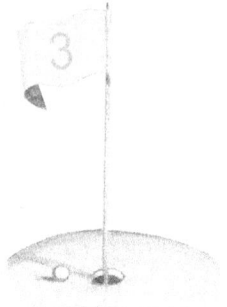

Overwhelmed

(2004-05)

There is an old saying about raising kids: the first child changes your life; the second child takes over your life. While the second year of the child's life demands patience, in the third year, patience just isn't enough. Aidan had learned "no" very early in life, but we hadn't felt the full brunt of a "no" until he was a fully-mobile and fearless two-year-old. It was one thing to prevent Aidan from stuffing a cheerio in his nose. It was an entirely different thing to prevent him from running into the busy street. From his perspective, Aidan was being denied what he wanted to do—and screamed bloody murder.

So, of course, we did what many parents do when their first child has entered the terrible twos—we decided to have another child. I met the initial news with unbridled excitement. I like to say that our younger son—Elliott—doesn't have a birth*day*, he has a birth *weekend*. Of course, he was born on a single day, but that day was really 72 hours. On Friday of that weekend, Theresa had been having contractions for several hours, and I left work with the feeling that she would soon be in full-on labor. We talked several times during the day.

"The contractions have started." She calmly related.

"Wow." I not so calmly responded.

A few hours later. "The contractions are getting more organized."

"Okay, I'll be home right away." By the time I got home from work, she was in a lot of pain. My mother was in town for the week to take care of Aidan when we had to go to the hospital. I called her. "Theresa's contractions are eight minutes apart. Can you come over?"

"I'll be right there."

I came home to find my wife upstairs, taking a bath, trying to make the best use of water to ease the pain. "Please call Laurel. Let her know that the contractions are now three minutes apart." Theresa was so calm. I called our midwife Laurel and she told me to come right in to the hospital. Theresa was in so much pain; I couldn't drive fast enough.

When we arrived at the downtown hospital, a nurse met us at the door with a wheelchair. We walked quickly to the midwife unit. Laurel had just started her shift and met us there. It was kind of a routine from there: contraction/pain, breathing/coaching, rest/ laughing. I just observed as these women practiced the collective wisdom of thousands of years. Very rarely have I been so useless. But I would be there, no matter what. And then … it stopped. Labor, it seemed, had ceased. Three hours of intense labor at the hospital, on top of several hours at home, and everything stopped. The lights were bright, the room was cold—labor stopped.

Laurel said, "You have two options. I can give you something to restart labor, or you can go home." We knew about the relationship between Pitocin—the medication commonly used to start labor or make contractions more intense—and c-sections, and Theresa had already been through that once. "I don't want another c-section," Theresa firmly stated. So, we went home.

I can't say that I understood what she had gone through—it had been hours of intense pain. I'm sure she was physically exhausted. To encourage her to rest, the midwife had given my wife two sleeping pills. But she didn't look sleepy: she looked physically spent and, from what I could tell, dejected. *Going through that kind of pain for a purpose,* I imagined her thinking, *is worth it. Go through that kind of pain only to be sent home? No way.*

We arrived home 15 minutes later, and wouldn't you believe, her intense contractions resumed. In the bright lights, machine-dominated, and intensely impersonal hospital, Theresa's body shut down. But as we crossed the threshold into our warm, personal, and machine-less home, everything restarted. She was in so much pain. But we couldn't simply go back to the hospital. So, for many hours, Theresa continued to get through the pain of contractions every few minutes. Our conversations were reduced to short phrases. "Some water, please." "Right away." "Aidan, okay?" "Yes, he's asleep." "I can't sleep." "Can I get you anything?" The contractions were back to three minutes apart, and very intense.

"Laurel, it's Matt again. Theresa's contractions are back to three minutes apart."

"Okay, come back to the hospital." It was now Saturday at 2:30 in the morning. This second visit to the hospital seemed more hopeful, as the middle of the night contractions had to be moving Theresa closer to giving birth, right? No, not really. But they didn't want to send us home just yet, so they gave Theresa a shot of morphine for her pain and set up a pull-out bed for me, and we slept for a few hours.

I wasn't able to sleep very well. While it was clear that my wife's frustration was growing with the seemingly pointless pain, she also needed to sleep, and I couldn't help her with that. So, we agreed that I would go back home to meet Aidan for his Saturday morning routine, and she would try to sleep at the hospital. It's a strange fact about the hours (or in this case, days) before the birth of a child—our minds were so focused on what's in front of us. There is no past or future … there is only the present.

Aidan, who had spent the past day with his grandmother, largely unaware of what was happening, was just up for the day. Two-and-a-half is an age when everything is immediate, and there is no explanation for absence. I had been gone. It didn't matter why I wasn't there; the fact is I wasn't there. I walked in and was met not with joy that I was home, but a deep and extended cry that he had, apparently, been holding in for the two days of our absence. I held him and tried to prepare him for the fact that I would be leaving soon. My mother did her absolute best to comfort our son; but he was scared and being at the hospital for the birth of his brother was a bridge too far for his young mind.

Theresa called a bit later: "I need you to come back and pick me up." There was resignation in her voice.

I didn't ask her why. "I'll be right there." It was obvious that labor had stopped again. So, I returned to the hospital, and picked her up. The birth of our son would have to wait. I drove her home in complete silence—what could be said? As had happened the day before, as we entered the house, labor started again.

I broke the silence: "I'm going to call Marjorie," our doula, who had planned to meet us at the hospital. It was Aidan's bedtime by now, so I focused on his needs. I don't know how I got through reading his books for the night—I probably dozed off every page. But somehow we got through it, and he was asleep. Marjorie spent hours with Theresa, helping her through every contraction. I slept. To this day, my wife and I talk (argue?) about why I slept that third night. I don't know how she went a third night without sleep—I suppose she had no choice. But I simply couldn't keep my eyes open another minute. I slept through the most intense hours of her labor. I know I should have been awake to support my wife. I know I should have been present for her. But I slept.

I don't know what Marjorie said to or did with Theresa—I probably will never know. But when I woke up with the sun that morning, something had happened to Theresa during the night. Where before she was scared, in pain, and exhausted, this morning she was confident, relaxed, and in control. She hadn't slept, and no doubt the pain was just as intense. But she had moved to a different mental place. Calmly and with great determination, Theresa asked, "please call Laurel and tell her we're coming in." I dialed the number, and was about to speak when she stopped me: "please hang up and take your coat off." I looked at her, puzzled and concerned. She read my face and explained, "I'm not ready. He's not ready. I don't want to be sent home again." So she and Marjorie worked through another hour of contractions.

And then, it was time. I called. "We're coming back in."

When we arrived at the hospital for the third time in three days, the Midwife Unit was closed, so we were sent to the OB Unit. It was 6:30am on Sunday. The nurse suggested a "whiff" of Pitocin to try to advance labor. My wife agreed, and we spent several hours in the room, as Theresa experienced the most intense contractions so far. Her eyes showed it—she was reaching her limit. The experienced nurse was clear: "You need to make a decision. Labor isn't advancing. You are exhausted, and you have to sleep. Do you want to sleep here or at home?" Theresa could sleep in the hospital, and I could be just a phone call away. It was around 10:00am, and I was heading home, again. Theresa would call me when she woke up, and I would spend the day with our son.

Theresa called me about six hours later: "please come get me." She sounded worse than before. She was beyond, beyond exhausted. She needed this labor to end. She had nothing left. Five minutes later, she called again. "I'm going to sleep more." Okay, what should

I do? Aidan and his grandmother had gone shopping, so I didn't need to be home. But there was no reason to make the drive, yet. I dozed. An hour later: "please come get me."

I called my mother. "I'm going to get Theresa."

"Oh, no. Is she okay?" I needed to let my mother know what was going on, but the last thing I needed was for her to show to Aidan that she was worried about his mom.

So, I said, "she's absolutely fine. Great." We hung up. Over the next 15 minutes, as I drove back to the hospital in our version of Groundhog Day, Theresa met her goal of not returning home for the third time. I walked into her room. "My water broke. They just gave me an IV and an antibiotic." I hugged her, and I could tell that she had shifted again. It was the final stage, and she knew it. But little did she know how long that final stage would be. We slowly walked the hallways of the hospital. She rolled the IV stand and I held her hand. I called my mother to say goodnight to Aidan—he would have to spend another night with his grandma. He spoke to Theresa for the first time in three days. "I love you Aidan. Have a good night with Grammy." He cried. He missed us so much and didn't understand why we couldn't be home.

Laurel, whom we hadn't seen since her last shift, was back on call. She came in the room. She explained, "despite the fact that your water has broken, and despite the three days of contractions, your labor hasn't *progressed*." That word. It was like an indictment. Like Theresa had done something wrong. It stung her. "The OB doctor is starting to pressure us to have a c-section to ensure the safety of the baby. Labor like this can't go on much longer." Theresa began to cry softly. She had nothing left.

Laurel said, "You have three options: 1) Do nothing and hope the pain is bearable and that labor progresses; 2) Take NuBain, a drug that will relax your mind and maybe your baby; 3) Get an epidural." Theresa looked at me. I had never seen her so completely and totally spent.

There was so much going on in our sleep-deprived minds. We had spoken at length about her desire not to get a c-section again. Her recovery from the first c-section was long and painful. She wanted a natural birth. And we also knew that the likelihood of a c-section increased dramatically with an epidural. But NuBain was not an option—several of her sisters had taken NuBain and hated the loopy feeling, and Theresa did not want to lose her ability to focus and communicate. And doing nothing hadn't been working for three days. "I can't do this anymore. I'm sorry." She was crying with a voice I'd never seen before. She had nothing to apologize for; she had been through so much the post three days. I uttered, "of course," and comforted her. So, with uncertainty, anxiety and relief, Theresa chose option three.

The next 45 minutes—from the moment the epidural was ordered until the doctor entered the room—were beyond unbearable for Theresa. The contractions were the most intense yet, and all she could think about was the relief that the epidural would provide. The minutes couldn't have ticked more slowly. "Where the !@#$%^ is the doctor!?" she screamed through pain. And then the doctor arrived. After a few minutes of maneuvering to find the right location for the shot, there it was: the infamous epidural. Theresa found immediate pain relief.

And thus began one of the most surreal three-and-a-half-hours of my life (and surely hers as well). For days, there had been only commotion, with Laurel, Marjorie, occasional nurses and me in the room, and Theresa writhing in pain every two to three minutes. With the epidural, and the cessation of immediate pain, she was finally able to settle down. With days of sleep-deprivation and the most intense physical pain, her body just collapsed on the bed. Everyone else left the room. On her way out, a thoughtful nurse shut the blinds and turned off the lights, and all the sounds were shut off except the fetal monitor. The room became eerily dark and quiet. Theresa fell asleep immediately. I surely dozed off as well, despite the discomfort of the hospital chair.

Laurel checked in about once an hour to make sure everything was okay—it was. Theresa continued to sleep. Then, about three-and-a-half hours after the epidural, Laurel came in again. Theresa woke up, so Laurel decided to check for progress. "It's time," she announced. As it turned out, the epidural had been exactly the right thing to do. Suddenly, I was awake. Marjorie and the nurses poured in, as if pulled by a mysterious power. They moved Theresa into position, and I moved out of the way. I was physically in the room, but I had to give her space—space to get through this, space to work with the women in the room who knew exactly what they were doing. I just watched in awe.

It didn't take much longer—maybe 15 minutes of pushing. I'm sure Theresa was filled with a mix of utter exhaustion, impending relief that the ordeal was almost over, and incredible excitement to meet our son. As he emerged slowly, it was clear that Laurel and the nurses were intensively focused on their jobs—it was a well-coordinated symphony of birthing. When our son emerged, the nurse with this particular responsibility immediately cut the umbilical cord and brought him to a small table near Theresa. He wasn't breathing. I was five feet away, with my heart in my throat. I could hear Theresa ask the midwife, "Is he okay?" The midwife said "yes," but I was watching, and *okay* is not a word I would have used. The nurse inserted a long tube down our newly born son's throat, and I shook. It took about 10 to 15 seconds, and he let out a gag, then a cough, then a hearty cry. The nurse cleaned him up and brought him to Theresa's chest, where he wanted to remain for the next six months.

When Aidan was born, he was very happy to be on my chest. While I couldn't feed him, Theresa would feed him and quickly turn him over to me, where I was able to help him burp, change his diapers, and rock him to sleep. Things were just plain different with Elliott. He was happy eating, but when the handoff came, he was miserable. He didn't want me to hold him, to burp him, to change his diaper, and he would never fall asleep in my arms. Try as I might, he just wanted to be with his mom. It is possible that because Theresa had been recovering from a c-section, Aidan somehow sensed that his mom needed the space to recover. By contrast, she experienced a pretty quick recovery after Elliott's marathon birth, and maybe he sensed that. I don't know. What I do know is that I was clearly pretty useless in the opening months after Elliott's birth. So, I did what most fathers probably do in that situation: I was Aidan's main companion. While Elliott was nursing with his mom, I was helping our almost-three-year-old eat. When Elliott was sleeping in his crib, Aidan and I were exploring the park. When Elliott needed his mom, Aidan needed me. And that was our routine.

Bethpage Black (Farmingdale, NY)

Overwhelmed is the emotion I felt most often facing the reality of raising two kids, one of whom screamed every moment he was away from his mom. I also felt overwhelmed as I sat on a train, returning from a glorious day on Long Island. It wasn't the same type of feeling—one grounded in sleep-deprived, always-on exhaustion, the other grounded in gratitude for the opportunity.

I don't know if I've ever been as excited to play a golf course as I was to play Bethpage Black. Maybe it was because Bethpage Black had been the site of the 2009 U.S. Open and 2002 U.S. Open, Tiger Woods' eighth major championship. Maybe it was because of the sign meant to intimidate golfers just behind the 1st tee: "The Black Course is An Extremely Difficult Course Which We Recommend Only for Highly Skilled Golfers." Maybe it was because I had made the long journey to the golf course to escape a day with Theresa's seven sisters who had gathered in Manhattan for the wedding of one of them. Maybe it was all of these reasons, and many more. Who knows? I was shaking with excitement.

I woke up at four in the morning, wide awake and ready for the journey. It was a rare weekend: we had fenagled my mother to be with our kids so Theresa and I could fly off to New York City for the weekend. We would be leaving on a Thursday, with a Saturday wedding, and a return to home on a Sunday. Travel on Thursday and Sunday. Family on Saturday. Friday? Open. Before we left, Theresa told me the wedding weekend plan: on Friday, we (*we!?*) would be spending the day with her sisters, all seven of them. No brothers. And while I have no deep problems with any of them, and I like some of them more than others, what is crystal clear to *all of us* is that I'm not well-suited to spending the day with all of them. I reasoned, "sister days are an important part of *your life*. I need another plan." She agreed. What's a husband to do? A full day in New York, with no kids and no responsibilities ... play golf, of course. But where? Bethpage Black was my first choice, as the best public course in the area. I had read about how hard it was to get a tee time—golfers spending the night in their cars—even though it was public. So, maybe not the Black course. I knew they had other courses, so maybe I would go there, try to play the Black course, and—if I couldn't get a tee time—I could always play the Red course, or any of their five courses. Or, maybe somewhere else? I did some research and couldn't find another course that I could reach by public transportation and within a few hours. I packed my clubs for the flight to New York, determined that I was going to play at Bethpage State Park.

I set my alarm for 4am, and 15 minutes after I had woken up, I set off on the streets of Manhattan with a small carry bag on my back, bound and determined to reach Bethpage State Park. I'm sure I looked like a crazy person, walking down the street in lower Manhattan, well before dawn, with golf clubs on my back. Maybe I *was* a crazy person. I didn't care. I had my headsets on, and my craziness was no more or less apparent than the throngs of others who were up, doing their own thing. I took the subway to Penn Station, where I managed to figure out how to buy a ticket on the Long Island Railroad to the Farmingdale Station.

Getting on a train with golf clubs is a strange sensation, at least for me. Typically, I drive to a golf course with my clubs already in the trunk. While I routinely play public golf courses, the golfing endeavor isn't exactly public. On a typical golf day, the only people I interact with are golfers themselves. Not so on the LIRR, where everyone I saw gave me a look when they saw my golf clubs—it was a combination of confusion (what the hell are *those?*) and dismissal (what kind of *idiot* are you?) and outright hostility (get those *things* out of my way!). I didn't care. I ignored the glaring looks from passersby and settled into my seat for the roughly hour-long train ride. I dreamed of being the "highly skilled" golfer as the sign referenced. I dreamed of hitting a solid first drive. I dreamed of getting on the course. The closer we got to Bethpage, the lower my requirements—from *I want to break 80* to *I just want a good first shot* to *please let me get a tee time.* Was this the craziest waste of a day imaginable?

I decided to pretend that it was definitely going to happen. I checked on Google Maps. Just 1.3 miles. The app alerted, "taxi recommended." As I left the train, a line of taxis was waiting. Surely I would hop in one of them. Nope. I was going to walk the course, I reasoned, so I might as well walk the two-and-a-half miles round trip between the train station and the course. It looked "doable." I left the train station and weaved through a few flat neighborhood streets. *This is going to be fine—easy peazy.* Yet as I turned the corner, my confidence quickly dissipated. Each block seemed steeper than the previous one. Straight uphill, for about a mile. I took a deep breath and dug in for the climb. A few minutes later, I noticed, out-of-nowhere, that I had a companion. No, not the four-legged kind that so often follow golfers trekking across land unfit for clubs. No, this companion was the two-legged variety, too close to be simply passing by, but too far to be in conversation. So, I paused. "Do you want to pass?"

If you've ever seen the movie *Fargo* then you know of the Steve Buscemi character: Carl, a bumbling criminal who ultimately ends up in a woodchipper. While Buscemi's character was the victim of that particular crime, what I remembered about the film was Buscemi and a woodchipper, not who ended up in it. And here, less than five feet behind me, was Mr. Buscemi! … or a spitting image of him. Whoever he was, and whether he had a woodchipper in his history, he was here now, and I had a set of golf clubs on my back. He also reeked of whiskey—yes, the sun had only arisen about 30 minutes before my encounter with Mr. Buscemi's twin—and was quite friendly.

"Heading to Bethpage?"

"Um, yes."

"I'll show you a shortcut and get you on the course."

We talked for the next half-mile as we walked up the hill. Buscemi somewhat slurred, "I used to caddie at Bethpage. Here the number one rule: if you hit it in the rough, just use a 7-iron and punch it back on the fairway. Don't even think about advancing the ball."

"Okay," I said. "I'll try to remember that."

"Let's go down here. It's the back entrance."

I don't know what showed on my face, but I started to think about how quickly I could get that 9-iron in my hand. The bag, after all, was strapped to my back. I let him lead the way. At the very least, I wanted a few seconds notice before he reached for whatever he was planning to use against me at Bethpage's back entrance.

But lo and behold, there we were, walking through the service entrance to Bethpage's golf courses. Buscemi kept walking me up the hill to the starter's shed. "Wait a minute," he told me and pointed me to stand back. He walked over to the starter's shed and had a few words with the starter. She looked over at me with what seemed from a distance to be skepticism, and then Buscemi came over and said, "we're in."

I didn't know if he was bullshitting me—if I had a tee time or if I was about to face my own *Fargo* moment—but he walked me another couple hundred yards farther and told me to go into a small building where he said I would pay for the round. It was nearly 7am by that point, and Buscemi told me that I had a tee time. I was stuck between fear and exhilaration. I walked into the small building, waited about 10 minutes in a small line, and arrived at the tee time desk. It was only at that moment that I realized that I had a problem: *What the hell should I say? Buscemi got me a tee time? That guy out there spoke to the starter and told me we're in? I'm just a fool from out-of-town and I have no clue what to do?* I decided that I should have what I perceive as a New York conversation: quick, blunt, and all-business.

"I'm looking for a tee time on the Black course for a single." Too hard to explain Buscemi.

The tee-time agent said, "we have a singles system for the Black course. One tee time per hour reserved for singles. Plus, we will add singles to any groups with fewer than four golfers. Stay close to the starter's hut and listen for your name." I paid and did as I was told.

At Bethpage, there is a space near the back entrance they call a driving range. It's not much of a range. It's mainly a place to stretch your body and hit a few wedges. I decided to go over to get my back warmed up as much as possible. I headed down the hill to the driving range and figured out how to get a small bucket. Then, I proceeded to try to focus (mostly unsuccessfully) on stretching my back and hitting wedges and that trusty 9-iron that I had at the ready. I heard many names called in that 30 minutes of warm up, but none were mine. Then, all of a sudden, my name was called to report to the starter's hut.

My heart began to race—is this the news I was hoping for? I don't know, but I almost ran the five-minute walk back to the starter's gate and breathlessly told the starter my name. She looked me over and seemed to remember that I was the guy that Buscemi had told her about. "Do you know him?," she enquired. *What do I say to that? If I say yes, will that get me on the course? If I say no, will that get me on the course? Was she friend or foe? Was Buscemi friend or foe?* I didn't know if she was his ex, mortal enemy, or close friend. I sensed that my answer might have a huge impact on whether I was playing golf that day. So, as in all moments of indecision I have had as a father, I decided to tell the truth. If not knowing Buscemi before this morning prevented me from getting on the course, so be it. I might have thrown away my ticket to Black, but I wasn't going to lie to get it.

"Um, not really. I just met him on the walk here and he offered to help."

I could visibly see the relief washing over her face as a small, wry smile broke out on her face. "You're in the hole." I was in. I would tee off on Bethpage Black in 20 minutes. I just had to wait for the group on the tee, the group on deck, and then it would be my turn. I said a hearty thank you.

So, with no sign of Buscemi and a tee time in hand, I turned around and walked over to try my hand at a few putts on the practice green. As I would discover then, and would experience throughout the round, I had never putted on greens as fast as these. I came to understand first-hand what roll out meant, as my first 10 or so putts went cruising past the hole. I just pretended I was putting to the next hole.

Every serious golfer knows that the sign on the 1st tee at Beth-page Black warns that the course is "extremely difficult" and is only meant for "highly skilled" golfers. I didn't yet know what was meant by this level of difficulty, but I was about to find out. Designed by A.W. Tillinghast as part of a Depression era public-works project, the Black course opened in 1936. It began as, and continues to be, one of the best public examples of classical golf architecture. Tillinghast, whose work in the United States from the turn of the century through the Depression was extensive, is most revered for his designs of Somerset Hills (1917), Quaker Ridge (1918), Baltusrol (1922), Winged Foot (1923), San Francisco Golf Club (1924), and Bethpage Black (1936). His three designs at Bethpage are clearly the most notable public courses on the list. While the pros played the course from over 7,400 yards, the three other singles and I would be teeing it up from the middle/white tees, which still measured a healthy 6,600 yards.

On the 1st tee, however, the tee box is so tight that the chosen box is a distinction without a difference. We would all be playing right in front of the sign, with a larger-than-usual crowd watching to make sure we were "skilled" enough to play the Black course. I don't know what would've happened if I had hit my drive 20 yards or missed the ball completely. Luckily, I didn't have to find out. But I don't know if I've been more nervous than that first drive. Predictably, I didn't swing through aggressively enough, and my ball, though hit well, faded into the right rough. I'm sure that rough gets a ton of play from golfers like me, who are more skilled in their minds than in reality.

Nevertheless, we were off, and I was so excited. It's a steep climb down from the 1st tee, and then a long walk up the fairway. I could see the 18th fairway off to the left, and some of the thickest rough I had ever seen in between. As I would come to realize repeatedly during the round, Bethpage Black defines what it means to get it back in play. I did find my ball on the right side, and all things considered, the lie wasn't terrible. I was able to get a 5-iron on the ball and played it under the tree branches in front of me. While the ball didn't have enough juice to get all the way to the green, it came pretty close. I was able to hit a nice chip to about four feet and magically sunk the putt. My compatriots—none of whom had parred the hole—congratulated me on the first par of the round. There wouldn't be many more.

As we walked under the road, Billy, one of my partners for the day, asked me how often I played the Black course. "Never," I responded.

"Really? Well, you're in for a treat. Look back there," he said as he pointed behind us and to the left. "The 15th hole is the hardest hole on the course. The front nine is much easier than the back." I didn't know what to say. Was he congratulating me for my fine save on the 1st, or mocking me for enjoying it? It may have been both.

We arrived on the 2nd tee and I was first up. We sized up the 350-yard hole. I knew that driver was not the right play, both because the dogleg left would mean certain right rough for me, and because the fairway looked impossibly narrow. I pulled 3-wood and hit what I thought was a good shot. Unfortunately, my straight drive was just a bit too long for the curve of the fairway, and I landed straight in the right rough, my ball dropped down deep in the grass.

Earlier, Buscemi had directed me to use a 7-iron to punch back to the fairway any ball that found the deep rough. At the time, I had dismissed his edict as nothing more than drunken hyperbole. But as we arrived at the place where we had all seen my ball land, and none of us could initially find it, I started to believe him. We did find my ball, nestled down in about six inches of rough. I pulled out my 7-iron and I did in fact simply punch it back out to the fairway. Thank you, Buscemi.

From the fairway, I faced a 125-yard uphill shot to the elevated green. With the pin in sight and nothing more, I took an uncertain swing and came up out of my shot, sending the ball long and low. From the back of the green, I had only a chip to get back on to the putting surface to about 30 feet. Two putts later, and I was in with a double bogey. I shook off the bad result as best I could. Billy had a magnificent par save. I give him a get-to-know-you fist pump and we walked to the 3rd tee.

From the tee box, the 160 yards to the pin seemed benign enough. It was a straight shot, with bunkers and rough to carry. Billy, however, assured me that the green was very difficult, titled severely from back to front, and the sand and rough were no bargain. If my playing partners were trying to be helpful with their advice, I wished they would have saved their attention for themselves. But after seeing Billy and the other two miss the green, I stepped forward with my 6-iron, taking an extra club to face the wind that had seemed to pick up right as I was getting ready to tee off. I hit a great shot to the green, just about 18 feet above the hole.

As we stepped off the tee, Billy asked me why I was at Bethpage. "I'm escaping a day with my wife's seven sisters." That's a conversation starter if there ever was one. The requisite questions: "Seven sisters?," "No brothers?," "Where was your wife born in the order?," and the accompanying comment, "I feel for her father!" I've told this factoid to numerous golfers over the years and the questions (and comment) are always the same.

I laughed. "One of her sisters is getting married, our kids are off with grandma, and I have the day to myself while the women have their sister time."

"Good choice!" Billy confidently announced. I agreed readily. When we arrived at the green, I could see the steep slope they had been referring to. I would have to putt straight down the hill. Although I did manage to two-putt, I barely touched the ball and watched it roll, and roll, and roll down the hill. It was the first time in my life that I had really experienced roll-out in a round.

My second par in the first three holes. Ever so briefly, I actually felt confident as we walked down the hill to see the magnificent 4th hole. Billy said, "here's your first wow! moment." I agreed: the 4th hole took my breath away. The entry point is fairly narrow, with trees on both sides of the tee. But looking past the trees, the view is stunning. It's difficult—nearly impossible—to figure out where to hit the ball. It's as if there are only islands of fairway, and more sand and rough than anything else. Billy pointed straight away: "Just land it there." I squinted to see what he meant—yes, I think I can see some fairway. I would have guessed Billy was in his early thirties, clean cut with all the latest golfing paraphernalia. Blue pants and a white belt screamed "pro," but his game was clearly not as advanced as his likely success in his profession.

Walking with Billy, I switched the topic. "Have any kids?"

"Not yet" he uttered, "first one is due later this year. Any advice?" I found my ball in the thinned out rough right and long of the fairway, and assessed my situation. I didn't think I could advance my ball more than 100 yards, and I wasn't convinced that it would get up and over the hill to the next segment of fairway. Anything short would leave me stuck in the rough, or more likely at the bottom of the cavernous bunker ahead. I also might pull the ball sharply, into the left rough where all hope for finding my ball would likely be lost. So, I did the sensible thing: I followed Buscemi's advice and punched out back to the fairway. The medicine didn't taste great, but I had to take it.

Billy and the other two were also punching out, so no time for conversation. I was thinking about what I would say to Billy, who had just asked me for advice for a soon-to-be-father. After all, it had all happened recently for me, so one would think that I would have a lot to say. But what do you say to an expecting father? *It's the greatest thing in your life? It's easy? You'll be so exhausted you can't imagine?* I hadn't thought about what to say. My third shot left me 10 yards over the back of the green. A chip and two putts later, I was in for a well-earned bogey on a very tough hole.

For the next 10 holes, I struggled off the tee, visiting the knee-deep rough on multiple occasions. A few highlights, like a great 4-iron to the 8th green leading to a two-putt par, a solid drive and 3-wood to the tough 10th green led to another par, and a great 8-iron on the par-three 14th that produced my best draw ball flight of the day. During those holes, I declined to give Billy advice and instead asked him how he was feeling about becoming a father—I had decided to listen more than talk about fatherhood. At first, he was reserved and used words like "excited" and phrases like "looking forward to it." Later, after opening up a bit, he shared, "the thing I'm most worried about is I will lose myself. I will be unrecognizable to myself in a few years." I knew what he meant.

"Yeah, that's core," I replied. "I don't think I can be a good father if I can't be myself. It's really hard to be a good father at all. It's even harder to be a good one who stays true to himself." I'm not sure I knew exactly what I was saying. *Hard not to be exhausted? Hard not to treat my kids the same way my father treated me? Hard to keep my pre-fatherhood identity? Did I even want to?*

As we walked down the hill toward the green, I thought of the journey I had taken to be there on this day. From the 4am wakeup, to the subways and trains, to the hike up the hill with the was-he-or-wasn't-he a body chipper Buscemi, to the parade of poor shots, I was here on the 14th green with a 10-footer for birdie. *Don't blow it.* I don't know if I could have hit a more cautious putt—I settled for a par.

Maybe to get me out of the doldrums, or maybe to intimidate us (for what?), Billy announced that "now the course gets hard!" Well, I was plenty intimidated by the course already, and I was good at the whole catch-and-release thing, so I went back across the road ready for the final four. As we turned the corner, we saw a large plaque in the ground announcing the tee where the pros played the 2002 US Open. I had watched that tournament just a few years before, not realizing that we were witnessing the last major battle between Tiger Woods and Phil Michelson (Tiger won by three strokes).

But I wasn't thinking of the future as we bore witness to the impossibly long 15th hole, I was thinking about the impossibility of it. *They hit it from here!?* It just didn't seem possible. We bantered our way forward, with requisite oohs and aahs, and camped out instead at the still-robust 430-yard white tee box. I think my mind was on the pros, and not on myself, because my swing was quite lazy, with plenty of arms and not enough body as I came across the top and put the dreaded slice on my ball.

With some of the thickest rough on the course to the right of the already mystical 15th, I put on my mountaineering boots and set off to find my ball. From this point, however, the best all of us could do was a 7-iron (Buscemi strikes again!) perpendicularly back to the fairway. From there, we all looked at the mountain—ahem, green complex—looming ahead, knowing that the 200 yards remaining required more height than I could produce. Billy took his second dose of medicine and hit a wedge 100 yards to set up another wedge. I wasn't so prudent, pulling a 3-iron and expecting a hero shot that there was no chance I had in my bag. Predictably, I came up very short, landing—and stopping—on the steep upslope. I slashed a pitch up the hill and over the green. Two uphill putts later, and another double bogey.

The 16th was even longer, but thankfully downhill. And yet, this 457-yard par four from the white tees was simply cruel. I needed a change in perspective. I convinced myself that it was a reachable par five and played a really good drive. It wasn't perfect—it still had plenty of fade on it—but from the elevated tee and the straight fairway, I saw my ball floating through the sky and landing sweetly on the right side of the fairway. Billy and I reconnected going down the hill. He was much more at ease talking. He said, "I've been so focused on myself for the past decade. I finished college, went straight to medical school and became a surgeon. Even when I met my wife, I didn't really have to give up anything. I'm worried that's what fatherhood will bring." I was glad for his candor, and I knew the feeling. We men are so used to being able to put ourselves first.

I said what I felt: "You know, I didn't realize just how much I would *love* putting someone else first. I didn't realize that losing a bit of my self-centeredness would actually make me happy." Billy smiled, somewhat doubtful I'm sure, but I think he heard me. And as we arrived at our balls in the fairway, I realized that it was true: as overwhelmed as I was, being a father made me happy.

With 250 yards remaining to the green, however, I was not optimistic about carrying the bunker fronting the green on the right. There was an opening on the left, however, so I aimed my 3-iron there. I struck what I thought was an excellent shot, but I landed well short. A good pitch, the two-bounce-and-stop variety, would give me great look at par. But it wasn't meant to be, as my cautious pitch came up 15 feet short. Two more putts—that was my theme for the round—and I was at the bottom of the cup for yet another bogey.

So, we turned into the wind for the par-three 17th. At just under 200 yards, to a two-tiered, peanut-shaped green surrounded by deep rough and even deeper bunkers, this would be the most difficult par three on the course. I chose my hybrid, hoping that a high shot would be held back just enough by the wind to stop my ball on the green. It wasn't a smooth swing, however, and my Titleist went right of the green and came to rest in some of that ankle deep rough right of the green. I made bogey, but was excited for the finishing hole.

After climbing the hill to the final tee box, I remembered Buscemi telling me that he'd see me after the 18th green. *Did he really mean he'd stick around?* I put the thought out of my head and hit a fantastic tee shot to the middle of the fairway, reflecting a kind of smooth, worry-free swing that I hadn't really seen all day. Billy and I walked down the hill and onto the fairway, reminiscing about each of our favorite shots of the day. We were a good group—the four singles who had somehow easily split into twosomes—who loved to tell tales about the great shots, and quickly forget the bad ones. We laughed that the golfing gods had to allow the four of us one hole to all be in the fairway.

The second shot on the 18th is straight up a large hill, with bunkers left and right, the one on the right jutting into the green severely. I thought I hit a perfect 7-iron, but it was just a bit too far right, and it landed at the top of the deep bunker and rolled back down. As I walked up the hill and surveyed the damage with a smile, I told myself that I had to experience Black's bunkers one final time. I would need a full swing to get my ball up and out of the bunker, but I had plenty of green to the left to work with and gave it a mighty cut. The ball came out high and long, landing and stopping on the left side of the green. Although the putt dove down to the right, I assessed the speed well enough and needed only a three-footer to close out the round. I made it, and I shook hands with Billy, talking about the next time we would meet on the Black course and wishing him the best with fatherhood. Then, I looked up to see Buscemi's buckteeth smiling wide. *Shit.*

I walked off the green in the only possible direction—up the hill—and Buscemi practically tackled me with excitement. "How was it?"

"Great" I said, with more recognition than enthusiasm. *What could he want?*

"Can you get me that drink that you promised?" With those words, I had the vague recognition of promising to buy him a drink. It's the kind of promise that people make in the middle of a drink-induced haze—what my high school friends called beer goggles. I was drunk before the round, for sure, drunk on the hope of playing the Black course. Now that it was over, I was hungry and wanted to get my boys some souvenirs from the pro shop. But I believed that I had made that promise to Buscemi, and one to keep promises, I went into the restaurant with him and bought him that drink. The bartender asked me if I knew Buscemi. "No, I just met him this morning."

The bartender looked at me a long time and explained, "this is his gig; this is how he drinks." I finally understood. I was Buscemi's mark for the day. Tomorrow, there would be a new mark. There was no woodchipper planned, just an alcoholic who had found an innovative way to get his fix.

I paid my tab, gave Buscemi his drink, and walked out as fast as I could, saying something vague about having to get back to the city. With my clubs in tow, I made a pitstop at the pro shop, then began my hike back down the hill to the train station. I didn't look back, figuring that Buscemi no longer needed me, and at that very moment my cell phone died. I had found my way to Bethpage via GPS; I would have to find my way back to Manhattan the old-fashioned way. So, I hiked down the endless hill, and after many false turns, I found the train station. From there, I rode the train in a kind of Tillinghast haze, a bit less overwhelmed having survived the legendary Black course.

As I rode the train back in, I was excited to see Theresa and join the rest of her family, but I also realized how much I needed this adventure. I had taken a train ride on blind faith, accepted help from a stranger, met a soon-to-be father, and it paid off. I was exhausted, but from something other than caring for our child. I had managed to do what Billy was afraid of losing—I took some time for myself—and I was grateful for it. It reminded me how much of a sanctuary that golf can be in the life of a father, and how much we need it. I was equally overwhelmed by fatherhood and Bethpage Black, but the day had been for me. I could have done a lot worse.

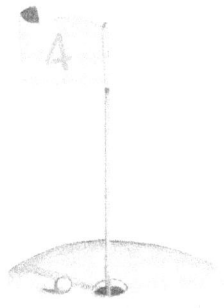

Care

(2005-06)

We were very excited. After a long search for a day care, we had found Seward Child Care Center close to our home. Our first day care was at an older woman's home. She was a warm and kind woman who seemed to love the dozen or so kids at a variety of ages that she hosted in her home every day. Yet one day, we had to pick up Aidan early. We arrived to find all the kids glued to the television. When we asked the woman why they were all watching TV, she told us it was "TV Tuesday." We took Aidan out that day and never returned.

So, we searched for a better alternative. Theresa and I listed our day-care needs: spending time with kids his age, playing, reading, napping, and eating. Well-supervised but with the freedom to explore his world. We wanted him to meet new friends, learn about new worlds, and be safe, comfortable, and happy. We wanted him to be able to get dirty, to learn how to clean up, to run when it was safe and sleep without interruption. And it couldn't be us. I was already back to work, and Theresa would be soon. We found it in spades at Seward. It seemed perfect. It was a building specifically designed for child care, right in the middle of a quiet neighborhood. There were three main rooms: the Teddy Bear Room for 15 months to age three, the Polar Bear Room for three- and four-year-olds, and the Penguin Room for the oldest kids the year before kindergarten. Aidan would be a Polar Bear, if we decided to send him there, and Elliott could go to the Teddy Bear Room soon.

Seward was well-known: a popular choice, it often had a waitlist. We would have to act soon if we wanted to send him there. It wasn't a hard choice—the space was perfect. The Polar Bear Room was a large space, with a clear nap area, age-appropriate toys, plenty of sun, right-sized chairs and tables, cubbies for every child, perfectly sized sinks and toilets, and an idyllic play space on the property. It was also a short walk from a large park and slightly further to the mighty Mississippi. We knew the moment we arrived that this was right for Aidan, and only took a minute of conversation to decide to fill out the application. He was admitted shortly thereafter.

But while we were excited to see the space, knowing that it was the kind of place where he would thrive—with kids his age, clearly engaged and caring teachers, and a perfectly structured daily space for him—he was not excited. As much as a three-year-old can convey it, he told us in no uncertain terms that he didn't want to go. He abhorred change, and this was a big one. We put on the "you'll love it!" routine, but he wasn't buying it. So when I had the (mis)fortune of being the one to take our son to day care the first day, I found myself giving him a pep talk: "You're going to love it! There's so much fun here. There are amazing toys. There's a fun monkey bar and sand box. The food is really good. And you'll meet new friends!"

He looked at me with a what-the-hell-are-you-smoking look, a look that I would see over and over again. He was not to be persuaded. We had taken him out of the Tuesday TV day care, where he could ride a big wheel in the backyard and eat junk food (and watch TV!). Mostly, we took him out of his comfort zone.

We arrived at Seward right as it opened. They allowed parents of first-day kids to stay for a while, to help their kids adjust. He held my hand while I introduced him to his teacher—I had no idea that a three-year-old could squeeze that tightly. Becky was warm and welcoming. She asked if she could show him around.

"Can my dad come?"

"Sure," Becky replied. She gave me a look as if to say *that isn't ideal—why don't you tell him that he should explore the place with me?* But either because I sensed that he wouldn't do it without a fight, or because I wasn't ready, I accompanied him on the tour. First, we went over to the reading area, where there was a comfy rug and books galore. Becky explained that sometimes she would read to the kids, and sometimes they would pull out picture books. Of course, they couldn't read yet, but they could certainly look at pictures.

Next, she moved the 10 feet over to the art area, where there were myriad art supplies, and several kids were drawing at the table. Aidan, never much interested in art much to his artist-mom's chagrin, looked at the tables with a mix of fear and disinterest. But I was excited. The kids were happy and engaged, and it would be a place where he might discover some well-hidden interests.

Next, the food area. Aidan perked up a bit. Becky showed us the snack and lunch area, the cubbies, the bathroom, and the kitchen. There were picture instructions everywhere—how to turn on the water, how to wash hands, how to clean a plastic plate. I knew we had made the right choice, but I could tell that Aidan was as skeptical as ever.

Then, Becky brought us outside. There were swings, monkey bars, balls, and a sand box. Kids weren't outside yet—they would go outside every morning and every afternoon, for an hour of play time. Aidan looked at what normally would be his happy place and could only think of his fear. Somehow, he must have sensed that the tour was ending and I would be leaving soon. He wasn't having it.

We walked back to the Polar Bear Room, where more kids had arrived. There was a great mix of boys and girls, with lots of excitement in the room. It was overwhelming for Aidan. He asked to be picked up and held. I did some more encouraging: "You're going to have so much fun! Daddy has to leave now. I have to go to work."

The dreaded words. My son began to cry. Some kids slowly build up, from a barely audible whimper to a solid cry to a scream. As a three-year-old, Aidan was much more Tesla than Prius—he had plenty of torque. Becky came over immediately, taking Aidan from my arms. He was screaming bloody murder the second I handed him over, and it only got worse from there. She took him over to the reading area and picked up one of her favorite books. She called the other kids over for morning reading time. I don't know how they heard her over my son's building-shaking screams, but somehow they did. Kids are amazingly resilient.

I knew this was a moment of truth. If I went back to him, I would be conveying to him that all he needed to do was cry and I'd come back. So, I couldn't go back. I had to keep walking.

It wasn't easy. For three years, I had responded to his cries to comfort him. I knew that it had made a difference—Theresa and I could soothe the most serious tears with a simple hug. At this moment, though, I knew I had to ignore him, and trust that he would settle down with Becky and the other kids very soon. He had to know that I was going to leave each day, that he would be fine, and that he actually might have a great time. But the only way to help him to learn that hard life lesson was to keep walking, so I did. I

still carry those screams in my mind, and the knowledge that I intentionally didn't comfort him.

I will never really know what that first day was like for him. When I picked him up after work, he was definitely happy to see me—there's nothing quite like the feeling of a three-year-old seeing you and coming running for a big hug. But it wasn't the kind of save-me-from-this-awful-place hug. It was more of an I'm-glad-to-see-you hug. I asked Becky how the day went. She said "great!" and handed me the daily report. The teary faced emoji was checked—he had clearly cried some of the day. But the notes were generally positive. He had eaten normally, used the bathroom himself, played outside, and seemed to do well with the other kids. I don't know if it happened that day, or soon after, but it seemed that he would be making some friends. I let out a long, deep exhale.

I don't know when it happened, or exactly how, but I noticed that Aidan was hanging out with two other boys at Seward: Noah and Bruno. It's a funny thing about how young kids make friends. They don't announce it or plan it, they just do it. They start doing things together and become friends. Our son was spending more and more time with Noah and Bruno, and even started talking about them at home. Soon, we found ourselves meeting their parents—Cindy and Karl, Kate, and Regina, at pick up or drop off, all noticing that they were forming a mini-Three Musketeers. We resolved to find time to get the kids together outside of day care, and lo and behold, these two boys become my son's best friends for the next eight or so years. We become close friends with the parents, sharing hundreds of play dates, travelling to state parks together for overnight camping trips, hosting and attending many, many birthday parties, playing on park baseball and soccer teams.

The boys grew up to be very different, and their friendships didn't last once they entered middle school. But for the idyllic years from the Polar Bear Room through the end of elementary school, Aidan had found his people.

The Classic at Madden's (Brainerd, MN)

We've heard of some of the famous golf course architects. From classic figures such as Old Tom Morris, Donald Ross, Alister MacKenzie, C.B. Macdonald, Seth Raynor, and A.W. Tillinghast, to modern architects such as Pete Dye, Robert Trent Jones, and Bill Coore, even former star players such as Jack Nicklaus, Ben Crenshaw, and Arnold Palmer, and contemporary architects such as Tom Doak, Gil Hanse, and Tom Fazio. Many golf course architects become household names for those of us who love golf. Scott Hoffman, in all likelihood, is not one of them. Yet the course he designed and managed for many years in northern Minnesota, The Classic, is one of the most brilliant layouts in the United States.

The property is part of Madden's Resort, a typical northern Minnesota summer resort catering to families. With a variety of child-friendly activities and a property largely devoid of speeding cars, this resort attracts families from across the Northern Plains states. Yet for golfers, before the arrival of the Classic in 1997, Madden's played second fiddle to other area golf courses designed by more famous architects such as Palmer's Deacon's Lodge and Jones' Dutch Legacy.

Now ranked 59th in the *Golf Digest* America's 100 Greatest Public Courses, the Classic is one of the premier tracks in the country, no matter its remoteness, and no matter how unknown its designer. The course is tough. Stretching over 7,100 yards from the tips, with narrow fairways pinched by towering northern Minnesota pines and plenty of water, even the most accomplished players will be challenged at the Classic. And not being one of those accomplished players, I stood on the practice green thinking about breaking 80 ... or even 90. The practice green sends an immediate message—don't expect a flat lie on the green anywhere. It is one of the steepest, most undulating and penal greens I've ever experienced. I struck my first putt—a slick five-foot downhiller—slightly too hard and watched in hysterics as it rolled and rolled, ultimately coming to rest at least 50 feet below the hole. It might have been easier to putt on Everest. At least the laughter at my horrific first putt kept me loose—I would need it.

Hoffman had an incredible piece of property to mold. The grounds are hilly—I'm not sure if they are Augusta National hilly (I've never set foot on those hallowed grounds)—but a walk through the Classic is as tough as the playing conditions. And the 1st hole, what appears to be a benign 500-yard opening par-five, is no slouch. Mercifully, I had chosen to play the black tees, one step up from the tour tees, for about 6,700 yards. It would be plenty of a test. It was also a test I would be taking alone, as the group of friends I was scheduled to play with had been called to various family duties.

From the tee box, the 1st hole is deceiving. Looking straight ahead and up the hill, only the first 250 or so yards of fairway are visible. On the left side of the fairway sits a large and deep bunker, right at the hill's peak. Since it was uphill, I was unlikely to crest the hill … I just wanted to avoid the bunker. Yet at this stage in my golfing career, I had two main shots off the tee: slice or fade. I would choose a fade. I had warmed up well this day, and felt loose. Yet unlike the wide-open practice range, the driving areas on the course were much tighter—hemmed in by massive tree lines. Hoffman's brilliance here is showing the teeth of the course and hiding the safe zones.

My time had come to hit away, and hit away I did. The opening drive was what I would call "decent." It wasn't a booming drive by any means, and it definitely had more fade than desired. From the tee, I couldn't tell if my decent drive would end up stymied behind a tree, or sitting pretty in the fairway. I proceeded with cautious optimism. But with extra width to the fairway on the right especially in the 230-yard wipey fade zone, I was fine just off the fairway, still on the uphill.

The second shot challenges every aspect of a golfer's game. The fairway is narrow, maybe 25 paces across. It travels up then down and cambers left and right, twisted like a corkscrew roller coaster. Too far left, and the ball would disappear in the thick trees. Too far right, and the more open trees would likely lead to a found ball, but one where a game of tree Pachinko was the only option. Needless to say, the shot had to be straight. I looked at my lie—thin rough, with the ball above my feet. Although the lie was likely to send the ball left, my swing was likely to send the ball right. I needed to split the difference. Relying more on the realities of my swing than the impacts of the lie, I aimed slightly left of center and grasped my 5-iron. The lie wouldn't allow a 3-wood, and I couldn't see the advantage of added length. I played to my strengths and sent the ball off toward the left of the fairway with a clear fade. It landed on the downslope and trundled down to the bottom of the hill, remaining in the fairway, just barely. It would be about 80 yards to the green for my third shot.

Like many golfers, 80 yards is a tough distance for me. My 60-degree lob wedge can sometimes travel that distance, but only if the conditions are perfect, the green is even with the fairway, and I strike it perfectly. More often than not, it comes up short of 80 yards. Alternatively, I can play a three-quarter sand wedge. Finding the "three quarter" point of my swing, however, is a challenge. And this shot came from a very tight lie, almost straight uphill. It would play closer to a full 100-yard sand wedge, but I worried that with a false front, that I would get the ball to the correct surface and spin it back down the hill, likely to my feet. I was uncertain but had to commit.

I was between clubs, so I took a little off a sand wedge. My swing felt good, and the contact was excellent, but it came up short. Fortunately for me, while the ball started to reverse back down the hill, it rolled just to the right, stopping at the collar of the right green-side bunker. A chip I could handle to the pin, and a tap-in par. So far, so good.

Just a short walk from the 1st green, through a stand of trees, down to the flat 2nd tee. Again, Hoffman does an amazing job hiding the safe zones and showing the dangers. A large lake sits just off the right of the tee box and juts into the sight lines ahead. The feeling is that the entire shot is over water, with a pin perched just a few feet past the water line. The reality is much more benign, with plenty of room to the left of the water, and a large green angling short left to long right. Clearly, Hoffman wanted to punish the long draw and the short fade. I would have to hit mine solidly to clear the water, but with enough height to hold the green. I did it, sort of.

The hole measured 150 yards, so I pulled my 8-iron. I took a few easy practice swings, tried to ignore the lake in my peripheral vision, took a deep breath of fresh northern air, and put the club to the ball. It was a solid strike, with only a slight fade pushing it to the right. I missed the green, but just barely, with my ball coming to rest in the rough just to the right. As I walked to the green, I looked over the expanse of the lake. With no other golfers close by, it felt like I had the course to myself. I could hear the trees rustle, but far above. I heard birds, but had no ability to identify their calls. I just soaked it in. I wish my sons were with me, just to realize how great life could be. I'm sure they would find this kind of serenity somewhere in their lives, but it was sure hard to beat the feeling of this golf course, this day.

In all this calm solitude, many thoughts came to me. *I wonder what kind of men they will grow into? What can I do now to help them become the kind of men they want to be? Should I push them, like Earl Woods pushed the most famous golfer on the planet? How much should I comfort them? What can I say so they will listen? How can I listen so they will talk?*

These thoughts fill my mind with uncertainty, not the type of conviction I would need at The Classic. I found my ball nestled in the rough just short-right of the green. The pin was in the back, a solid 20 yards from my ball. I pulled my sand wedge and judged whether I could make solid contact. This was the type of lie where a flub was eminently possible. There seemed to be layers of grass behind the ball, and any contact with the ground before the ball would ensure that my ball would travel five yards at best. I took some practice swings, committing to the feel of accelerating through the ball. A deep breath. *This is the type of shot I have to be able pull off. No excuses. It's like driving: you can't be indecisive. You have to make a decision, act on it, and live with the consequences, whatever they are.*

I nearly holed the chip. I looked around—not a single person within earshot. No one saw me pull it off. Was it a dream? If so, where were the crowds? I heard the applause in my mind and acknowledged the crowd with the best tour-pro impression I could muster.

As if building to a crescendo, Hoffman perched the 3rd tee box on a mini-peninsula, overlooking another large part of the lake. The shot presented yet another visual conundrum. As the crow flies, the shot is probably only 250 yards, from a peninsula tee to a peninsula green to the right. Getting the ball to stop on the narrow strip of green, however, is nearly impossible. The bailout is to the left, where the fairway appears wide enough to land, but also easy to miss. Left and long are massive northern pines, short and right is the lake, then a 40-yard-wide bunker, and then two pine trees, standing alone on the right side of the fairway like pre-teen boys at their school dance. The play is a draw off those two trees, landing just left of the trees in the fairway. Unfortunately, I don't have that shot. I would have to start the ball at or over the trees to the left and fade it back to the fairway, taking care not to slice too far, either into the trees, bunker, or water. As I mentioned, Hoffman understands the psychology of danger on a golf course. He puts you in challenging situations and forces you to make decisions, and to avoid the hazards, you have to commit.

With a full distance from tee- to-green of only 330 yards, I knew that a 200-yard shot would be fine. Instead of a relaxed tempo that would send the ball high in the air, coming to rest in the fairway, I produced a nervous and choppy tempo and a ball that corkscrewed directly at the two trees, coming to rest somewhere to the right of them. *Wherever it came to rest, I will be fine. It's a spectacular golf course, with a stunning lake to my right and nothing but the sounds of birds. I would take it, wherever it is. I'll just play it. Figure it out when I get there.* My thoughts were swirling, oscillating between my boys and my round. *How can I ever answer the big questions about my boys? There's no one I can turn to who has done it. No father, or grandfather to consult for advice. Just Theresa and I figuring it out when we get there.*

I walked along the lake, lost in my thoughts, looking for errant Pro V1s on the edge of the lake. As I approached the trees, I scanned all around for that little white ball. No luck. Then, I spotted it in the middle of the long bunker, perched on the sand like a conch shell, beckoning for my attention. I looked for the green. A straight shot would have to come out cleanly from the bunker, carry about 80 yards of water, and come to rest somewhere on the peninsula green. It would be a full wedge shot, with more like a hope and a prayer than any particular skill. It takes focus to hit the ball cleanly enough out of the sand from this distance. I grabbed my wedge, descended into the bunker, dug in my feet, choked up on my club, and took a final look at the pin. My shot came off cleanly, and while it was a bit too short to reach the meat of the green, it did clear that water and come to rest on the collar. *That's what I'm talking about!* I laughed at myself as I gave a Mickelson-esque fist pump for absolutely no one's entertainment. This was most definitely not the 13th at Augusta from the pine straw. But it was my own little miracle shot.

The short walk to the green gave me the opportunity to search for a bald eagle, which I had heard earlier somewhere high in the trees, wondering who I was and whether I was friend or foe. My ball was easily recognizable on the collar, just 22 feet from the pin. I took a deep breath, read the putt from four directions as if it meant something, and proceeded to underestimate the degree of downhill, leaving myself a five-foot comebacker. Had I completely forgotten the practice green? Was I really going to throw away a par after that miraculous bunker shot? It was a confident putt, with just enough juice to drop in the cup on the front side. *Phew!*

Unfortunately, the rights off the tee continued and my hot-ish start was quickly sunk. A double, three bogeys, and two pars brought me to the turn in 41. My early round distracted thoughts—stuck between thoughts of my sons and thoughts of my round—were sufficient to sink my chance at par. *Three holes in, three pars. Was my first par round in play? ... I love my sons so much, but I have no idea how to be the father they need. There's no training for this. I can't go to the fatherhood practice green. I can't take a lesson. Are they destined to be effectively fatherless, as I was? ... Today was the day! I hadn't been hitting great shots off the tee, but I had some outstanding recovery shots and luck seemed to be on my side. Maybe this was it!*

It's strange—in golf and life—what we choose to view as important. Was it really important that Aidan brushed his teeth every night? I was on him like a fly on shit, making him think it was the single most important activity in his day. Maybe it was, maybe it wasn't. What about Elliott? Did it really matter that he ate well before bedtime to protect his teeth and gums? In the grand scheme of raising sons, these were relatively minor daily reminders. But they sure felt important to me each day, and my boys would hold onto the unmistakable feeling that if they didn't do these things, there would be serious consequences.

Back to the golf ... Did it really matter that I had a hot start? Did it really matter that I blew my chances over four tough holes? As I moved to the back nine, I reassessed my prospects for this day. *It was a solid start in which 72 seemed within reach. I'm just five-over. Maybe now I can break 80 ... a 38 would do it.* As I've learned over my golfing life, these kinds of thoughts are devastating to the focused, stay-within-yourself and live-in-the-moment mind. I was filled with these unhelpful thoughts as I meandered through the woods to the next tee.

On the scorecard, the 466-yard par-five 10th seems like a typo. Even those of us who struggle to drive it more than 250 yards could be flirting with an eagle. From the tee box, the downhill slope of the fairway makes the par five seem even more reachable, but this par five is much more complex. The teeing grounds are hemmed in by towering trees, like a body entering an MRI machine. I don't suffer from claustrophobia, but this tee shot gave me no sense of comfort. As if the swallowing trees weren't enough, a small creek runs down the right side, and then crosses the fairway about 25 yards short of the hole. The next time I played the course, I knew to play less than driver. There is nothing to be gained being farther down the fairway. But I was not knowledgeable and prudent, I was ignorant and distracted and sent my drive high, far, and too far right. While I could see the first bounce, and maybe the second, the third was decidedly in the trees to the right.

I was able to find my ball, but it was completely stymied behind not one, but three tightly packed trees. There was nothing to do but pitch out sideways and swallow hard. I did it, and had about 220 yards remaining. From this distance, a solidly struck hybrid would certainly clear the creek, but the green looked like a postage stamp, and I didn't want to risk losing my Titleist. So, I swallowed hard again and wedged it down to 100 yards. Another strong wedge—almost a carbon copy of the last one—managed to find the back-to-front sloping green, about 25 feet from the pin. I enjoyed the view—a creek deep in the woods with this magnificent golf course cut amid its beauty. After two tentative putts, I was in with bogey.

From the fairway of the 11th hole, I could see that the green was elevated, pear-shaped, and two tiers. With the pin on the left (lower) tier, I knew I had to be precise with my pitching wedge. I hit it well, but with more distance than planned, I had a ticklish 10-footer down the hill. I fought beauty-distraction, like trying to write with my wife in the room, and somehow managed to nudge my ball down to makable range, where I tapped in for bogey.

With four pars and three bogeys over the final seven holes, I played closely to my almost-single-digit-handicap. As I walked up the 18th fairway, a steep hill through the woods, I wondered: *Why had I put so much pressure on myself? Why would I possibly care about the score? No one else cares what you shoot. The only thing that mattered was how much fun I was having. Too much of the glorious round was spent chasing a score. What's wrong with me?* All of those thoughts flowed through my mind as I realized just how uptight I had felt. Catch and release. I swung my lob wedge with almost cloud-like ease and landed smoothly on the green. I almost made the 30-footer, prompting a polite applause from the foursome watching from the balcony. They probably saw my lousy 4-iron as well. Anyway, I walked off with an 82.

Looking back, sometimes it's great to play a round alone in the woods, finding fun in my own thoughts, apart from the social demands of our lives. I thought about Aidan's time adjusting to day care and finding comfort away from me and Theresa. These are hard but necessary truths. We have to be able to take care of ourselves, no matter how hard it is or how lonely it feels. I couldn't help my sons learn that lesson by comforting them every time they needed me. Sometimes, I had to walk away. As for how I played, I had a mixture of focused swings and others where I lacked commitment.

But lesson learned: in golf and in fatherhood, it's almost never clear and easy, and execution is always in doubt. But once you've done your research, you just have to make a decision. The most important thing to do is be committed.

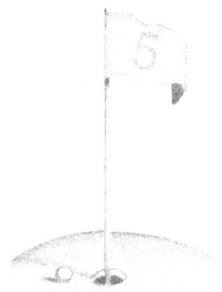

Sleep

(2006-07)

Aidan was a terrible sleeper. Theresa and I told this to each other dozens of times. We stated it as a fact of his nature. He wouldn't sleep through the night for most of his first year. Even in his second year, he woke up constantly. We tried everything: comforting him, leaving him, blankets, no blankets, music, food before bed, no food before bed, soothing foods, sleeping near us, sleeping away from us. We tried it all and nothing seemed to work. He just wouldn't sleep through the night. We asked every question of everyone we could—from our pediatrician to our family members to our friends. We tried just about every suggestion they made. But we never asked *why*: Why didn't he sleep through the night? We had chalked it up to personality traits, or constipation, and most often, just a fact about Aidan. We marveled at Elliott, who slept much better and through the night from a very young age. We knew our boys were different, but we didn't know why. All of that changed when Aidan was four, when we spent the weekend at my in-laws.

At their house, we had two beds pushed together, and Aidan slept in one of the beds with us while Elliott was in a crib. Unlike any night since the first few months of his life, we actually spent the night in bed with him. Notice, I didn't write "slept" in the same bed, because the one thing we most certainly did not do that night was sleep. He slept fine, although he still woke up constantly. But watching him—and listening to him—all night long made it readily apparent that he couldn't breathe very well. I don't know if children can suffer from sleep apnea, but I know certain adults cannot get enough oxygen and wake up often throughout the night. Whatever was happening, it was clear that he was waking up because *he couldn't breathe.*

This is one of the many realizations we have had that sits with me long after the discovery. As a father, it's hard to avoid the woulda-shoulda-coulda second-guessing. But I did it constantly. *How did I not notice? How could I have not thought of it? I should have known. If I had noticed, I could have brought him to the doctor much, much sooner. How many more sleep-filled nights would he have had? How much more sleep would we all have had? If only I had paid closer attention to my son. When he was waking up, he was telling us something.* I carried all of these regrets, and others, with me as an early father. I've since learned to let go—the woulda-shoulda-coulda way of thinking doesn't help anyone. It doesn't make me a better father. It doesn't help make my sons' life any better. It's just a pathway to guilt and regret.

But at the time, I was racked with guilt. I called our pediatrician and made an appointment. Aidan was most worried about the shots. Too often, the only thing he remembered about our visits to the doctor were the pokes on his arm. Sorry, but the suckers don't soothe the memories. "Do I have to get a shot?" Tears welled up in his eyes.

"No, you don't need any shots today."

"Good." I didn't tell him this visit was about something much more serious than a few shots. Instead I said, "wanna get a milkshake after the doctor?"

An hour later, we're sitting in a small room, talking to our pediatrician. Dr. Hobbs smiled, and after some relaxing chit-chat about being dads of boys, he leaned in closer to Aidan. "Open wide."

Aidan, who was not a small child, has a very small mouth—always has. Who knows why, but "open wide" is an oxymoron for him: he opened narrow. The doctor pushed in a tongue depressor and let out an audible gasp. He announced, "I think I know what's going on. ... His tonsils and adenoids are *huge!*" Aidan looked at the doctor with a completely blank stare that are so common with young children. There are certain words that they are looking for that will elicit an immediate response. Shot=tears! Milkshake=cheers! He understood that the doctor was talking about him, and I think he knew what *huge* meant—at least that it had something to do with big. But he had no clue what the other words meant, and he didn't know if it meant more shots or a larger milkshake. The doctor tried to explain to him: "there are parts of your body inside your throat that are supposed to be small, like a small grape. But in your body, they are really big, like the biggest lollipop you can imagine." My son's eyes widened as he began to imagine a giant lollipop. I don't know how big it got in his mind, but I'm thinking *Charlie and the Chocolate Factory* big, Veruca-Salt big. When he realized that the doctor was saying that this giant lollipop was inside his throat, he started to cry. I held him and tried to help him understand that it wasn't as big as he imagined—maybe golf-ball sized? That didn't help, but he now knew it was bad.

Dr. Hobbs put on his talking-to-the-parent voice and gave me a tentative diagnosis: "your son has obstructive sleep apnea. During the night, when he's lying on his back, his tonsils and adenoids come together and obstruct the flow of air. He has to wake up to breathe. I need you to take him to see an Ear, Nose, and Throat doctor as soon as possible to decide what to do next." I listened to the words and knew instinctively that he needed to have his tonsils removed. He couldn't go on this way. We couldn't go on this way.

Although I felt enormous guilt that it had taken this long, I was relieved that we were finally on our way to a solution. We went to the ENT doctor, who confirmed the diagnosis of obstructive sleep apnea. The doctor gave us a choice: "have the tonsillectomy and your son will likely be sleeping normally very quickly with no complications, or you can elect not to have the surgery and hope the rest of his body will grow enough soon that he probably will have no trouble sleeping."

Theresa and I talked through the decision. "I feel like the word *choice* is a trap," I said.

"What do you mean?," she asked.

"Do you choose to have the surgery? Feels like they're really asking if we love our son."

"Yeah. 'He needs surgery' feels like, 'If you loved your son, you would have noticed this before he was four years old!'"

Theresa agreed. That feeling of guilt would apparently not give us any peace. We wouldn't make the mistake of doing too little this time. We were going to err on the side of doing too much. Even if he might ultimately grow out of it, what would be lost in the years ahead? And more than anything, we just wanted him to sleep. So, surgery it would be.

He was too young to be nervous. After all, getting nervous depends on knowing what the hell is going on.

I tried to explain to Aidan not just that everything would be okay, but better. "We're going to the hospital to sleep. Daddy will be with you the whole time. When you wake up, the things in your throat will be gone." He started to cry.

"I don't want to go!," he announced.

"I know you don't want to go, but after you wake up, you'll get as much ice cream as you want!" That stopped him in his tracks. He'd never heard of all-you-can-eat ice cream. Now we're talking. Theresa and I shared a smile. Bribery with food always works. For months we had tried to cajole him to use the toilet with no success. The day we added a chocolate reward, he was potty-trained for good.

We showed him our mouths and tried to help him see what tonsils looked like. If this had happened now, we probably would have shown him a video of his own tonsils in action. But this was in the pre-smartphone era, so we decided to make it an adventure. He got to bring his favorite blanket, and we promised that endless cup of ice cream. In all, he finally seemed willing to go along for the ride.

I, on the other hand, was nervous as hell. Aidan was the active type, and so he had gone through dozens of minor injuries in his short time on this earth. We were quite used to hugging and kissing the wounds and making sure everything was healing as it should. But this was another matter entirely. This was a *hospital* and he was going to be put under during the surgery. And while I would be with him before and after the surgery, I most certainly would not be with him during the surgery. I had met the doctor, and I generally trusted the hospital staff. But still, there are always the horror stories, and I couldn't help but fear that I was headed for one.

We drove to the hospital, parked, and checked in. Aidan was given a wristband and a coloring book. I was on autopilot, and it was all heading toward the moment I will never forget: sitting in a pre-operating room, my son laying in my arms, with the anesthesiologist and a nurse sitting next to us. Aidan had a distinctive look of terror, but he didn't say anything. I think he kept expecting me to stop whatever was about to happen. The doctor explained, "I'm going to put a mask on your face and then you will fall asleep." When Aidan gave a puzzled look, the doctor continued: "The mask has a special air that will make you fall asleep." He still looked terrified. But not a word came out of his mouth.

I reassured Aidan: "It's going to be okay, I promise. I will be right here the whole time." I lied. I preach honesty and integrity to my kids—always tell the truth, even if it hurts. But when I really think about it, I have lied to my sons to try to make them feel better. I didn't tell him that I was going to leave the room as soon as he fell asleep. I didn't tell him that I am not allowed in the operating room. I didn't tell him that I would be in a waiting room, filled with all the other anxious parents, counting the minutes until he was done, several hours later. I didn't tell him that it would hurt, probably a lot, when he woke up. I didn't tell him any of these things. I just told him that it would be okay, that I loved him, and that I would be seeing him as soon as he woke up.

I waited, and waited, and waited. No news, no sign of him. It seemed like every other parent was called, and I kept waiting. This can't be good. And, then, suddenly, I heard my name. Everything was a blur for the next few minutes, and I tried to locate my son. The nurses had no doubt seen the look—the look that says, *I'm nervous as hell but can't find a socially acceptable way to express it.* I walked out of the waiting room, looked around every corner, and there was no sight of him. And then, though two swinging doors, a nurse emerged rolling a bed with Aidan asleep, looking far too small to be someone coming out of surgery.

He was rolled into a recovery room, with me at his side. The nurses who kept coming in were ostensibly there to check to make sure Aidan was still asleep, but I think there were really checking to make sure I wasn't panicking. Although it seemed interminable, it was probably just about 15 minutes longer until Aidan started to wake up. Groggy, with a very scratchy throat, Aidan looked at me. I gave him a big smile, said "good morning!" and explained where we were. He looked more confused than concerned, and I told him that good stuff would be coming soon. The nurse came in and told him right away that he could have a popsicle. Aidan lit up—it's amazing what frozen sugar water and food coloring can do. After a popsicle and some time playing on the provided iPad (a newer experience for our boy), Aidan started to complain about his sore throat. About the same time, the doctor came in to check with him. "Aidan has to stay in the hospital overnight unless he can eat something more than popsicles in the next four hours." I had told him we would be going home right after the surgery, so he looked at me waiting for me to tell the doctor that he was wrong, and that we are going home soon. Whether because of his intense desire to get some of the promised ice cream in his stomach, or his dread at having to spend a night away from home (despite my assurances that I would stay with him), Aidan pushed through the pain in his throat and had as much food as they would give him. He started with ice cream, then graduated to apple sauce. I think he would have eaten a steak if they would've let him. But sure enough, after four hours of eating and drinking and playing video games, we were given the green light to go home.

Of course, having parents dote on your every need, while eating unlimited ice cream, is a dream come true for a four-year-old. And Aidan made the most of his opportunity. He must have developed a complex list in his mind, because upon arrival at home he gave

Theresa his ice cream wish list. We had no idea how he knew some of those flavors, but I safely delivered Aidan home and was off to the store to buy his throat soothers. And wouldn't you know it, after a few days of soreness, Aidan was able to sleep through the night. We were all soothed.

After that surgery, Aidan was like a different kid. Where before he was almost always tired and grumpy, he started genuinely laughing throughout the day. He would run and run and laugh and laugh. Elliott—who was one by this time—chased his brother with a crawl, then walked, then ran. They were so bonded, attached in a way that we wouldn't see again for many years.

But I wasn't quite there. The hours of sleep deprivation, worry, and work stress were adding up, putting me on edge. I was more and more irritable, more and more impatient.

Aidan was doing laps in the house one winter day. It was his exercise. His brother was taking a nap. "Too loud," I said. He made more noise. "Too loud!," I said louder. He laughed and ran, giggling around our four-square home. Living room, laugh. Dining room, laugh. Kitchen, laugh. Around and around he went, louder and louder. Elliott was sleeping. I was sleep deprived. Louder and louder. My head was ringing. Louder and louder. I was spinning. And then, silence. I snapped. The terror in Aidan's eyes shocked me. I hadn't hit him, just grabbed his arm with such force that his giggles evaporated. Only screams of fear, and sadness, and distrust.

I saw his fear. It screamed at me louder than his tears. But I also saw my father in myself: the father I had sworn I would never become, the father who had screamed at everyone he saw. The road rage, the screaming at the referees at Capitol Center. The screaming at my mother, the screaming at my sister. And most of all, the screaming at me. For what? For leaving my bag on the ground, for loving the sports car that I saw in the parking lot. For giggling with my sister in the backseat. I didn't have outward wounds, but the inner wounds were deep.

I didn't have a way of understanding my father's moods, his anger, and whether it was me or something else causing it. I was so young. I came to know it as pathological lying; as emotional manipulation, as abuse. It didn't matter what it was—he was always right and his child was always wrong. As I got older and called him on his lies, the lies got bigger and bolder. I hadn't experienced screaming, he would say I was making it up. He hadn't knocked me down, he would say I tripped. I came to believe that his gaslighting was the most severe in the world.

I promised that I wouldn't put Aidan or Elliott through that. I would always tell them the truth, no matter how difficult. I would never raise my voice to them, no matter what I was feeling inside. I would never make them feel small, even when I needed to feel big. I would raise them up, not cut them down. And yet, here I was standing over my four-year-old son, with terror in his eyes. I couldn't believe that I had done it. I couldn't believe I had snapped. How could I ever put that genie back in the bottle? Maybe I was the one who needed surgery.

Troy Burne (Hudson, WI)

I'd like to say I'm the type of golfer who plays a consistent game. I'd like to say that I hit most fairways. I'd like to say that I sniff most greens in regulation. I'd like to say that I consistently break 80, with more rounds closer to my life goal than to the rounds exceeding 80. I'd like to say that breaking 90 is something I only need to worry about when I'm playing the country's most difficult courses, such as Bethpage Black and Torrey Pines South. I'd like to say that at every 1st tee I'm calm, focused, and ready to play my best. I'd like to say that high heat and a fierce wind are merely bumps in my road to golfing excellence. And I'd like to say that my day at Troy Burne in western Wisconsin was one in which all of these things came together and I played an outstanding round.

The story of my day at Troy Burne is about facing the fact that more often than I'd like, I don't hit enough fairways or greens, I don't have a smooth, repeatable swing, I arrive at the 1st tee anxious and out-of-sorts, and I don't handle the heat or wind well. Simply put, my day at Troy Burne was tough.

I arrived that late morning with great expectations. I knew of the course from following course designer Tom Lehman, who began as a journeyman pro from Minnesota and developed into an accomplished tour player who capped his five PGA Tour wins with an impressive win at the 1996 Open Championship. That week, Lehman played like the World Number 1 golfer he would become in 1997: the peak of a three-year stretch when he easily could have won two or three more majors (he held the 54-hole lead at the US Open for three consecutive years). As he matured as a golfer and moved to the senior tour, he began to design golf courses. Although the Dunes course at the Prairie Club in Nebraska gets more press, his first and possibly one of his best designs (with co-designers Dana Fry and Michael Hurdzan), is Troy Burne in western Wisconsin.

And while my expectations were high, so too were the temperatures: about 95 degrees as I warmed up on the range. I quickly realized that the only thing preventing me from dousing my towel with my own sweat was the strong, sustained south wind—great for wicking sweat, not great for a ballooning ball flight. The first few warmup shots were disastrous worm burners. I had 10 minutes to settle down. I eventually found some semblance of a swing. I left for the practice green to roll a few putts.

I overheard the starter warning golfers that the greens were "running fast, at 11" or so. A few practice putts later, I could see what he meant. This was no muni that Lehman had constructed. I would find large, undulating greens battered by high temps and brisk winds. I didn't know how I would stop the ball. So I went to the 1st tee, with little confidence from my warmup session at the range, compounded by great uncertainty on the putting green.

I shook hands with my playing partners, a father-son pair from the exurbs of St. Paul, Minnesota. As we were waiting for the group in front to clear, I overheard the starter and the father talking. "There's so much chaos in the city, where *those people* live."

"Yeah, it's so dangerous. I don't know how people can live *there*."

They mentioned where *there* was—four blocks from my house, four blocks from where Theresa and I were raising our children. A comfortable place to live. Yes, with people of all kinds, from all backgrounds. But no chaos, no danger to be found. I felt my frustration from a terrible warmup bleed into a tension from opposing world views. I would have to get it together, or this would be a very tough round. Somehow, my legs held together long enough to make my way to the tee box, and after a few deep-breath swings, I launched the first drive of the day.

Troy Burne is noted for large fairways, large bunkers, and large greens. While not a big track by international standards, it's plenty large for a course that draws almost entirely from eastern Minnesota and western Wisconsin. Yet the enormous fairway on the 1st hole, a healthy 549 yards from the Championship black tees where I would be playing from today, was not wide enough to contain my drive—or my spinning emotions, the same type of spinning that I had unleashed on Aidan that day. My drive sailed far to the right, landing in the thick rough and disappearing immediately. The downwind orientation of the hole didn't adequately counteract my straight push, so I set off with my eagle eye on the spot and hoped to find my ball not too deeply nestled.

I had learned from my day at Bethpage that a shot from very deep rough is probably best understood as a simple punch out—advancing the ball much more than that was simply not an option. So, while I found my ball, I didn't like where I found it, and had nothing to do but punch out with a 7-iron. I didn't even make it all the way back to the fairway. From still thick rough, I looked ahead and saw a beautifully long and undulating hole, with an impossibly wide fairway. *How could I have missed it?* My confidence was plummeting with my mood as I pulled my hybrid and hoped to send the ball below the imposing limb of the large tree on the right. I had to keep it low and managed decent contact as my ball flew low, failing again to take advantage of the heavy wind. My ball came to rest 200 yards from the hole. As I walked down the fairway, I reviewed the beginning of my round—terrible warmup, frustrating conversation, sliced drive, punch out, low hybrid. I was sitting three on a par five, a full 4-iron to the green. *It's okay. Catch and release. Yes, some bad shots. But a good shot here and I'll be putting for par. A bogey on the opening hole is fine.* At least that's what I told myself. My body knew better, as a good swing was nowhere to be found as of late. I rushed yet another swing, and while the contact was much better, my hands came through a bit too fast and my shot sailed left, landing in some thick rough short of the green. Four shots, and still not on the green.

As I am apt to do, I quickly adjusted my expectations. *Get up and down for a bogey.* This kind of thinking has a great benefit—rather than sinking myself deep into golfing despair, where I rue the fact that I'm not a very good golfer on this day, I remain optimistic about what is possible. My mind shape-shifts to stay in the moment. The chief downside is that I think far too much about the score, and not enough about the shot. I arrived at my ball and judged 30 yards to the green. I didn't bother to walk up to the green. I didn't bother to find out how many paces the pin was sitting on the middle right. I didn't bother to try to read the green. I just told myself, get up and down for a bogey. While I caught the chip flush, I hadn't planned on the nearly 25 yards of roll on the green that I would need to get to the pin, so it came up woefully short. The bogey putt was easily 40 feet, which I judged well, but not exactly, and tapped in for an opening double.

One hole in, and I had already put myself in a tough spot. And I hadn't faced any of the upwind holes. But onward I must go, and I struggled my way around the course in an outward 47—four doubles, three bogeys, and only two pars. I had played the 4th hole extremely well. Playing in the opposite direction of the 3rd, I faced a right to left wind, which is a much more comfortable wind for those of us who fight the rights. I wasn't going to gamble with driver on this 310-yard hole, so I pulled hybrid and planned to draw the shot with the wind. I came close, hitting a perfectly straight shot. My first fairway of the day.

"Nice shot," Jim said—I had almost forgotten Jim and his son Nick since I overheard his bias.

"Thanks," I replied, feeling a little more human for the first time. I bounced down the fairway and arrived at my ball, sitting up, almost exactly 100 yards from the pin. With the green uphill and a deep bunker in front, I decided to take my gap wedge rather than my sand wedge. I'd rather be long than short. I struck the wedge well, although a bit left of the pin. And, as shots to the left often do, my ball rolled to the back of the green. No matter—I had my first GIR of the round. After two putts, I was excited to have one well-played hole, at least so far, under my belt. Too bad it would be the only one on the front.

As I waited on the 10th tee for Jim and Nick to use the facilities and get a snack, I asked myself some questions to get my mind off my poor play: *Could I find something that I have in common with Jim and Nick? We're going to spend the next two hours together—I might as well enjoy it. Jim and I are both fathers—of course.* It was hot; it was windy. Those things wouldn't change. My swing was what it was this day—I wasn't going to fix it over the next nine holes. *What could I control?* Only my attitude. I was pissed, and it showed. Playing golf upset does no one any good. Trying to avoid bogeys or worse often produces bogeys or worse. Instead, I would have to change my attitude. *Swing easy. Swing for birdies. Forget about the score! Try to find some connections to this father-son twosome.* Jim and Nick returned to the tee and the group in front was clearly struggling. I would strike up a more substantive conversation, whatever our differences.

"Do you play a lot of golf together?" Jim's eyes lit up.

"It's my favorite thing to do." I judged that Nick was in his mid-teens, maybe 15 or so. As I would discover years later, getting a 15-year-old to play golf with his dad was a feat in and of itself. Jim was obviously doing something right.

"You play well," I said to Nick. It was true—his score was roughly the same as mine ... all three of us were in the mid to upper 40s on the front.

"Thanks," he replied.

"What's your secret to keeping golf fun for your son?," I asked Jim. He was clearly someone who liked to talk about himself, so I could see my question put him at ease.

"I don't know. ... We have fun together." It was clearly true. They were both having fun. Although I could see that Nick was frustrated by bad shots, Jim was able to laugh at his own bad shots, and that clearly rubbed off. There was no pressure in that twosome—just a lot of fun.

I was thinking about how much I admired his ability to have fun as I was getting ready to tee off. I noticed that just as the wind was mercifully behind us, I was swinging free and easy. I hit a magnificent drive down the right side of the fairway. I even worried that my 270-yard drive would reach the normally-out-of-reach fairway bunker on the right. Fortunately, there was enough of an upslope right before the bunker that my ball stopped just short.

We walked down the fairway together, for the first time in the round, and talked about being fathers. Jim asked the standard questions: "How old are your kids?," and "Boys? Girls?" I told him about my young sons, how getting to this course was a special treat, and how I someday hope to bring my sons here. I can't say that I liked being with Jim—he wasn't the kind of person I would become friends with, but our conversation made the back nine much more pleasant.

With only about 110 yards remaining on the 385-yard hole, I decided to try to play my approach shot low. The green was perched just short-right of a large lake. Anything left or long would be wet. Also, fronting the green was a large bunker and deep mounds. Without wind, I would play the ball high and let it land and stop. With the wind, I was worried that anything high would fly too far and into the water. So, with a three-quarter swing with my gap wedge, I sent my ball low, straight toward the green. Unfortunately, it had too much speed, and after a hard bounce, rolled off the back. I was in a decent spot, however, and was able to chip back up to the green and watch my ball roll to within a foot for an easy tap-in par. Nice start to the back.

I felt great standing on the tee of the picturesque 11th hole. A short par three, downwind and against a backdrop of tall pines, I could see my draw off the creek to the right onto the green. I knew that the green was surrounded by bunkers, but I was able to hone in on the green. Although the wind was still howling, I didn't want to leave it short and was convinced that the shot would play to my normal distance. I hit a very solid 8-iron, beginning right at the pin. Unfortunately, I pulled it slightly and the ball landed on the left side of the green, took one bounce left, and rolled deep down into the greenside bunker. As I walked to the green complex, I did my best to enjoy the trickling water in the creek, running low due to the long drought. *Bad luck, that's all.* I kept trying to talk myself into that elusive positive attitude. My bad luck was compounded as I found my ball buried deep in the thick sand. I could do no better with my lob wedge than punching the ball out of the sand, leaving me a tricky downhill chip with a creek on the other side of the pin. I decided to keep my ball dry and play away from the pin, leaving me an uphill 20-footer. Two putts later, and I made my fifth double of the round. The test of mental fortitude continued.

I call the feeling I had as I stood at the top of the 12th tee "despondent acceptance." On a day with more doubles than pars, and a slew of bogeys, I tried to restore the loose feeling that I had conjured on the 10th tee. I sized up the large lake on the left side, realizing that any hooked shot would be wet. I also realized that the 12th was listed as a par five but only measured 452 yards. The 9th was longer, and a stroke less on par. *This game is absurd,* I thought to myself. So with not much more of a thought, I gripped and ripped and hit my best drive of the day.

Now, think for a second about what it would take to hit a pitching wedge on my second shot to a par five ... I'm no Dustin Johnson, mind you, but that's exactly what happened. My drive was truly incredible. I don't know where it came from—certainly not a Bryson-esque workout regimen. But the ball rolled out to over 300 yards, leaving me with only 140 to the pin. Knowing the wind direction, and seeing the lake curve around and behind the hole, I didn't want to be long. So, I chose pitching wedge and hit a high, drawing shot to the left portion of the green. Making the 30-foot eagle putt wasn't likely, but it was a legit *eagle* putt. I missed it, but tapped in for a stunning birdie in an otherwise miserable round.

The good shots continued down the hill on the 13th. The wind was decidedly left to right, and so a solid draw with my 7-iron held the left side of the green. Two putts later, and I was in for another par. I was almost starting to feel good about myself. I was almost starting to enjoy the sweat dripping from my cap. I was almost starting to forget the five doubles in the first 11 holes. I was almost starting to feel like a golfer again. *Almost.* But those were the last well-played holes of my round, as I struggled through the final five with three doubles and two bogeys, and I finished with a painful score for a golfer seeking par: a 91. I shook hands with Jim and Nick, knowing that I would be safe and comfortable at home, no matter the assumptions that Jim had. But I had assumptions of my own, the kind that only hurt us. I assumed that Jim had nothing to offer, but I had witnessed him having great fun with his son. And his son seemed so at ease, even with his on-course screw ups. Jim was doing something right, and I had to channel more of his fun loving, catch-and-release attitude with Aidan and Elliott.

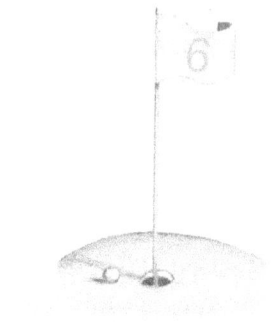

Friends

(2007-08)

"We're going to Mamaroneck, we're going to Mamaroneck."
No, not to play Winged Foot—this was reality, not a
dream. No, the four of us were on the Metro-North Railroad to
visit my friend Nick and his young children. I was dragging Theresa and our five- and two-year-olds through the public transportation maze of NYC and suburbs to see Nick and his family.
Although I hadn't seen him since our kids were born (his kids
were younger, but his family would prove more prolific), he was
a close friend whom I met at a very consequential time in my life.

At some points in their lives, Aidan and Elliott would be in the
same stage in life as each other and would enjoy the same things.
When they were both into baseball, we could do anything baseball-
related and both would be happy. When they were older, they would
go off driving together, or head to the gym, or play catch, or just
hang out. But at certain times, the two boys were in such different

stages that it was almost impossible to find something to do that would satisfy both. This was one of those times.

Aidan had recently begun that magical period between ages 5 and 12. He had left behind the terrible twos (*and threes and fours*) and was willing and able, curious, and content. We just had to make an adventure out of it, and he had the stamina to make it through just about anything (and could even tie his own shoes!). Elliott, however, was not yet there. Having recently embraced the word no, he was quick to insist that he could do it himself, whatever it was. Open a 50-pound door? "I want to do it." Cross the street without holding hands? "I can do it myself." Hold the train ticket? "It's mine."

With a curious Aidan, an insistent Elliott, and a remarkably willing Theresa, I was really looking forward to seeing my good friend Nick. A decade earlier, I had a first marriage that ended in a painful, ugly divorce, and Nick was my most important friend when I was going through it. His friendship was instrumental in helping me get through it. In some key ways, I wouldn't have met Theresa, and we wouldn't have had Aidan and Elliott, had it not been for Nick.

I met Jennifer—my first wife—in college. She walked into the house I was renting with a few friends, ostensibly to pick up my housemate Andrei with her best friend (Andrei and Tanya were dating). Andrei was my soccer teammate and close friend in college—the type of friend who would always be up for an adventure. He was also the type of friend who thought every day was April Fool's Day. One day, Andrei decided that it would be funny to climb my Trek mountain bike to the very top of a 40-foot oak. I came out of class, despondent that my bike had been stolen. As I began the long trek home, a fellow teammate saw me.

"Have you found your bike?," Jason asked.

"Um, no. How did you know it was missing?" He started to laugh. This was no stolen-bike laugh. I smiled. "What?"

"I saw Andrei climbing with it. There was a crowd watching him."

"Where?," I asked, quickly surmising that this was an all-time prank.

"On the other side of the quad, near Wilder Hall." I took off, using my well-earned soccer fitness to sprint over to the suspected tree.

I looked up and saw nothing. A nearby student pointed just to the right of where I was looking, and I could just make out a piece of metal. There, at the top of a 40-foot tree, my Trek 950 was hanging.

I immediately set off up the tree. I pretended that I knew what I was doing—I had never climbed that tree, and probably no tree for more than a decade. But my college-age mind would not give him the satisfaction of asking for help. I never looked down, never thought about the dangers. I just kept climbing, got to my bike, and slowly made it down. The crowd of 30 gossiping peers had apparently been watching me the whole time. I smiled, gave a quick bow, and never mentioned the incident to Andrei or anyone else again. I wouldn't give him the satisfaction of a confrontation.

Thus, when Tanya—whom I had met only twice and knew nothing about—stopped by to pick up Andrei a few months later, I was notably subdued. Tanya came in the house, we said our hellos and they left, just like that. A minute later, Andrei came back in and asked me if I wanted to go. "She says you're cute and wants to know if you want to come with us." Another April Fools joke? Reality? It was an hour drive to Cleveland, where they had chosen a restaurant. I didn't have another plan, so I eagerly got my coat.

We had a great meal, full of laughs and drinks (for them), and by the end I was the designated driver. I drove the four of us home, my future first wife in the front seat, and Andrei and his girlfriend Tanya in the back. All three were asleep. I was the responsible one, or so I thought. After just a few months of romance, I had proposed— well, sort of. It wasn't a get-down-on-my-knee moment—no, that proper proposal would come later in my life. It was more a "I think I'm falling in love," "we should get married," "okay, that sounds like fun!" set of moments. Suddenly, we were at the local mall looking at engagement rings. The stupid things we do in college. My friend Jason got it right: "are you fucking crazy!?" But in the moment, and with the naïveté and arrogance of the early twenties, I was swept up. While the wedding wasn't going to be for two years, I was all in.

The whirlwind of those first years was spurred on by three great events: college graduation, spitting me into a world I was woefully underprepared for; the death of my aforementioned friend, Jason, the only one with the wisdom and courage to name my insanity; and a trip to Ireland to play soccer, while Jennifer studied Irish literature. Throughout those years, we were brought closer by circumstances, obscuring the complete dearth of a real relationship.

When we returned from Ireland and faced the reality of daily living, with real jobs, the loss of a friend, and nothing new in our lives save the manufactured wedding, we fought a lot. I don't know how many walls the engagement ring bounced off of during that year, but suffice it to say that her throwing arm was getting pretty strong, as was my ability to dodge a diamond ring flying at high speeds. The end was clearly in sight, yet we had both made a commitment to marry, and we had family and friends coming to wish us well. So, we both put on our best acting display—her from many years of training, me on the fly—and went through with the wedding. What a mistake, as it only put a second mini weapon in her arsenal, and I learned quickly how futile it was to try to dodge thrown wedding and engagement rings at the same time.

But we persisted, egged on by a foreboding sense of responsibility and an enduring hope that we were just going through a phase. I finished my job, she graduated from college, and we moved for my graduate program. She would get a job, and I would study, and study, and study. And after a year of further misery, it was over. She was moving to New York City to study drama, and I was staying in the Midwest. And that's when I met Nick.

Nick was a year behind me at school and arrived just when I needed a new friend. I needed someone to talk philosophy with, to lift weights with, to play soccer with, and to forget the fact that I had just invested three years with the absolutely wrong woman. I dated—plenty —during those years. And those dates helped me recover my emotional stability. But I also needed a friendship that would help me forget about the past and the future, and simply live in the moment.

Nick and I went to the gym a lot. I got stronger in those two years than any other time in my life. I look back at photos of that time and I can hardly believe how ripped I was. And we laughed a lot.

"Big deal," Nick quipped. "It was just a mistake. Haven't you made mistakes?"

"Of course, but this was a big mistake."

"Yeah? So, what. You think you won't make any more big mistakes? Life is full of them." Nick was right: it was just a mistake. And like any mistake, the best thing I could do was to learn from it and let it go.

We talked about relationships. Nick had dated, but not much. That would come later. For now, he was focused on his studies, and we were focused on lifting. We made a list of relationship musts to count our reps.

1. Attraction. Of course, that has to be first;

2. Conversation. We have to be able to talk;

3. Ease. It shouldn't be so hard. Making a relationship work need not involve dodging precious metals;

4. Mutual. It has to be fully and completely mutual. You can't "persuade" someone into a long-term relationship. You both have to feel it, completely and totally;

5. Acceptance. There are no mulligans. Whatever mistakes I made in the past, I can't relive them. I can't change them. We have to accept each other fully for who we are.

We lifted lots of sets of five, and I internalized those musts. Nick helped me to focus on these essential needs, fully and completely.

So it was with great excitement that my family and I travelled to see Nick, to meet his wife and young children, and to introduce him to Theresa, Aidan, and Elliott. I wanted to share with him this new stage of our lives, where we weren't wondering about the future, we were living it. I had found my match—as had he—and we wanted to share it.

I was highly motivated to keep my boys engaged during the journey to Westchester County, New York. The journey began with us walking through the streets of lower Manhattan with Elliott in a stroller. If you've ever spent any time in Manhattan with a stroller, you know that getting around with that bulky beast is an exercise in emotional fortitude. We avoided construction sites as best we could. We arrived at the subway station, only to realize that there were no elevators or escalators. I grabbed the front of the stroller, Theresa grabbed the back, and I told Elliott that we were going for a rollercoaster ride, with Aidan close by. Occasionally, a friendly New Yorker would lend a hand when the stairs became particularly challenging, but for the most part we were on our own.

At this point, in the sixth year of my life as a father, I had come to believe that really there was only one, important job: keep our boys fed. Everything was better when they had eaten, but keeping them fed was no small feat, especially when we were away from home and doing our best to lighten our load. Keeping the boys safe from germs—fuhgettaboudit. We didn't go so far as to pick up snacks off the subway floor, but I'd be lying if I didn't admit that I thought about it to stop the crying. *Why do two-year-olds throw all their food on the floor? Aren't they hungry?*

But to get to Mamaroneck, we had to take the train, and to get to the train, we had to get to Grand Central Station, and to get there we had to ride the subway. So, here I was, desperately trying to make the eating and the subway riding and the long journey into a memorable game that would pass the time. We played "I spy;" we stared out the window at the darkened walls, searching for graffiti; I gave him a horsey ride on my lap; and yes, we resorted to electronics for a particularly long wait at the train station. And we fed them just about anything we could get our hands on that wasn't going to lead to a frantic excursion to the scary bathroom.

And that's how we ended up on a train to Mamaroneck, with me desperately trying to compose an awful song that would help us pass the time. *What else rhymes with Mamaroneck? "Heck," already been used. "Neck"—yes, we can work with that. "Deck?"—we'll see.*

We're goin' to Mamaroneck
We're goin' to Mamaroneck,
We can't go without our neck!

We're goin' to Mamaroneck,
We're goin' to Mamaroneck,
Let's hope that Nick has a deck!

We're goin' to Mamaroneck,
We're goin' to Mamaroneck,
Everyone have their shoes on? Check!

We're goin' to Mamaroneck,
We're goin' to Mamaroneck,
There better not be a wreck!

We were laughing at the absurdity of our impromptu song, and the hand gestures we made to fit the lyrics. But lo and behold, after much discussion of the possible rhymes for Mamaroneck, some very awkward songwriting, and more than a few laughs, we had arrived at our destination. We made our way out as our train neighbors gave us looks of annoyance and appreciation. Soon we found Nick and his family, picking us up appropriately in a mini-van and we set off for their home.

As we settled down into a thoroughly interrupted conversation, Nick said, "we aren't talking about someday anymore. We're talking about now." I knew exactly what he meant.

As our wives began their own conversation, I said, "Homeowners? Check. Good jobs? Check. Rambunctious kids? Check."

Nick responded, "Attraction? Check. Conversation? Check. Ease? Check. Mutual? Check. Acceptance? Check."

I asked, "What do you find most challenging about being a dad?" I think Nick knew the question was coming.

"Time," Nick offered. "Between my job and my marriage, it's tough to find enough time to really know all three of my boys. They need such different things. Each one has his own personality and ways of being in the world."

I said, "tell me about each of your sons," hoping to hear not only about them, but also about how Nick was coping with fatherhood.

"I've got an athlete, a lover, and a fighter." Just then, the athlete came running in with Aidan, asking if they can go outside and play. Our oldest kids scampered out, and the younger ones sat on our laps. And with that, the brief window into Nick's experience was supplanted with chasing the little ones. Although we didn't get the time to know each other's wives, it was clear right then that we had both checked all our boxes.

The Wilderness at Fortune Bay (Tower, MN)

There are a pair of courses in northern Minnesota, designed by Jeffrey Brauer, for which only one word suffices: massive. I haven't played any of Brauer's other designs, so it's difficult to know whether this is his style, or just that this region—known as the Iron Range—affords such size and scope. But the Wilderness at Fortune Bay, a casino course if there ever was one, is just a gargantuan track. I encountered this course essentially on a whim, and what an encounter it was. Even though I didn't play from the tips, I spent most of the round wishing I had more distance in the bag, but so thankful for the chance to play one of the truly big courses in the upper Midwest.

I woke up early that morning to leave the yurt where Theresa and I had decided to spend a few days alone, away from the boys. Yes, we chose a yurt. No running water, no bathroom, but enough solitude to refresh us for months. We used the community bathroom down the hill, carried a five-gallon jug of water to drink and wash, and listened to the morning symphonies of the various bird species. Between pulling ticks off our dogs and dodging the mosquito swarms, we had plenty to do.

I woke up early and drove to the casino, and soon luckily found the pro shop. After exchanging a few words of banter, the pro spoke those magic words golfers love to hear: "the tee box is yours." Today, to save time and energy, I was taking a cart. I took in my surroundings as I drove to the 1st tee, so excited to be here. High in the sky, two hawks rode the thermals. The pines lining the fairway felt like they were 100-feet high. The air was crisp and clean, and there were no other golfers in sight. At least at first, I had the golf course to myself.

And what a golf course that Brauer designed here, along the shores of Lake Vermillion. The 1st hole is no gentle handshake. Instead, Brauer lets the golfer know the scale of the track immediately. Measuring 649 yards from the tips (I would be playing the one-up blue tees, still a healthy 6,772 yards total), this split-fairway hole appears infinitely long. With the upper fairway standing about 10 feet above the lower fairway, separated by ubiquitous granite, it feels entirely possible to get lost. I stood on the tee, surveying the first shot and giddy with anticipation. *What would the rest of the day bring?* I'm not a loner, and I'm not lonely. But one of my favorite things to experience is the full measure of a golf course alone. I miss the camaraderie that comes with golfing with friends and family—those are some of my greatest golf memories. But there's also something special about the time alone, with only the birds and the trees to bear witness to my golfing endeavor.

Because most of my attention was on the trees towering over the 1st hole, my swing didn't show the kind of necessary commitment. The ball came off the clubhead tentatively, seemingly unwilling to venture off into the depth of the fairway. As the ball landed into the steepest part of one of the rolling hills, it seemed to crawl up the hill, into the rough. With no playing partners, I got to my ball quickly, with little time to reflect on what I could've done differently and how I could be more committed to my next shot. That left me a long way out, in thick rough, with the ball well above my feet. I have learned over many years to take seriously the relation-ship between my feet and the ball—too many fat shots with the ball above my feet, or shots that sail far to the right when facing a slice lie. I pulled my hybrid, adjusted my shoulders to match the pitch of the hill, and aimed left. My shot was very good, as the ball stayed on the left side of the right fairway—the split fairway resumed about 200 yards from the green—leaving me a long shot to the green.

I rode up to my ball and realized that I was behind a foursome, currently putting on the green. Although I realized that I might be in for a long round, I did my best to ignore what might be coming and focus instead on the shot to come. The large green complex was perched high above the right fairway—I had no way of seeing the green from my location. The shot was into the wind, about 150 yards uphill. I decided I needed an extra club as I waited for the foursome to putt out. Every round has several key moments, when a good shot quickly builds confidence, while a poor shot can suck that confidence dry. I took several deep breaths, and visualized the shot. There was a steep false front on the right side, so I knew I had to commit to a draw. With the green clear, I took another deep breath and focused on the shot. Stay committed. As the ball came off my 7-iron, I knew I had struck it extremely well. It rose fast and high, left of my visualized target. I worried it was too good, maybe over the back of the green. Alas, knowing the result would have to wait—I could only sit with the confidence of a well-struck shot.

As I arrived at the green, I realized my well-struck shot had found the sweet spot of the green. While I do my best not to get attached to outcomes—my NATO theory of life (*Not Attached To Outcome*)—it sure felt good to discover that my ball had landed 30 feet to the left of the pin and had rolled to the back of the green and taken the bowl back down and to the right toward the pin. It came to rest about 10 feet from the pin. I allowed myself a fist pump. And then I committed one of the worst sins in golf—I imagined how it would feel to begin the round with birdie. This putt, downhill and slightly right to left, was right in my wheelhouse. I knew I could make it.

I read the putt from behind the ball, and behind the pin. I read the putt by splitting my legs wide about half of the distance. I did my impression of Australian golfer Adam Scott's AimPoint method—only for my own entertainment, not really fully understanding how to do it. I knew I would have to respect the downhill, and I knew it would have to be a cup or two outside the hole. I took my Scotty Cameron back, maintained speed to the ball and struck it exactly as I had intended. The ball slowly but surely made its way down the hill, curling in toward the hole. Unfortunately, I had overread the putt, and while the speed was spot on, the ball stayed right a few inches. An easy tap-in par.

I arrived at the second tee, perched high above a beautiful hole, framed by massive trees and a large bunker cut into the right side of the fairway. As I waited for the foursome to move ahead toward the green, I thought of the near miss on the 1st hole. It's so difficult as a parent not to think about what you should've said or done. *If only I had done it differently, the outcome would have been different.* It's so difficult not to play the woulda-coulda-shoulda game. If I had been able to tee off right away, I think I would have successfully put the missed putt behind me. But a quick round was not in the cards this day, and so I was left with my thoughts. *Aidan is starting school soon. Will he be ready? Am I showing Elliott enough attention? Does he feel ignored? Does he know I love him with every fiber of my being? Does Theresa know how much I love and appreciate her? Everything was good in my life, but was I showing it?*

Whether it was the slumped shoulders feeling of a missed chance for an opening birdie, or the thoughts of my wife and sons, my next swing was not the most committed one. While I struck the ball in the center of the clubface, my drive faded into a perilous part of the right bunker. Although not my best swing ever, it was good enough that on most holes, the ball could finish on the right side of the fairway with a clean look at the green. But golf isn't like that; you can't choose a tight dogleg right for your slices and a sharp dogleg left for your hooks. And no matter how good my drive might have been, it landed at the front of the bunker and buried itself in one of the more picturesque fried eggs I'd ever seen. It was hard not to just shake my head and smirk while I admired the view.

Like the 1st hole, the second green is set well above the fairway, surrounded by deep bunkers. I realized that with a buried lie in the bunker, and a hill to climb to get to the green, there was little or no chance. I decided to pull a wedge and focused on the not-so-simple task of getting the ball out of the bunker. I dug in my feet, dropped my hands off the top of the grip, and settled in. I knew I had to swing in control, but also to keep my speed through the sand. I did it well enough, but I hadn't paid any attention to the landing spot—what was I thinking?—and the ball landed squarely in the rough in front of the bunker.

About 150 yards from the pin, I again pulled 7-iron. My shot would have to clear the bunkers in front of the green, and the rough was thick enough to give me pause. Yet it also appeared that I might catch a flyer, and that's exactly what happened. I struck the ball well, slightly left of my target, but it sailed over the green. I found my ball sitting up in the rough on the upslope over the green. Because the pin was set in the back of the green, and the green sloped back to front, there was simply no way for my chip to stop near the pin, leaving me a 23-footer back up the hill. While the putt was generally well struck, it was somewhat indifferent read, and I missed the putt below the hole. A short tap-in later, I recorded a double bogey. Ouch.

Catch and release. These are the words I constantly say to remind me to let things go. Yes, I had missed a very makeable birdie putt on the first. Yes, I had the poor luck of getting buried in a fairway bunker and laid up poorly into the rough. Yes, I didn't account for a flyer lie and sent my well struck shot over the green, resulting in a double bogey. I was two over when even par was eminently possible. None of that had anything to do with the 3rd hole, which I faced from the tee. *Catch and release.*

As I drove up, the four men in front of me were engaged in playful banter with the woman selling drinks (beers, it became clear). One of them waved me over and invited me to play through. I jumped at the chance, not wanting to spend the entire round behind these men.

"Take your time." "Show us the way." "Knock it close." "Buy us drinks!" I too wanted to see my 1st hole-in-one fly through the air.

The tee was a healthy 193 yards from the green, which had two distinct tiers. Most of the green was below a steep ledge, with balls that go up the ledge coming back to a pin located on the lower tier. Today, though, the pin was tucked in the back of the green, on the top tier. I pulled my 4-iron, believing that even though it was a downhill shot, I would need all of it to get the ball to the back of the green. Also, a steep drop-off on the right side of the green with a pond short focused my attention on aiming left. I struck my Mizuno well, but too far left as the ball sailed toward the hill just to the right of the cart path. It took an inauspicious bounce onto and then over the cart path and came to rest just left of the path.

Although I tried not to rush, anytime a single golfer plays through a larger group, there's a feeling of urgency to get through the hole, no matter what the foursome says about taking your time. I took a quick look at the green and realized that I had a good backstop behind the hole, so I just needed to get the ball onto the green and the ball would not likely leave the putting surface. I was pin high, so I pulled my lob wedge, assessed the lie, and sent the ball high in the air toward the pin. The ball landed safely on the green, but the backstop wasn't quite as steep as I had imagined, and the ball rolled onto the fringe. No matter, a downhill putt was easy enough on this green, as I put my ball on the right trajectory and ended up six inches from the cup. Bogey. Three over after three. I waved to thank the guys for letting me through.

What followed was a streak that appears every once in a while: seven straight pars. This was some stability I could get used to. I played extremely well, missing only the 5th, 6th, and 10th greens, but got up and down for par. But good things must come to an end, and my par streak came to a screeching halt on number 11. This long, uphill par four seemed to challenge my shot-making. From the moment I arrived on the tee, I didn't feel comfortable. Maybe it's the forced carry, or the deep rough on the right, or the uphill that makes a long hole even longer. Whatever the cause, I hit my worst slice of the round, deep in the rough on the right. Although I found my ball, it was so deep in the thick June rough that I could only punch a 7-iron back to the fairway. This still left me with 190 yards uphill, and my 4-iron came up well short. I wasn't even on the green in three shots. My fourth shot, a flop shot over the bunker, made it to the green. I missed the tricky seven-footer down the hill, then holed the comebacker for a double bogey. Talk about breaking the streak.

After a solid par on the picturesque 12th hole, where I hit a high draw over the pond to a green that's shaped like a ghost grabbing a bicycle seat, I came to the signature 13th hole. With massive Lake Vermillion running along the entire left side, the fairway seemed more a grazing ground for ducks and geese than a golf hole. Not particularly wanting to take down a waterfowl in the middle of my round of golf, I grabbed my 3-wood, hoping to play a draw left of the flock. Since the hole played only 325 yards, and even less if I could cut the corner, 3-wood was plenty. The shot came off my club perfectly, in fact maybe too perfectly. From the tee, I couldn't tell whether I had hit it straight into the fairway, or if I had cut off too much of the corner and my ball was destined to fall down the hill into the lake. Once I saw it bounce, more left than straight, I realized that I had landed at almost exactly the border between flat fairway and steep rough. I was lucky to find my ball hugging the left edge, in the aforementioned rough. That left only a sand wedge from about 100 yards to the pin. With a careful, but comfortable swing, I put the ball up in the air with neither fade nor draw, and my straight shot landed just a few feet from the pin and stopped! It would be a tap-in two-footer for my first and only birdie of the round. Birdies are not easy for me to come by, so I made a show of it: I waved to my avian audience now reconstituted on the fairway and smiled my way to the next tee.

The final five holes saw me pepper some great shots with some slightly off fades that left me in bunkers where I couldn't save par. It also included a near miss at greatness. As I walked up to the 17th tee, I remembered that the pro had told me that the 17th was the designated $10k hole-in-one-contest hole. The hole was straight, only playing only 145 yards from the pin. I had dreams of glory. But as a single, I wondered how they would know. Would they believe me? This is a casino, they can't possibly take my word for it. I looked around, hunting for some hidden cameras that must be recording every shot. *For $10k, Filner on the tee. He takes the club back and launches ... a beautiful high draw headed right for the pin. This could be it, folks. A miracle shot.* It flew straight ... over the pin into the greenside bunker behind. I really thought it was going in. From the greenside bunker, I had a downhill lie and couldn't put any height into the shot, which rolled out to 15 feet past the cup. With a solid putt up the hill that came up just short, I was left with a two-footer for par. As I walked off the green, I laughed at my performance—I hope they enjoyed it. As I walked off the 18th green and started to count the score in my head, I realized that I had shot 39 on both nines for a great score of 78.

Did I have regrets over some bad shots and bad breaks? Of course, but after that double bogey, I'm happy with how I picked myself up. Between bench press reps, Nick and I had repeated the mantra: *you can't change the past—you can only learn from it and move on.* I was proud of the fact that I had heard Nick's voice clearly after my tough start: I didn't get too down on myself. I caught-and-released the bad shots and for once I was having fun. Good things followed.

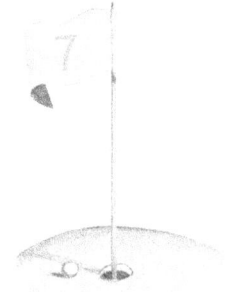

Risks

(2008-09)

A idan and Elliott were six and three, and Theresa and I needed a regular night out. They were old enough that a skilled babysitter could handle them. While they would cry on our way out, we knew that our sitter would know what to do. We had learned early on that the worst thing we could do was to go back, whether it was to give them another hug or to grab something we forgot. So we said quick goodbyes and left without looking back.

We were going to meet our friends at a local sushi restaurant in Minneapolis' Warehouse District. We knew the neighborhood well, because both of us had worked close by. After the 20-minute drive in freezing temperatures, we found street parking down a hill from the main street of the restaurant. It was only a few minutes' walk. We met our friends and had a delightful dinner, all except for the uni. Our friends loved *uni*, the Japanese name for the edible part of sea urchin—namely, the gonads. Yes, the part of the sea urchin that is edible is the sex organ, the part that produces roe. It's bright orange, with the consistency of a thick sour cream. And the taste—yes, we tasted it—was truly repulsive, at least to my pallet. The only thing I've tasted that's worse is durian fruit in Vietnam. But that's a story for another day.

It's a funny thing when you become close friends with your kids' friends' parents. You don't choose them, and you often don't have much in common. But you assume that since you chose the same school for your kids, and since your kids like each other, you must be able to be friends. We spent hours with Kate and Regina talking about our young kids, taking them to parks and lakes, watching them play sports and—in my case at least—coaching them in soccer and baseball. But when it came to cuisine, we had some lines with them that we wouldn't cross: call it our *uni* line. After tasting a pea-sized piece of *uni* so we could cross it off our list, never to be tried again, we both less-than-subtly stuffed our mouths with an obnoxious amount of rice. I don't know what the looks on our faces betrayed, but as we confided in each other later, it was a truly repulsive moment.

Right as we were frantically stuffing our mouths with rice, Kate announced, "we've decided not to get Bruno vaccinated." We swallowed.

"Um, what?" Theresa asked.

"We don't trust the pharmaceutical companies, and we think there's too much evidence that vaccinations cause health problems," Regina continued. We'd known Kate and Regina for a couple of years, since we started day care. We had so much in common with them. We chose the same day care, and we were planning to send our boys to the same neighborhood school. But we also knew about the vaccination requirements for the school, and we flatly disagreed with them about vaccines. Theresa and I caught each other's eye. *What do we say to that? Vehemently disagree? Say nothing? Change the subject?* Their son Bruno was Aidan's best friend—we cared about him as well. How could his parents endanger him with measles, mumps, polio, and other diseases we didn't quite know? And yet, and yet. We were sure that our friends disagreed with some of the parenting decisions we made. Did we really want to argue with them about every decision? I summoned my best mutual respect voice. "Aidan and Elliott have already received all their scheduled vaccinations. We think the risk of the diseases is far worse that any risk with a vaccine. But we respect your perspective." I think it was important to register our disagreement, without being argumentative. That seemed to end the conversation.

We were all quite content through the rest of our dinner, and the four of us left the restaurant at a leisurely pace. We all walked down the main street, talking as if we were without kids for the first time in a while—because we were! As we arrived at the corner, about a lob wedge from our car, I noticed something moving inside. From a distance, it looked like the shadow from a streetlight inside the car. As we got closer, however, I realized that there was a man in the car. Without a single thought, I took off toward him at full speed.

Now, if you're a dad who hasn't gone out in a while, you'll likely put on some of your best shoes for a night out. And if you know anything about winter in the northlands, you know that the sidewalks and streets are basically never fully clear of ice and snow during the winter. This combination of slippery dress shoes and frozen ground make for a treacherous run down a hill to a car that—yes, it was really happening—was currently being robbed.

At roughly the same time that I was doing my worst impression of a hockey player down the hill at my full, middle-aged speed, two things happened: 1) the guy in the car noticed me and urgently began to abandon the car; and 2) Theresa, noticing me running and the guy getting out of our car shouted: "Are you fucking crazy?!?" Yes, actually, I was. My crazy ass kept on running after the thief, as I slid down the hill. I guess I thought I could catch him, but after a brief chase, he fled into a dark construction site. When I reached the end of the street, I abandoned my ill-advised chase and slowly walked back up the hill toward our car. By that time, Theresa and our friends had reached our car, broken glass everywhere. The thief had broken our driver's side window and—based on the internal damage to the dashboard—had been in the middle of stealing our navigation system.

If you had asked me as we left the house that night whether I would trade my unimpressive car for my life, of course I wouldn't have given it a second thought. If you had asked me whether it was worth injury or death to keep navigation in our car, of course I would have said no. If you had asked me whether running toward a thief who was in our car without any plan was a smart decision, I would have replied of course not. For some reason, though, I wasn't thinking about our kids, or our insurance policy, or the risks that this man posed to everything that was important to me. I just reacted.

To this day, I still have no idea what I would have done if I *had* caught him. All-in-all, the risk could be seen as a dangerous waste, but something inside me was glad I reacted, not willing simply to accept the fate that we had been given on this cold night.

Yet at the same time, I knew that this was one of the most idiotic risks I had ever taken. I am a responsible husband and father, or so I thought. All of that could have disappeared in an instant if that thief had a weapon and was willing to use it. I don't know what types of crimes he was capable of committing. I had no idea. And because of my stupid ego thinking I should do something, I had put my life at risk, and potentially abandoned my boys. *Could I have done anything more damaging to my boys than stupidly allow myself to be killed? And what lessons would I have taught them? And what kind of trauma would it have caused to my wife if she had witnessed me gunned down over a stupid car? What were my priorities?*

And I wasn't the only one thinking these things. The car ride home, with the smashed window, was silent. Of course, both of us were upset about the car, and the manner in which we had encountered the damage. But the discomfort was primarily due to my egotistical and dangerous act. "I just don't understand what you were thinking," Theresa scolded. She asked the question, and my response was far too typical: "I was trying to catch the asshole who did this to our car." That dark cloud would hang over us for awhile.

Around the same time, with Aidan comfortably placed in first grade at our local public school, we decided to move Elliott to day care in the same building. Not only would it be a much easier drop off, but we could also make day care seem more like school, and

Elliott wanted to do everything Aidan could do. Elliott's favorite phrase was "me too." His brother was on a slide: "me too." His brother was eating in a big-boy chair: "me too." His brother got to stay up late: "me too." It was our daily routine. But, unlike his brother who detested change, Elliott was excited to go into Miss Kathy's room for school.

For Aidan, day care was painful for all. He screamed when we first chose day care, as if we were leaving him for good. By contrast, Elliott seemed right at home from the first day. He didn't quite say "get out" to me on the first day, but it was pretty close. He seemed to wonder why we were even there a second more than needed to drop him off. He jumped right into whatever the kids were doing. Storytime: "I'm in." Get your hands wet and messy in the sand pit: "give me a bucket." New kids: "hello old friend." Elliott was right at home with other kids, eager to play, eat, sleep, and listen. Whatever was thrown at him he embraced. And so, the opportunity to go to a new day care in the same building as his brother was like a gift from heaven.

Every day we walked the six blocks to school together. Most days they were excited and ready for school. We packed lunches every day. When Theresa was the lunch maker, she almost always found a way to stash a surprise treat. Sometimes the treat was a piece of kiwi; sometimes it was a cookie; sometimes a well-designed edible art creation. My lunches were far more mundane, with a sandwich, some carrots or fruit, a drink, and a dessert. They never elicited so much as a compliment or a complaint, but the boxes always came home empty. These were the days of routines. There were few dramas, and I enjoyed the simplicity of our lives. We knew that we had begun the calm between the two storms of their childhoods.

The Quarry at Giants Ridge (Biwabik, MN)

Jeffrey Brauer's most acclaimed course in Minnesota is the Quarry at Giant's Ridge. The course was built on an old, industrial, silica-sand quarry. According to the Minnesota Department of Natural

Resources, silica sand "is composed of almost pure quartz grains" and is processed into "frac sand," used in fracking by the oil and gas industry. While Minnesota has a long history of industrial production of natural resources, oil and gas has always taken a back seat to iron-ore production. As a result, some of the sand quarries have been retired. What an opportunity for a golf course!

The Iron Range of northern Minnesota is known for many things: brutally cold winters, reddish brown water, and Bob Dylan (who is from the nearby town of Hibbing). On this particular morning, I found myself being attacked by swarms of giant mosquitoes on the driving range. I covered my body and clothes with bug spray and grabbed a club. I estimated that I had 30 seconds in a single spot before the swarm would find me and these undeterred mosquitoes would draw some of my blood.

I don't know about most golfers, but there seems to be no connection whatsoever between how I warm up and how I play. Some days, I warm up well and make a mess of the course. Other days, my good warmups bode well for a strong round. The opposite is also true: some poor warmups carry onto the course, while on other days I get the bad practice shots out of my system. I don't know why, or how, but I had a remarkably good warmup this day. It may have been the mosquitoes, which prevented me from standing behind the ball for more than a second. Or maybe it was the fact that I was so excited to play Jeff Brauer's masterpiece. Whatever it was, I was hitting baby draws with my driver on the range. Unsure of what was to come on the course, I decided today that I'd try to avoid unnecessary risks. Playing it safe would be my mantra.

I left the range and took the short walk over to the 1st tee. Although I had ambitions of playing the blue tees (at 6,700 yards, with the back tees tipped out at over 7,200 yards), I settled on the white tees, which played a reasonable 6,100 yards. No need to be macho today. After a sloppy opening bogey, I walked through the woods, where a new colony of mosquitoes was waiting for a tasty breakfast. When I arrived at the 2nd tee, however, I stopped my swatting and my eyes lit up. There are more famous holes in the world, and there are other holes that make golfers gasp in delight.

For me, the 2nd hole at the Quarry at Giants Ridge is one of the most jaw-dropping holes I've ever played. From the tee is a giant vista, with fairway in front and at least 60 feet below, a stand of trees and rough to the right, a curve in the fairway up and to the left—and, far in the distance—a large green embedded in so much sand it looked like beachfront property. It's a massive hole, and one that I aimed to conquer through solid strategy.

Once I caught my breath and returned to the reality of golf—I would have to maneuver my ball through this undulating terrain, somehow directing my ball to the fairway, then up and over the ridge to the left, then over the bunkers surrounding the green. With my previous sliced drive decidedly on my mind, I took my best anti-right swing I could muster (the baby draw swing from the range was just a memory). I sent the ball high and far, for me at least. But while the slice was contained, it was only barely so as the ball faded right toward the thick rough.

As I arrived at my ball, what looked like flat rough from the epic tee box was actually the side of a large hill. I found my ball easily enough in the rough, but it was at least six inches above my feet. I was reticent to simply chop out, so I decided to take a risk. I steered my ball away from the trees and found the fairway, 185 yards from the center of the green.

Okay, I've recovered safely from a mediocre tee shot. I solid 5-iron will give me a putt for birdie. Such thoughts are always dangerous, because they inevitably lead to an uncommitted process. As a result, my high 5-iron was actually a bunker-seeking missile, landing square and sliding forward in the left greenside bunker. It was a silly risk I took. I would have to get up-and-down for par.

While I had improved immensely over the years, my bunker play is one area where I am decidedly lacking. Rarely do I enter a bunker with anything more than a hope to get it on the green. I know the basic rules of bunker play—place your weight forward, open your clubface, slide the club under the sand two inches before the ball, hear a *thump*. I know all of it. Doing it, however, is an entirely different thing. Usually something in that sequence gets out of whack, and I leave it in the sand or crush it well over the green. I took far too many practice swings—fortunately, there was no group lurking behind—and stepped down into the sand. I shuffled my feet, opened the club face, pushed my weight forward and tried to take a smooth swing into the white sand. And lo and behold, the club entered the sand a few inches behind the ball, sending sand high and the ball forward toward the green. While the putt would be a solid 11 feet—I had played for the fat part of the green, hoping to give myself as much leeway as possible—it was a putt for par. I left the putt below the hole, never really giving it a chance. But it was in, for a grinding bogey. Two holes, two over. Not the start I had imagined as my swing grooved into place while fighting mosquitoes, but, as they say, it could have been much worse.

I played very well for the remainder of the front nine, with five solid pars and only two missed GIRs. Playing it safe was the message of the day. While I didn't card a birdie, I was pleased with a solid 40 on the front. The sun had emerged while the holes opened up from the woods, and I was now comfortably shedding layers. I began the back nine with similarly solid play, with two pars and a bogey—three-over the past 10 holes—a streak of the kind of golf I'm most certainly capable of, but too often fail to achieve. Caution was working in my favor.

I was happy with the state of my game as I climbed up the hill to the tee of the infamous 13th hole, the signature hole at the Quarry. This short par four demonstrates how Brauer can trigger a golfer's worst instincts. From this elevated tee, much of the green is visible from the tee. From the white tees, it's only 275 yards, so it seems easy and straight-forward. The design seems to obscure its dangers—a stand of trees for any slices seems far too close to be in play. From the tee, what seems like flat, benign rough surrounding the green is really thick rough and an elevated green. Most golfers will be tempted to swing away with driver, and most of those who take the risk and hit driver will find themselves sweating to a bogey or worse.

I didn't take the bait, but I wanted to. Down the hill, just about any decent drive is liable to wind up on the very large green, or at worst a short chip shot away. But I had committed to managing risk, and wasn't confident that I could either hit it straight enough, or that I would have the distance to carry to the green. Whatever feeling I had on the range was long gone, left only with a feeling that driver is bringing five or worse into play. So I did the prudent thing and pulled a hybrid, sending my ball comfortably down to the right side of the fairway, with only a lob wedge for my approach. From the bottom of the hill, the shot becomes blind, with at least a 15-foot carry back up the hill, but I was glad to be far enough back to make a bigger swing. I aimed for the middle of the green and left myself with a 30-footer. Another easy two-putt par left me feeling satisfied that I didn't take the bait, as who knows what would've happened if I took off more than I could chew.

I played within myself for the remainder of the round, carding a second straight 40, and failing to break 80 by a single stroke. Nevertheless, I knew that with all the danger that lurked out at the Quarry, if I played more aggressively, it could've been a 90. I walked off the 18th green knowing that I probably shot the best I could, with what little I had that day.

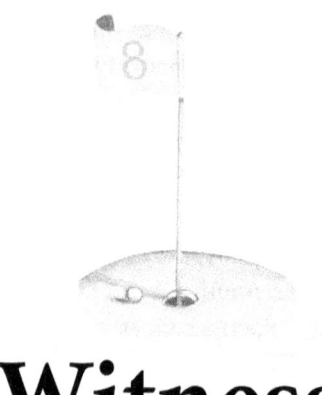

Witness

(2009-10)

I didn't meet the Real Deal, at least not in the formal sense of a handshake. But I was in his presence for one of the most momentous days in our lives. I wanted Aidan to see what greatness truly meant in as many shapes it takes. A father knows that his boys will one day have to look beyond just his dad for a model of what they can be, what they're capable of achieving. It's an exciting time to see the world through your children's eyes, to look on in amazement at some larger-than-life figures and the expanse of our diverse world, rediscovering it all over again.

So, on a cold January day, we spent many hours freezing outside, The Real Deal one row in front of us, as we tried desperately to see over his 6'2" frame. Fortunately, the object of our attention was far enough, and high enough away that it didn't really matter. I could see the man's head, if not the expression on his face. Behind us was a reported 1.8 million people, almost all of whom were standing.

We were sitting behind Evander Holyfield, with Aidan, now a seven-year-old, who was cold, thirsty, tired, and not particularly interested in the inauguration of President Barack Obama. Four-year-old Elliott was home with his grandmother—not cold, probably not thirsty, and likely also a bit tired. But we were determined to persevere through the elements to bear witness to this monumental event.

Periodically, I looked back at the National Mall. Having grown up outside Washington, DC, going to "the Mall" was not a shopping visit for me. From school trips to the Smithsonian to dates along the Tidal Basin, I had spent my fair share of time at the Mall. I loved it. I loved the history, the monuments to democracy, the sense that this is the people's park. When I needed inspiration as a 16-year-old, I would drive down to the Lincoln Memorial and sit inside, reading and re-reading those hallowed words. I had worked at the Department of Housing and Urban Development, and had used the Mall as a commuting depot. In short, I knew the area well. I had never seen it so crowded—in fact, crowded is not the proper word for it: it was jam-packed. There were seas of people everywhere we looked, all there to witness and celebrate. And it was celebratory. Unlike inaugurations before and since in which there was a dour acceptance of the present and the future, this inauguration was filled with hope.

Watching the peaceful transition of power, when former President Bush shook hands with newly inaugurated President Obama, I was struck by a profound sense of stability. A country that could witness two archrivals shake hands—and witness the former president share a mint with the new first lady—was a country that would endure. Although our history is replete with violence against people of color—from slavery, to Jim Crow, to segregation, to redlining, to mass incarceration, and more—it has also shown itself to be resilient in the face of anti-democratic forces. There always have been these forces, and always will be. But I had a clear sense this day that I was part of the consensus-total 1.8 million people bearing witness to the strengthening of our democracy. Whether or not you supported President Obama in 2008, you could unify around the peaceful transition of power, you could absorb the civility.

Bearing witness to Obama's inauguration was not the only important event that we attended. This year would be a year of travel, some trips more distant than others, when we would do our best to help Aidan and Elliott experience the vastness and diversity of our country, to show them what's possible. We travelled to DC, Silicon Valley, and South Padre Island. Each trip brought us new experiences as our boys opened their eyes further to the country around them. Maybe most memorable among them was to watch, for the first time, the defeat of a giant.

In 2009, I had the opportunity to bring Aidan to the PGA Championship at Hazeltine National. A stunning course in the exurbs of Minneapolis that I have never played, Hazeltine's mission statement is clear, "to build and maintain a golf course suitable for the conduct of national championships." And they have clearly succeeded in that mission. Designed by Robert Trent Jones and opened for play in 1962, Hazeltine has hosted, among others, the 1966 and 1977 US Women's Open Championships, the 1970 and 1991 US Opens, the 2002 and 2009 PGA Championships, and the 2016 (and 2029!) Ryder Cup.

Aidan, Elliott, and I joined a group of First Tee golfing kids at a local muni and rode a bus to the PGA Championship visitor lot to see the first practice round. It was also my first time at a PGA Tour event, so I took in the sights and sounds among the throngs of fans, including my two boys. We decided to pick several holes for the day, watch for about 45 minutes, and then get as many autographs as we could. That meant a first stop at the sales tent, where we would stock up on hats, t-shirts, and other memorabilia. Doing my best to keep this day fun, we sought out specific players—the older kids wanted to see Tiger Woods, who was nowhere to be found. They looked for Phil Michelson, who walked by with a wave, thumb pointing toward the sky. Aidan and Elliott didn't know any of the players, but they seemed to like the excitement of the crowds. Some of the pros stopped to sign, while others didn't give the kids a moment's notice.

The boys compared their signatures—they wondered who had gotten more. Of course, they didn't recognize any of the names, but it didn't matter. The quest was the important thing. We found the kids' zone, where they could try their hand at a few putts, watch videos, and otherwise be entertained. But I just wanted to see the golf. I wanted to see the swings, the trajectory, the landing spots. I stood in awe as I watched diminutive South African golfer Tim Clark launch a drive 300 yards, with a sound and ball flight that I couldn't fathom. I watched defending champion Padraig Harrington, with his distinctive gait and everyman style, grind on a chip around the 6th green. I watched amazed by the massive speed created by the young Rory McIlroy, who had only turned pro two years prior and was seeking his first win on US soil (he had won the Dubai Desert Classic for this first professional win earlier that year). My "kids' zone" was the course.

We returned each day of the PGA Championship to watch the larger-than-life players. Length off the tee was a premium at Hazeltine, and while there was plenty of water on the course, the penalty for inaccuracy off the tee was relatively minor. With Tiger Woods in his prime, and a field searching for answers, the tournament seemed poised for another Tiger Woods victory. And that's exactly how it started, with Woods taking a two-shot lead over Padraig Harrington. Witnessing that greatness would be a treat for all three of us.

Elliott was too young to fight the larger crowd on Thursday, but Aidan was excited to go. While walking with Woods and Harrington meant that I was in the back of a seven-deep crowd (although I did bring a two-step stool, which allowed me to see over heads from the back), Aidan could easily squeeze past taller fans and reach the ropes. And reach the ropes he did. He was greenside at three of Woods' five birdies (the 2nd, 7th, and 15th); I was more concerned at that point in making sure that I could find him after the putts dropped. Day one was a thrilling day of watching Woods' magic and Harrington stand tall, only one back.

On day two, we joined the same group of kids on the bus, then arrived at an even more crowded course. The crowds around the surging Woods were too massive, however, so we followed the lesser-known players. After just a few holes, while I was thrilled to see the lesser-knowns—who were still awe-inspiring—hit massive drives, flush crisp irons, and putt lights out, the kids were losing interest fast. Maybe it was the more intense winds that knocked them off their stride, or maybe it was the sights and smells of the food tents, but the boys needed to be fed. I felt like a denied child, straining to catch any glimpse of any swing on the course from the food tents. But the kids were happy, and that's what mattered. While we didn't get up close, we saw Tiger Woods ended the day with a seemingly unsurmountable four stroke lead over Padraig Harrington and four others. That lead would be reduced to two when they began the final round, over Harrington and the relatively unknown South Korean golfer Y.E. Yang.

On the final day, I managed to talk Aidan into coming one more time. I promised Tiger Woods sightings, and an ice cream after the round. He succumbed to the post-round promise, and we decided to go on our own. After the drive, bus ride, bathroom break and food, we arrived on the 1st hole about 30 minutes before the leaders were set to tee off. The crowds were massive and despite my best efforts, I couldn't find a spot where we could easily see outside the ropes. That's when I spotted a lone tree on the right side of the fairway, about 250 yards from the tee box. I asked Aidan if he could climb the tree. He looked at me, both excited and nervous: "Is it okay?"

"Yeah, it will be fine," I replied. I gave him a boost to the base of a branch, about six feet up. I then grabbed it as best as my middle-aged body could, and somehow maneuvered my body up into the tree. It took us about 10 minutes to find a tolerable position where we could relax our bodies and still see the golf course, just in time to look up to see someone hit their drive down the fairway—it was Padraig Harrington, sitting only two shots off the lead. We stayed and watched a tiny Woods and Yang hit from the top of the hill, as the balls flew down the hill.

And for the next few holes, we just followed the final group. Aidan was able to squeeze his way past the crowds and right up to the ropes, seeing (but not remembering) some of the most important shots of the final round. I saw very little, worried again about finding him after each shot was finished. But we heard the crowds, oh did we hear them! We heard the stunned roars as Y.E. Yang halved the deficit with a birdie on the 3rd, and the moans as Woods missed makable putts on the first three holes. With a bogey on the par three 4th, Woods and Yang were tied, and we could feel the shocked electricity of the crowd.

At the most remote part of the course, Aidan had a perfect view greenside as Woods made par and Yang dropped a shot, seemingly restoring the world to as it should be with Woods in the lead. Yet with the crowds growing, we decided to skip ahead a hole and go to the area short and right of the 7th green. While Woods and Yang were playing the 6th, we watched as the penultimate groups, including Harrington, played the 7th. It's an amazing par five, with water left and a length conducive to going for it in two. Most players did, and we saw a few amazing shots.

I'm not sure why—I'll never be sure, although the wave of crowds following Woods and Yang probably had something to do with it—but we decided to vacate our spot near the 7th green in favor of finding a spot in the stands on the par-three 8th. Unabashedly using my son as currency, we managed to squeeze into a spot just in time to watch Harrington tee off. We could see a red shirt, but this time worn by the confident Harrington. He was playing a safe if uninspiring round, with pars through the first seven holes. With a brisk wind heading left to right, we watched as Harrington's ball sailed right, hitting off the bank and into the pond. With his head down, Harrington walked forward to what appeared to be a drop zone. We watched him hit his third shot, and in the air it looked like it was coming straight for us. We heard someone yell "fore," and I put one hand on my head, another on Aidan's head. Harrington's ball landed in the rough, 20 feet in front of us.

The crowd buzzed as we watched Harrington make his way to his ball. Most of us knew that Woods was in the lead by one stroke, with Yang and Harrington only a shot back. With his third shot in the deep rough (we couldn't see his ball from 20 feet away, if that's any indication of the thickness of the rough), Harrington was facing double bogey to fall out of contention. He seemed unperturbed when he arrived at his ball, took was seemed like no time to get set, and then hit what appeared to be a flop shot. For whatever reason he launched his ball at least 10 feet farther than he wanted, flying his ball straight into the pond. The crowd, including me, let out a terrible groan.

Harrington grabbed another ball from his caddie and dropped at the same location where he had just hit his second ball in the water. Lying five, Harrington could not afford another water ball, so predictably left his sixth shot still in the rough. We let out another moan, as we came to realize that we were watching an historic meltdown. Harrington composed himself somewhat, hitting his seventh to four feet and burying the putt. We had just watched the defending PGA champion, who was sitting only one shot off the lead, make an eight! My son whispered to me that he thought he could do better than an eight on this hole. He was probably right. But we sat quietly and watched Yang come through with par, while Woods bogeyed. With pars on the 9th, the two made the turn tied, three shots clear of the surging youngster Rory McIlroy and seasoned pros Lucas Glover and Henrik Stenson.

As we recovered from the buzz of watching such an epic meltdown, I realized that we needed a strategy to see any of the remaining back nine. I could tell that Aidan was beginning to tire, so walking with the group was not an option. At the same time, going to the final 2-3 holes would mean a long wait—which I doubted he could manage. So, I figured that we should get a few holes in front of Woods, listen for the crowds, and try to find a spot. After first trying for the 11th and 12th holes, we could see the green of the 14th, which seemed like a decent hole to make a pit stop. It was not yet mobbed, so my son and I could snag a decent spot greenside.

We had learned earlier in the week that players were attempting to fly the green on this short par four, but this was our first time seeing it close. We were seven groups ahead of Woods and Yang, so we got to watch 14 players go for the green. It was fun seeing these pros in the distance, and waiting to see a ball fall out of the air. In most cases, we couldn't see the ball until it hit the ground, so Aidan and I made a game of guessing where we thought it would land. That kept him busy for the 70 minutes or so, until we saw Woods and Yang tee off. Both players were off the green, with Yang closer on the fringe. Woods played a great pitch to about six feet, putting the pressure on Yang.

From our vantage point, we could see Yang but couldn't see his ball, which was a bit on the upslope greenside. We watched as he sized up his chip with what looked like his highest lofted club. We watched as he took the club back and stopped. We watched as Yang reset and finally stroked the ball, with almost no follow through, and then watched his ball roll smoothly and straight toward the cup. We joined the crowd, first in making that distinctive *will it?* sound, and then a loud roar when it went it. An eagle! On the 14th hole of the PGA Championship! Woods had to make his putt to stay in range, which he did, prompting a polite, if less-than-excited applause from the crowd. Everyone dashed from the green.

I'd like to say that we walked with Woods and Yang to the 15th hole. I'd like to say that we were in the 18th fairway to see Yang majestic hybrid that landed just a few feet from the cup. I'd like to say that we were greenside as Woods tried to chip in to salvage a birdie to force Yang to make his putt. I'd like to say that we were in the stands watching Yang lift his hefty bag over his head to celebrate this historic victory.

Instead, after the excitement of the 14th, Aidan asked, "can we go?" I looked at him, torn momentarily between *do you know what is happening?*—a monumental golf moment—and empathy for my seven-year-old son. I chose Aidan. I chose to miss out on the final four holes of one of the most exciting PGA Championships in history in favor of caring for my son. We walked back to the gates, stopped for the promised ice cream, and headed onto the bus to our car. We listened to the golf tournament on the radio and talked about the greatness we witnessed. I wouldn't have had it any other way.

Whistling Straits (Sheboygan, WI)

As most dads can attest, if you want your children to witness great golf, they aren't going to witness it by watching your game. Us mere mortals need to find our own level of greatness—for us—as golfers and as fathers.

Two years previously, my grandfather Elmer died at age 95. He had taught me the rules of the game, taught me how to grip the club, taught me to keep my head down, and to chip with a 7-iron. Mostly, he had taught me to love golf, and for that—among many other things—I am eternally grateful.

Pop Pop had been a lifelong golfer. He loved the game and had shot his age when he was in his mid-eighties. While he had a penchant for being much tougher with boys than girls—he was kind to my mother while my uncles had to contend with his belt—I experienced him as a firm, but loving man. He was the kind of golfer who never hit it more than 150 yards, but always straight down the middle. I was the opposite as I got older—long and wayward, usually to the right.

"Keep your head down!," he would yell after I flubbed an iron. He would groan as I sliced another drive. No hugs from Pop Pop, but I loved it. I remember standing in front of the trunk of his massive Oldsmobile, looking at the shoebox full of golf balls. He would pull out the box as I waited with anticipation, hoping he would give me some of his balls. He always found a few to give to me; one grandpa's trash is his grandson's treasure.

When my kids were very young, like most fathers, I had very little time for golf. Between diaper changes, sleepless nights, doing my best to be present for Theresa, and all the responsibilities of full-time work, I just didn't have much time for golf. All that changed when my grandfather died. Our youngest, Elliott, was now almost five, and our lives started to open up. At the same time, I felt a need to honor my grandfather by continuing the tradition with the game that he loved. But I had played so rarely as of late, I felt a desperate need for lessons.

I went to my local muni and found a large banner advertising lessons with the head pro. I had never met Mike, but it turned out that we had a lot in common: we were almost the same age and we both had two kids. We hit it off immediately. We laughed at my grandfather's instructions ("head down!") and he taught me that "there's a difference between feel and real." And my rarely-able-to-break-90 golf game quickly improved to being able to break 80 on a good day. My vicious slice started to straighten out, my irons started to get some length, and most importantly, I learned to spin my chips, lag my putts, and generally to save strokes around the green. A couple of lessons a month with Mike throughout the summer help turn me into a better-than-decent golfer.

I was thrilled when Mike asked me to join him to play a local country club, where they had a pro-and-guest day. We met at the club, and Mike and I walked into the pro shop. He gabbed with the club pro whom he clearly knew and introduced me. In addition to being the head pro at our local muni, Mike had also just been hired as the head pro for the Minneapolis Chapter of the First Tee. One of his first tasks was to form a board of directors. Mike said to the head pro at this posh private course: "This is Matt Filner. He's on the board at the First Tee."

"Hello," said the pro.

Confused, I uttered, "um yes, nice to meet you." I'm not sure if my face betrayed my surprise or not, but I did my best to play it cool. As we left the building and headed to the 1st tee, I asked Mike about the board.

"Mike, I'm flattered and all, but what's this about the First Tee Board of Directors?"

"Will you serve on the board?"

"Well, what is it?"

"It's a group of people who oversee a non-profit organization."

"I know what a board is, Mike. What is the First Tee?" He explained that the First Tee was a non-profit that taught kids how to play golf while teaching them core values such as integrity, hard work, and perseverance. It was my kind of organization.

"I'd be honored," still shocked by the impromptu invitation.

"You're our first member. I'm naming you president of the board." I laughed out loud, but didn't say no.

And so began my decade-long involvement with the First Tee of Minneapolis, where I devoted countless hours to attending board meetings, supporting our pros and coaches at First Tee events, presenting kids with achievement awards, teaching kids a grip, how to putt, and the most basics of a swing before the pros took over, and generally doing my best to support the program. I also met golfers in our community who shared my passion for the game. We joined in a variety of events to support the kids, and I had an opportunity to join many of them on local courses, seeing them demonstrate the values that they had learned. Serving on the board also gave me the opportunity to play on a number of great local courses to raise money for our programs. I became a regular in the First Tee community.

I was particularly attracted to the First Tee because of the values they help to instill in kids, some of which were the most important values for me to teach my sons. Their list of clear: Honesty, Integrity, Sportsmanship, Respect, Confidence, Responsibility, Perseverance, Courtesy and Judgment.

Honesty. As a man who had suffered as the son of a compulsive liar, a person who would make up lies just to seem more impressive or to end a conversation, I knew that honesty was central to my life. I have told my sons repeatedly, "as long as you're honest with me about what happens, I will never be mad at you. It's when you lie that I will be really mad." It became a running joke when they were teenagers, but at a young age, it sunk in.

Integrity. My sons get sick of me repeating, "when you are alone, you should act as you would in the presence of others." Integrity is one of the highest personal values for me.

Confidence. Every day, I have tried to instill in my sons a sense of confidence, that they matter in this world.

Perseverance. I have told my boys over and over not to give up, to know that there will always be one more out, or one more shot. Yogi Berra's cliché that "it isn't over until it's over" is a mantra I repeat to their great dismay. These are my values.

Years after I began this work, I got an unexpected text from Mike: "WS on Thursday?"

"Um, what's WS?"

"Whistling Straits."

I nearly fell off my chair. I knew he was serious, and it was just like Mike to provide absolutely no buildup. I responded without even thinking about it: "I'm in."

There's a field of study in marketing and politics called "temporal decision-making." The theory goes something like this: when we need to make a decision that is temporally distant, we tend to think in abstractions. When we need to make a decision that is temporally immediate, we think much more concretely. So, for example, if I told you that I was sending you on a vacation to Hawaii in three years, you might think about beautiful sunsets, sandy beaches, and maybe the splendor of Kapalua's Plantation course. If, however, I told you that I was sending you to Hawaii in three hours, you would think about what to pack, who is going to walk your dogs, whether you are able to take off work, and how you'll get to the airport.

Having no time for abstract dreaming about Whistling Straits, I went straight to the concrete: *What commitments had I made for Thursday? How would we be getting there? What appointments would I have to reschedule? What would Theresa say?* I got started working through it.

First, at home: if I needed any more evidence about the amazing relationship with Theresa, she gave it to me: "Have a great time!

We'll figure it out." I smiled at her, knowing she meant it. The most important challenge was solved.

Second, at work: I checked my schedule. I called and emailed my colleagues and rescheduled every meeting. Second challenge solved.

Third, make plans with Mike. He would drive. We would leave Wednesday night, drive the five hours to Green Bay, stay overnight at the nearby casino hotel, and then drive the rest in the morning. All good. I got my clubs together and tried to slow down my heartbeat. This is really happening.

The drive that night to Green Bay was uneventful, and we managed to share a hotel room. Whether it was because of our shared excitement for playing Whistling Straits, or just exhaustion, we both slept well and awoke early, ready to go. The hour-long drive to Kohler was a slow buildup. The course, set on the Lake Michigan coast, is well-hidden until the entrance. And what an entrance it is. The winding drive from the county road to the clubhouse gives a distinct feeling of entering another world. The well-maintained pot bunkers on the entrance mounds signals the experience that is about to unfold. We were both so excited, with our cameras clicking away.

When you get to play a course like Whistling Straits, you don't think much about the conditions. As long as the course is open, you want to play. So it came as an utter surprise to me that the weather was—there's no other way to put it—awful. We were told it was 43 degrees with 20-mph sustained north wind—not the prevailing south wind of summer. So, the course would play in the opposite wind conditions as we might have seen on TV. Well, while I knew of Whistling Straits from the majors contested there, and while I knew the basic look of the course, I hadn't honed in on the hole directions, and which holes tended to play into the wind, and which were downwind. Needless to say, I know now.

I spent the better part of my time before teeing off trying to find some semblance of a swing. While Mike and I had spent years working together to prepare me for a course as challenging as Whistling Straits, my body didn't seem to remember any of the moves he taught me. On the range, every drive seemed to slice to the right. And with the wind, that meant a slice to the *far* right.

Mike walked by. "How's the swing?" *Awful*, I wanted to say. *Help*, I wanted to scream. But while Mike was a pro and my teacher, he was also a golfer, getting his first taste of Whistling Straits.

"Great!" I lied.

I tried everything I could think of to straighten out my drives, and the more I tried and the more I failed, the harder it got to focus on the course on which I was about to tee off. I had to leave the range—maybe I would find something on the putting green. Thankfully I had a lot more feel on and around the greens. I would stay there for the rest of the warmup.

Before this day, I had never played a Pete Dye design. Of course, I've heard of him and his "dye-abolical" courses, but it was entirely theoretical. That changed when I set foot on the Straits course along the western coast of Lake Michigan. The course has beauty, yes. But more importantly, it has brawn. Dye sets off your trepidation immediately from the practice green overlooking the 1st tee. As I stood on the practice green, nervous and worried about my wayward swing on this freezing October day, I couldn't help but look across the vista at what was coming: it's about a three-minute walk down and then up to the tee. It feels so far away, and so massive, like peering into a gauntlet, like you're entering Lake Michigan. Not a gentle handshake from Pete Dye.

Our caddie was an affable and enthusiastic young man who was torn between slowing us down to experience the majesty of Whistling Straits and speeding us up so we all could get a warm drink. But his ambivalence about spending his October day freezing his ass off did not damper my enthusiasm. Walking down the path toward the 1st hole felt a bit like walking into a historic ballpark, or even a great cathedral. If you've ever had the opportunity to venture inside Wrigley Field, or even the Sagrada Familia in Barcelona or the Palace of Versailles outside Paris, you should have a sense of the feeling of awe I experienced entering this Dye masterpiece. I'm sure that his Stadium Course at PGA West, TPC Sawgrass, Kiawah Island, Crooked Stick, are true masterpieces. They may even create a sense of awe-inspired wonder. But from my experience, no course creates this awe-inspiring feeling as completely as Whistling

Straits. But this feeling of entering a special ballpark is also coupled with the reality of having to *play* in that ballpark. Not in a year, or a month, or even a day. There were no practice rounds for me ... I had to swing away in five minutes. Where there is awe, there can also be fear.

Whistling Straits plays down and back along the coast of Lake Michigan, in the shape of a figure eight. The 1st and 10th holes dogleg somewhat easterly toward the water, while the 9th and 18th holes play back toward the clubhouse. As well, the separate nines don't play entirely in the same direction. Instead, Dye instituted a "cross-over" whereby holes 2 through 4 play south, then golfers are turned north for holes 5 through 8 and 11 through 13, and then, at the northern-most end of the property, golfers (*and sheep*) are turned back to the south for 14 through 17. If you're counting, that's seven holes north, seven holes south, and just two holes to the east and two to the west. And if you recall from my description above, we were playing in 43 degrees with a 20-mile north wind. Although I didn't realize it at the time, all of that meant that we would play seven holes in a row into the wind, with only a brief respite at the turn.

As well, while we were not playing the course from the tips—an astounding 7,790 yards—we were still playing a healthy 6,663 yards from the green tees. Yet despite its length, the 1st hole is actually quite reachable. At 370 yards from the tee, our caddie suggested a solid 3-wood, which would leave us with a simple 9-iron or wedge to the hole. "Just keep it to the right," he suggested. Well, on the practice green, I had no trouble keeping it right. In fact, virtually everything veered so far right that it wouldn't be found in the dunes.

At least that's what I was thinking as I arrived at the tee. Without listening, I pulled driver. I wasn't thinking of the wind, or the shortness of the hole, or the walk we were about to commence. Instead, I teed up my ball with what mental coaches could only describe as bad thoughts: *don't slice the ball, don't hit it in the junk,* and most importantly, *don't embarrass yourself.* I had apparently left useful mantras like smooth and tempo back in Minnesota.

You might be able to guess what came next: yes, my first duck hook of the day. I think my hands arrived at the ball a full second before my body and the ball curved left over left, into the junk. My ball was whistling, but certainly not straight. My friend and teacher Mike let out an unsurprised breath, walked to the tee himself, and proceeded to stripe his ball down the right side of the fairway. He grabbed two clubs from his bag and sent our caddie off with me to find my ball. We did find it, and I then struggled through several sand shots to finally reach the green in four. Two putts later I walked off with an embarrassing double bogey on the 1st hole.

I struggled with my swing over the entire front nine, with four double bogeys and five bogeys. I wished I could bury my head in one of the dunes. But golf allows only short breaks, and I would have to rediscover my love for the game quickly. We made the long walk past the clubhouse, and I bought sandwiches for myself, Mike, and our caddies. We took a moment to sit and eat and total up the damage. I had just shot an outward 49. Wow, those are scores that I hadn't seen since many years back, when I returned to golf. Only a brilliant back nine 40, in these conditions, would allow me to break 90. It was such a remote possibility that I talked myself into a completely different focus: *Listen to your caddie. Smooth swing. Forget about the score. Bear witness to this amazing place.*

As we reached the tee, I had a much better perspective. I felt lighter and could clearly swing faster. My drive on the 10th was good, but not great, left in the fairway on this short par four, well back. I would need a long iron to have any chance to get up the hill onto the green into this wind. And there it was: one of the best 3-irons I've ever hit, soaring up and over the mound and onto the 10th green. It was so good that my caddie, who had watched the miserable 49 on the front, let at a discernable "wow" of surprised excitement as my second shot pierced through the wind. My slightly tentative birdie putt came up short, but I had my first par of the day.

We still had to battle the wind for the next three holes—three straight bogeys—but my mind was much more focused as we arrived at the 14th hole. As we climbed the hill, I realized that we were turning back downwind. And suddenly, we collectively gasped at a remarkable sight: hundreds of sheep in the 14th fairway. With the wind howling above, the mounds surrounding the 14th kept the sheep warm and dry (not to mention their wool). A refuge was here, for sure.

I put the next drive into the fairway as well, and as we were walking down the fairway, Mike had to take a knee. I blurted out, "Are you okay?"

"My back just gave out." Mike had suffered from back problems for years, but the swing on the 14th put him over the edge. He was done, I mean really done. He didn't pick up a club for the rest of the round. Maybe it was my years of playing soccer, but I can't imagine not playing through that injury. I have no doubt that he was in pain, but this was Whistling Straits! But a pro knows, and Mike was done. He could only watch whatever was to come down the stretch.

I managed to scrape together three wind-aided pars on those final five holes, helped in part by Mike becoming my on-course coach. He helped me read the putts, choose clubs, and line up the shots. It was a lesson in careful concentration and full commitment to each shot. I hit another good tee shot off the 18th and marveled at the sight ahead. With the castle-like clubhouse in the distance, the 18th is a sight for sore eyes. We walked down the fairway, looking for signs of Dustin Johnson's famed "bunker" that cost him the 2010 PGA Championship (it has since been covered in fescue), and remembered the nuances of the day, the course, and my encounter with Pete Dye. From the fairway, I hit a great 3-wood, which had just enough tail on it to land right of the green, on the fairway. I had a 40-yard pitch, which rolled 20 feet past the pin. Two putts later, and I was in for a closing bogey. While my five bogeys on the back exceeded my four pars, the back nine actually showed me that I belonged.

As Tiger might say, I didn't have my "A" game that day, but I did the best with what I had. I was proud of how I turned things around. The course and conditions tested my resolve, and I committed myself to return with a much more positive and confident outlook, and a bit of recognition that I would never conquer the Straits.

Greatness is relative. Sometimes it's less obvious, and we have to train ourselves to know when we see it. I had played in the big ballpark, walked the same steps as the greats, and I had faced the fear and the glory; and I had a wind burn to prove it.

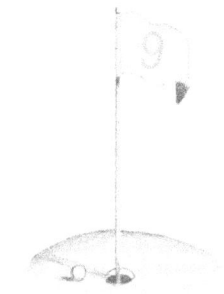

Priorities

(2010-11)

B efore I became a father, I knew I wanted to be a soccer coach. I had a lot of experience as a player: growing up in the Maryland suburbs of Washington DC, soccer was the sport of choice for many kids. I played basketball in the winter and dabbled in other sports throughout the year, but soccer was my mainstay. While not an accomplished player throughout high school, I developed well-enough to make it on to my Division III college team, where I experienced immediate success. Over the course of four years, I became my college's second all-time leading goal scorer, and first in assists and total points. I was awarded Academic All-American for the Midwest Region, All-Region, All-State, and I was named All-Conference every year while I started for four straight years.

Like many college graduates, I didn't have an immediate plan. I knew I wanted to work for a few years, before maybe getting a graduate degree of some kind. But I had no inkling of what, and I was burned out from an intense senior year of college. So, with little more than a dream, I decided to go to Ireland where I would try to play soccer professionally. Yes, that's right—I was going to try to get on a professional team, with no connections, no agent, no plan. I did have a girlfriend, and she was going to Ireland, so I figured that at the very worst, we would have more time together.

It was an inauspicious start, to say the least. After packing and saying goodbye to our respective families, we set off on a plane for London. The plan, as much as we had one, was to land in London, spend a couple of days with family friends adjusting to the time change, and the find a way—likely by ferry—to Ireland. We had about a week to do it. The flight was uneventful, and we filled out the requisite customs forms. We sleepily disembarked the plane and waited in the immigration line at Heathrow. My girlfriend Jennifer went through without a hitch. She was stopping in England briefly to visit friends, and then going to Ireland to study—simple enough. Then it was my turn. I expected the same result. The immigration officer asked me a few simple questions to confirm my identity as he examined my passport. Then, he asked what in retrospect were the most important questions, but at the time I hadn't given it any thought. "Why are you coming to England?" he asked.

"To visit friends," I replied.

"Are you two together?," he asked.

"Yes."

"So, you're going to Ireland?"

"Yes."

"What will you be doing in Ireland?" It was a simple question. If I had known, I would have said something innocuous and touristy, something like: "to explore," or "to read James Joyce," or "to play golf."

Instead, I answered honestly: "I'm going to try to play soccer." He looked up from the passport. It was probably one of the moments in his day that he remembers among the sea of lazy exchanges about tourism.

He responded, "for money?"

"Ah, yes, if they will pay me." Big mistake. The look he gave me was one I will never forget. It was a combination of *are you crazy!?* and *are you a criminal!?* and *are you a stupid American!?*

"Wait here," he said to me, as he got up off his perch. I looked at Jennifer and kind of shrugged my shoulders, realizing that I had made a mistake, but not yet knowing what, or why, or what the hell I could do about it. After about a 10-minute wait, as the line behind me became more and more impatient, his supervisor came out and said, "come with me."

"Can I have a moment to talk to my friend?" I pleaded.

"Yes," he impatiently responded.

I went over to Jennifer. I gave her the address and phone number of our family friends and said, "I don't know what's going on, but this might take a while. Please go. I'll call you when we're finished." She walked to get our bags while I obeyed the immigration official, therein beginning a daylong odyssey—my very own Joycean moment. I was taken to a holding cell, which was a desk-sized glass-enclosed room with two chairs facing each other and a tiny table. They kept me in the room alone for an hour, as the jetlag weighed upon me.

The supervisor finally came in with a serious look on his face. "Do you know why you're here?" I had no idea. As far as I was concerned, I was just coming to Ireland to try to fulfill a dream—isn't that why people come to Ireland? I didn't say that, of course. I shook my head. "You're here because you can't go to Ireland and get a job. While you are in England now, we have an agreement with Ireland to enforce their immigration laws. They do not allow foreign workers, no matter the profession. Do you realize that the unemployment rate in Ireland is 16%?"

I had no idea about any of this. I had grown up with high unemployment during the Carter years, but I was so young that I really didn't know what that meant. And I had no idea that the Irish kept foreigners out, unless their purpose was to create jobs with their money. They had no interest in someone coming to Ireland to take some of that money out. All of that was completely off my radar. I just wanted to play soccer.

"I don't need the money. I'll play for free. I just want to play soccer."

"Do you have any money on you?" I had a few hundred dollars in travelers' checks—those quaint paper documents that were actually used in place of cash and credit cards and Venmo back in the early 1990s. I showed him the checks. "That's not enough."

I stumbled for the right words. "I'll get my parents to send me money. Can I call them?" He looked at me—*likely story*, he was no doubt thinking. However, he did allow me to make a call. I woke up my mother in the middle of the night and managed to explain the situation. I tried to keep my sleep-deprived mind together. We hatched a plan.

"What if you commit to send me money on a regular basis so I could stay in Ireland for more than two weeks? What if I promised not to get a job?" It might work. My mother acquiesced. After the phone call, I motioned to the guard—yes, it was a bit like jail—that I would like to speak to the immigration official. He made me wait another hour at least, and then came in with a terse "what?" I explained our idea. "If we do those things, could I go to Ireland?"

"Let me talk to my supervisor." It felt a bit like negotiating when buying a car, when the salesman leaves the room to "talk to a supervisor" and proceeds to make up something, only to return with a definitive "no." He did leave and allegedly did have such a conversation, and predictably, another hour later, rejected our proposal. He would allow me to use the phone, however.

Over the next six hours, I made calls to family as we frantically tried to persuade the English immigration office, working with their Irish counterparts, to let this young, ignorant American enter their country. At around 5pm, the officer returned. "You're being deported." As if to drive home the point, he took my passport, put it on the desk in front of me, and pulled out his red pen. He drew a bright red "X" through the stamp that the first immigration officer had affixed before asking me that fateful question. My scarlet letter. "Please go with these two officers." The young immigration officers silently walked me back into the airport, to the gate, and we began down to the jetway. I passed hundreds of other passengers, who no doubt looked at me as a criminal being led by security onto a plane back to the States. As we were about halfway down the jetway, a young, out-of-breath immigration officer came running up to us with the magic words: *"you can stay!"* I couldn't believe my ears. It was all so surreal.

In fact, the Irish immigration office, in all their wisdom, had been convinced that I could come to their country. I'm not sure if they just came to realize that I was just a kid, not a job-stealing schemer, or whether a certain Member of Congress had intervened and convinced them not to make it an international incident, or whether they were just tired from a long day. But for whatever reason, the Irish government changed their mind. Our original immigration officer, who by now was at the end of a very long workday, told me, "you'll have to provide copies of your parent's bank statements to prove that they have the money. They will have to send you money every week. And you will have to contact Christie Moore, the head of the immigration office in Dublin." I also had to give them the address where I was staying in London, and they gave me only 48 hours to get to Dublin. If I hadn't met with Christie Moore in Dublin within 48 hours, they would come to this address, find me, and deport me on the next plane. "Do you understand?" I did. I let out a huge sigh of relief, gathered my bags, and set off to find our family friends.

When I got there, I told Jennifer and our friends the entire story. We had one night there, and then we had to head west to the coast and get a ferry to Dublin. I collapsed in bed, slept the full night through, and the next day we headed off. Once in Dublin, I called Christie Moore's office, told his assistant who I was and that I was in Dublin, and she instructed me to come to Mr. Moore's office first thing the next morning.

As we sat in a Dublin coffeehouse, we surveyed our predicament. "Tomorrow, I have to see Christie Moore. Today, we have to find an apartment." We searched the newspapers and found an advertisement for a small, one bedroom in Rathmines, on the south side of Dublin. After seeing this apartment in a newly built building, we signed the lease right away.

The next morning, I found my way to downtown Dublin and the office of Christie Moore. He was a gray-haired Irishman with rosy cheeks. "Come in," he offered as he smiled warmly and invited me into his bureaucratic office. So this was the man who made that fateful decision two days ago. We both realized right away that this was not a criminal enterprise.

"What brings you to Ireland?"

"I just graduated from college and my girlfriend is here in Dublin to study."

"Go on," he said in his thick Irish brogue.

"I want to fulfill a dream to try to play soccer outside the US," I relayed.

"But not for money, right?"

"Absolutely not," I replied.

"You're not going to get another job, right?"

"Absolutely not." He smiled, wrote something down in the file he had apparently been keeping since I arrived in London, and said the magic Irish words: "Have a pint of Guinness for me." That was the last I saw of Christie Moore.

Within a week, I walked on to a field near Trinity College where I saw a group of soccer players. It looked more like a pick-up scrimmage than a practice; I didn't see a coach anywhere. I donned my cleats and asked them if I could join. Although we all spoke English, they knew immediately that I was a foreigner and looked at me like they were ready to take it to the naïve American. That day, I played well, impressing them enough that I was no longer an American to be mocked, but a player to be recruited. They asked me to join their team, which turned out to be an alumni team of Trinity College Dublin. I played in a number of matches and ended up being their leading scorer, and then was recruited by another team. And then another. And finally, I was playing on a team full of semi-professionals. I had done it. I never took a paycheck, although I was provided with plenty of food and drink by the team. But I was playing soccer abroad—a dream come true.

*   *   *

Years later, I wanted to continue my soccer days by teaching my boys how to play soccer and then coaching them. From age five, I coached them as they played "swarm ball" at the local park. I discovered I had the ability to take a group of 10 kids and make them love soccer. We would play silly games to teach ball skills. I'd give them each a ball, show them some tricks, and then watch them laugh as they tried not to "break the egg." I'd give them a ball and we'd have races back and forth across the field, making sure the "egg" didn't get "cooked." With Aidan, it was fun, but it was clear that he was doing it to try to master a skill. He always had a look of seriousness on his face, afraid to make a mistake.

Elliott, by contrast, was fearless on the pitch. The ball seemed to stick to his shoes like a magnet as he managed as a five-year-old to dribble the ball across the field with it always under his control. Other players kicked and watched the ball; while still others couldn't figure out how to kick it at all. Elliott, however, kept his feet on the ball like glue. I didn't keep track of how many goals he scored that season, but basically the kids quickly understood that if Elliott got the ball at his feet, he'd score. Other parents were shocked at how well he dribbled. "You must be practicing," they told me. I responded, truthfully, that he had no interest in practice.

"He just does it," I remarked. It probably sounded arrogant, like Elliott just does this naturally. But although Elliott was remarkably good at soccer, it was clear that he didn't love it. He would come to games, happy to be there. But that love wouldn't stay with him. He didn't seek out a ball, didn't want to play at other times. Part of it surely was due to the fact that Aidan had now begun to play baseball, and we went to baseball games, not soccer games. As a result, Elliott was around baseball and wanted to emulate his older brother. But part of it was also just a lack of interest.

I can't explain why I fell in love with soccer at age five, or why my boys didn't. I gave them the same opportunities, at least in soccer, but many times it just doesn't stick. For me, it could've been that I was pulled out of baseball immediately, while my friends and I were kept in soccer. I don't remember it, but apparently when I was five I had a hard time hitting a ball on a tee. As a result, my mother decided that I wasn't good at baseball, and instead signed me up for soccer. I made close friends on the soccer team and persisted. By contrast, when Aidan and Elliott struggled to hit a ball off a tee, I bought a tee, and took them to the local park, and we practiced. I tried to instill in them a quest for *improvement*, not a quest for *perfection*. It didn't matter how good they were, it just mattered that they were trying to get better. It's hard to know why people choose to love the things they love, but my first love was soccer and theirs was baseball. And so I learned not to mistake my dreams for my sons' dreams. I wouldn't dream about what I thought my kids *should* do, or what I *wanted* them to do. Instead, I'd help them play the sport they wanted and to persist at it.

*   *   *

When Aidan's first baseball season was over, we set off to join my extended family for a get together in Washington State. Yes, a family reunion. Family reunions are tough for many, but for a spouse they are even tougher. And when the member of the family leaves to play golf while the spouse is left to take care of the kids with their extended in-laws—well, that's grounds for divorce. So, why did I do it? I love Theresa deeply, and I've always tried to be a fantastic husband. But for some of us, the golf addiction is real.

I asked Theresa, "Are you interested in going to Marrowstone Island in Washington State for a family reunion?" After a few seconds of silence, I lobbied: "it will be fun."

"Sure," she said. It wasn't much of a discussion. Our kids were eight and five, big enough to do many things for themselves, but not old enough to be by themselves. They would be with us—or with her, if I were golfing.

"I'd like to go golfing with my uncles and maybe Dave," I told her. I found out later that she interpreted that as golfing once with my uncles and brother-in-law. What I meant was golfing *every day*. With at least three golfers available every day to join me, how could I say no? In retrospect, quite easily. But I didn't, and thereby created the basis for a decade-long story of ditching my family. *But it was golf!*

The trip began smoothly enough. Now that we had two school-aged kids, they were more able than before to pack for a trip. Of course, while some kids are able to plan their wardrobe in advance, get their suitcases packed, and be ready at a very young age, we didn't have such kids. Our boys were more the throw-everything-in-a-pile-and-stare-at-it types. And we had piles. Their rooms were piles of random clothes, apparently residing at the very spot where they were removed last. Socks had no partners, and there was no such thing as a dresser—oh, the furniture was in their rooms, they simply served as decoration. The floor was their dresser.

After a few rough hours frantically trying to find everything needed to pack—even though Theresa had carefully packed both of their suitcases earlier in the week—we finally made it to the airport. Usually airports can be stressful, dealing with the ticketing, security and gate lines, the waiting. But by this point in our lives we had finally figured out the keys to successful airport travel: video games and food. We had long since given up the idea that we should limit screen time during travel. There simply was no other way to keep them engaged for long enough. We had tried playing cards—that worked, but for only a short time. And reading a book aloud was great, until the people sitting around you began to cough in disgust as their heard the same book for the fourth time. So we brought a backpack full of snacks, and each of the boys had a gaming device for the trip.

We managed to make it all the way—on planes, cars and ferries—to Marrowstone Island. An idyllic island in the northernmost section of Puget Sound, almost to the Salish Sea, Marrowstone is the kind of place people go to get away from civilization. While not uninhabited, the island has fewer than 900 residents. We would be seeing more otters and other water animals than people.

We arrived at the place where we were staying, gave our hugs to long-time-not-seen aunts, uncles, and cousins, and set off for the beach. There, we would collect driftwood, dig for clams, watch the otters play in the ocean. Elliott was most comfortable being carried, and Aidan wanted to run along the water. It was a blissful first day. After having our large get-reacquainted meal—and after realizing just how much the next generation had grown and the older generation had aged—we excused ourselves for our bedtime ritual. Books such as *Goodnight Moon, My Rotten Redheaded Older Brother*, and others kept us busy as we quieted down for the night.

The next morning, after I woke up early with the boys to get them fed, I brought both boys to Theresa. I announced, "I'm heading out to golf." I had made plans with my uncles and brother-in-law, but from the look Theresa gave me, I had apparently not shared those plans with her. Her eyes seemed to say, *you're leaving me with the kids, alone with your family?* Her mouth smiled and said, "see you later." It was an unenthusiastic goodbye to say the least. But drawn by my addiction, I didn't stop to ask her if she was okay, or if I could have communicated any better. I just left.

We had a fun round of golf on the island muni, with holes that weren't particularly challenging, but with beautiful surroundings and great company. We laughed at bad shots and cheered at good ones. We had a blast.

But the blast that I left on the golf course quickly became a blast of a different kind when I returned. The boys had been difficult to say the least, needing Theresa constantly. That's one thing when at home, where we have what they need and plenty of options for

adult mental breaks. It's entirely different on the road, when not only was Theresa stuck in a small cabin, but in the main cabin with the kitchen where she was expected to be social and conversant with her in-laws. And this would have been enough for a single day—that should have been clear to me from day one. But three straight days moved the annoyance of the first round to all-out rage by the final round. Theresa somehow kept her rage under control—she's not the type to throw dishes. But she was really mad. And I had my golf addiction to blame.

It took me longer than it should, but the trip underscored my failure to get my priorities right. I loved golf, for sure. But I love my family more. I have made some bad—perhaps cocky—decisions in the past, with soccer, and Ireland, and now the family reunion. While yet another round of golf is surely fun, what matters far more is having the self-awareness to wake up from your own dream, and be fully present for your family.

Irish Course at Whistling Straits (Sheboygan, WI)

As a general rule, at the end of April every year I would put away my winter gear, including the winter window scraper. On this morning in May, therefore, I'd have to get rid of the frost covering my car another way. I started the car and turned up the defroster. The thermometer read 37 degrees—it would be a cold one today at Whistling Straits. But first, I had to get there. Kohler, Wisconsin is a stunning small town with high-end shops and two truly world-class golf courses at Blackwolf Run. The drive from Kohler to Whistling Straits is a short one: just 20 minutes, through Sheboygan. But while the geographic distance if short, the economic differences are massive. From the wealth of Kohler to the working-class struggles of Sheboygan, back to the wealth of Whistling Straits, the drive is an economic rollercoaster. Sheboygan, home of companies such as Plenko Plastics and Old World Ice Creamery, seems to embrace its 1950s ethos, with small, well-kept homes. The wealth brought to the region by the Kohler corporation had not yet spread to Sheboygan.

Would it ever? Just outside of town, driving north on Lakeshore Drive, the homes and farms get bigger. And, of course, the massive Kohler plant. After three more miles, the mounds begin, and lurking behind them is Whistling Straits.

I casually and calmly parked my car, focusing on slowing my heartrate and believing that I had about 75 minutes to warm up. I slowly arranged my golf gear and sauntered over toward the clubhouse. While I wouldn't be playing the "big course," I still looked out over the dunes toward the ocean-like Lake Michigan. As beautiful as ever. Eventually, I made my way to the clubhouse. "Checking in for my eight o'clock tee time," I calmly shared.

The assistant pro checked on his computer with a confused look on his face. "Sorry, I don't see you on the tee sheet. Just a minute." He found his manager. "I'm sorry sir, I don't see your name at 8 am, and we are completely booked today." I knew I had reserved a tee time on the Irish course. *Could I have screwed up? Did they make a mistake?* Increasingly worried, I opened up my phone and found the confirmation email from the course. Phew! I showed it to the manager. "Ah, I see the problem: your tee time is 7:30am." I smiled and gulped at the same time. I would be teeing off in *20 minutes*. While I was relieved to find the time, I realized quickly that it meant I would have time to hit only a handful of balls before I had to make my way to the tee. It was tough to switch into high gear so quickly. It was a mistake I would regret for the rest of the day.

I've found that most of my 18-hole scores fall within a range of 80 to 84. Sometimes I play well and break 80, but other times I make too many mistakes and rise into the mid-80s. Today was one of those exceptional days, and not in a good way. I walked off the Irish course lucky for equitable stroke control, which holds my scores to a maximum of double bogey. The actual tournament score would have been 95.

I used to think I'd have a chance of being a scratch golfer, but it never happened. That dream, like others, would not become a reality. And I've learned to be more than okay with that. It's not about perfection, after all, but improvement—whether that's measured over a year, or a decade, or a life, or a day.

My playing partners for the day were three men—Joe, Steven, and Andrew—of approximately my age, from all over the country. Like me, each of these three golfers would inevitably have some great shots that day, and some terrible shots, and all types in between.

As I took my practice swings on the 1st hole—aimed straight at the giant blue lake—I felt tight. And my swing showed it, as I sent the first drive high and right, looking more like a faded 9-iron than a driver. My ball was easily identifiable in the thick fescue over the mounds to the right. My caddie Sam took a careful look at me. "You have a couple of options. The distance is 193 uphill. You could try to punch your hybrid or 4-iron. You could take a wedge and just pitch to the fairway. Or you could hit an 8-iron and try to place it for a pitch to the green."

My sense is that caddies are told to build the golfer's ego and create an atmosphere of positivity, rather than to tell them what they can't or shouldn't do. They are told to cheer on their player when a good shot appears—sometimes, seemingly out of nowhere—and to shake off the many, many bad shots that they must see. So Sam was faced with a dilemma: *should I allow him to pull his hybrid, knowing that the chances that he hits it through the fescue, over the mound, and with enough carry to keep it on the right side up the hill onto the green? Should I risk insulting him and tell him just take a wedge and get it back in play? Or, should I advise him to take an 8-iron, swing smoothly to advance the ball up the hill, and have a wedge shot to the green?* Personally, I've learned that my golfing game rarely finds hero status, and more often than not my hero shots end up in worse places. I gave him permission: "I don't have an ego here. What do you suggest?"

He tentatively answered, "maybe you shouldn't try the hero shot on the 1st hole." I quickly agreed and asked him what distance would put me about 90 yards from the pin. A smooth swing advanced the ball up the fairway well. I hit my next wedge shot it a bit too well and ended up on the back of the green. I cozied my ball down the hill to about two feet and tapped in for an opening bogey. Given the terrible drive, I was happy to walk off with only one stroke lost.

Andrew and I walked to the next tee together.

"What brings you to the Irish today?," I asked.

"Escaping my kids," he offered, with a mix of seriousness and playfulness that was hard to place.

"Oh yeah, how old are they?"

"Teenagers. I've got a boy and a girl, and they've turned into monsters. They hate me." Although I couldn't relate (yet) to the wrath of teenage hatred, I could relate to wanting to get to a golf course to escape for a while.

"I'm sorry to hear that. I hope today gives you a reprieve." I thought of playing golf in Marrowstone—*Had I been trying to "escape" my family? Is that why Theresa had been so mad?* The thought hit me like a ton of bricks. I had always thought of golf as something I just did for fun.

I played the first eight holes in five over, with a mix of fades, some great iron shots, and a few unlucky breaks. The par-four 9th hole heads back down the hill. On most short par fours, I had been foregoing my driver in favor of my 3-wood or less. For some reason, I decided to play driver. Sam was clearly displeased but agreed, and surprisingly I hit an excellent drive to about 90 yards in front of the green. When we arrived at my ball, Sam instructed me, "the green is elevated and there's a creek directly in front," which I could barely see. "Play an extra club and aim for the middle of the green." I obeyed and hit a fantastic wedge right over the flagstick, my ball coming to rest about eight feet above the hole. Sam gave me a read, and I stood up to the putt. I buried it and celebrated with a fist pump. It was good to get one back.

Although I wasn't going to set any records with the 40 on the front, I felt like I was playing well enough. As we walked toward the back nine, I had a chance to talk to Steven. Throughout the front nine, he had seemed quiet, absorbed with his golf and not particularly interested in engaging. But he was wearing a Milwaukee Brewers hat, so I decided to try to engage him with baseball.

"I'm more of a Twins fan," I smiled and gestured toward his hat. "Are you from Milwaukee?"

"Yeah, born and raised. My wife and I are raising our two kids a few blocks from where I was raised." Having married a Wisconsin-ite, I knew that it was pretty common for people from Wisconsin to spend their entire lives there. But it was so far out of my own experience, I decided to ask him about it. "Is it strange living so close to where you were raised?"

"Um, not really," Steven replied. "I've never really wanted to live anywhere else." Simple enough.

"Do your kids feel the same way?" I wondered. He smiled.

"I sure hope so. My oldest daughter is going to college in Milwaukee and my son just committed to go to Madison." I smiled. I wouldn't have pegged him for having such old kids, but it made sense. I was thinking about what it meant to stay so close to home. I've always felt antsy to leave—to travel to places like Ireland to experience different ways of life and to make some (terrible) mistakes. Here was a man who seemed utterly content with staying home.

With my mind on the idea of home, not on my poor round of golf, it's not surprising that my first swing resulted in a poor fade on the 10th hole, right into some thick rough, and continued with fades on the next two holes, resulting in three straight bogeys. Needless to say, the back nine had not started like the front ended. And that, dear reader, brings us to the 13th, Blind Man's Bluff, an absurdly difficult par three measuring 152 yards. The green is almost entirely blocked by the mound, with just a tiny tabletop visible at the far upper right corner. The green has multiple tiers, starting from the bottom tier on the front left and moving up, step by step, to the top tier on the upper right. The only place to find a pin placement that's visible from the tee is to use a 10-foot-long pin and place it on the tiny tabletop in the upper right. In other words, even the most magnificent shots will not be able to hold the top tier of the green, and most likely will roll out to 40 feet. Right off the green are dozens of bunkers, thick rough, and other hazards. That's fine enough on a hole with a green that can hold approaches. But the punishment for a good shot here simply doesn't match the crime. No one in our group managed better than a double bogey, each with at least three putts.

Definitely not the back nine I had dreamed of. While the remainder of the holes at the Irish course are good, even great, my play wasn't. I hit some terrible fades and slices, mentally anguished with a string of bogeys and doubles, with only one well-played hole breaking that streak. My drive at the par four, 425-yard 16th was the best of the day by far. While it wasn't far enough to clear the hill (that would have required close to 300 yards), I was sufficiently up the hill to reach a relatively flat area. Sensing an opportunity for some positive thinking, Sam said: "Okay, let's get focused on the shot. You're 175 yards to a back pin. But the wind is in your face. I think it's playing closer to 195 yards." With my limited experience with caddies, I've found that following their instructions usually results in better-than-normal outcomes. I obeyed, pulled my 4-iron and hit it about as well as I could. It wasn't enough to get to the elevated green, as my ball landed and stopped about 10 yards short of the green. But it was well-executed. Having just missed a gap wedge from a similar distance, I felt good about making amends and hit my wedge low, and with a couple of bounces it rolled out to less than two feet. A one-putt for my only par of the back nine.

With four doubles, four bogeys, and that lone par, I carded a dismal 48 for the back nine. Limping home was an understatement, but for some reason I felt refreshed. All it takes is a dose of reality and a shift in perspective. I chose to listen to my guide Sam, I chose to accept help, I chose to focus on what mattered and forgot what didn't. I was thinking about Steven's view of staying close to home. I was thinking about Andrew's need to "escape" his kids. It's really about priorities. I wasn't going to be Steven, as I'm far too interested in exposing my children to the diversity of the world. And I don't think I was trying to escape my kids, but when I left them alone with Theresa, that was the result. I would have to get my priorities straight as a father. I would have to be myself, and accept my boys as they are, even if they chose baseball over soccer. I would have to be present when they need me, and count my blessings when I get to spend the day on the coast of Lake Michigan.

The Turn

In every round of golf, there's a pause. You might stop in the clubhouse, a halfway house to refuel, perhaps a bathroom or even the trees to release. Some golfers tend to pause quickly, if nothing else to signify that they are starting the second nine. Other golfers take a longer break to rest their minds and their bodies. The origins of *the turn*, in case the concept is unfamiliar, traces to classic links courses, where the first nine was laid out in one direction away from the clubhouse, and the golfers had to turn from the *outward* nine in the reverse direction as they began the *inward* nine. For most contemporary courses, the turn often occurs with a return to the clubhouse. Either way, the turn is less about a physical change of directions now than a sort of pitstop—often the opportunity for courses to sell food and drinks to their famished golfers, but also a moment to pause, reflect, and reset one's mind. Often, this reset can result in a change in quality of play. It helps to take a moment to look at what you're doing, and what you can do to make things take a turn for the better.

*   *   *

When I think about my first 18 years as a father, there is no event, episode, decision, or worry that doesn't involve my wife, Theresa. And yet my storytelling is from my perspective by design—I wanted to tell my version of these years. Of course, she has her own version. In fact, several months after the births of each of our sons, we both wrote down our memories of their birth stories. As we shared and read one another's reflections, it was shocking to see how different they were. In golf as in life, perspective can be everything.

Theresa and I met when we were in our twenties. In August 1998, I moved from my job in Washington, DC to Minneapolis. I had come to the Twin Cities to write my first book—about Minneapolis neighborhoods—and work at the Center for Democracy and Citizenship at the University of Minnesota's Humphrey Institute. I found a great two-bedroom apartment in a classic four-unit building in the Elliot Park neighborhood of Minneapolis, just south of Hennepin County Medical Center. Living with a large dog in the heart of the city wasn't easy. Zoe, a four-year old german shepherd/husky mix, and my only concrete reminder from my first marriage, needed a lot of exercise, but there wasn't a nearby dog run. Instead, I took her on long walks through city streets, let her chase squirrels, but too often leaving her home alone.

At work, I met a group of graduate students who had a similar interest in public policy. I met these new friends for drinks often as they showed me around the city. One of the friends had a roommate, Nick, who is blind. Although I didn't see Nick very often, somehow we quickly realized we both had a shared interest in alternative music, and in particular the singer-songwriter Liz Phair. Nick was a huge fan of hers, as was I, but I also had met her. Well, sort of. Liz and I went to college together. As a freshman, I loved to hang out in my teammates' home—nicknamed the Blue House. I remember watching March Madness there. The house, full of soccer players, was a perennial mess. And yet one room almost always had its door closed. The one time I looked in, I noticed that it was remarkably clean. In this house, it stood out like John Daly in Loudmouth golf pants. And the resident of said room was none other than a young art student named Liz Phair, with whom I had shared a few brief hellos.

A few years after graduation, I first learned from my teammates that their former housemate Liz had recorded her first album, *Exile in Guyville* (1993). I found a copy and immediately loved it. The next year Liz released her second album *Whip-Smart* (1994), which I also loved. But the album that really captivated me was *whitechocolatespaceegg* (1998), which also happened to be the album that Liz would be performing at her concert in Minneapolis' First Avenue in October 1998. Nick and I resolved to buy tickets as soon as they went on sale.

I had never been to a concert with a blind person, and certainly not with Nick. So, I wasn't sure what to expect or how I could help. Nick wasn't the kind of person to beat around the bush, however, so he told me straight up: "I don't need much help. Just make sure I see when there are stairs, or other barriers that might be dangerous. Once we're at First Avenue, I don't care where we stand, I just want to be close enough to hear Liz." I admired his directness and his priorities.

To make sure we found a good standing spot (there were no seats at First Avenue), Nick and I arrived early. We found a spot on the upper floor where I could get a great view of Liz's performance, and where Nick could hear perfectly. We had to transverse a flight of stairs, however, so it took a while to get there. We made a pitstop at the bathroom, and the bar, and settled in for what I knew would be a great concert. Although it was quite a wait, we had a good time learning about each other. "How did you get into music?" I asked.

He laughed. "Well, I don't get much from visual arts!"

"Have you been to many concerts?"

"Hundreds. And I didn't see any of them!" Nick was a great companion, so it was an easy wait.

After an hour or so, Liz took the stage. It was magical. At some point while we were jamming to my former teammates' housemates' performance, someone behind me stepped on my heel, partially knocking off my shoe. I turned around and saw a gorgeous woman in a bright dress.

I was momentarily stunned. She said, "oh, I'm sorry. I didn't mean to kick your foot." She raised her arms at that moment to show that she really meant it. Her sleeveless dress exposed the most amazing arms I had ever seen, strong and muscular. I regained my composure. I smiled.

"You can step on my feet anytime you want." This was the first and only time in my life that I had exactly the right line come out of my mouth at exactly the right time. She smiled and we began a conversation. We talked about Liz Phair and I shared my story about college. We talked about music in general. We were lost in each other.

After a little while, I realized that Nick had been facing us the entire time, and that I hadn't introduced him. "Theresa," whose name I had now fully embraced, "this is Nick." They said their hellos.

Then, much to my surprise then, she said somewhat to me, somewhat to the room, "Don't you think he should be facing the stage?"

Nick was really into the music. "He can't see. He doesn't care what direction he is facing." Theresa looked at me skeptically.

We talked through the rest of the concert. After it ended, we resolved to keep talking. We had a few hurdles, however. I needed to get Nick home. And much to my surprise after having spent the entire concert talking to Theresa, she had come with someone else. We were outside when she saw the man whom she apparently had come with. "Can you hold on for just a minute?" she asked me. I waited for a few minutes while she talked to Joe. According to Theresa, she was under the impression that they hadn't been on a date, they had just driven together. I knew better, at least from his perspective. It was clear from his body language that he wasn't happy, but I was in the first moments of my lifelong love affair, so I wasn't going to give it much thought.

Theresa agreed to come with me in my car as we dropped off Nick. Then, we'd go out. And after, I'd drop her off at her car. My sister thinks that the reason Theresa trusted me was that I had come to the concert with a blind man. Theresa is confident that she knew, from that very moment, that I was the one. Whatever the reason, the three of us left together.

With Theresa in the back, we set off to get Nick home. After a few minutes, I came to a stop at a downtown intersection a bit too abruptly. "Whoa!," Theresa said from the back.

"Chill out, backseat driver," Nick responded.

"Well, if you had seen what I just saw!" Theresa made her place known from the start, and my budding feelings were quickly cemented. After we dropped off Nick, Theresa suggested, "one of my friends is having a party. Do you want to go?" We took a while to find the apartment, talking the entire time, and made our way in. Theresa knew the host, who welcomed her with a big smile. She knew no one else. And I, having only moved to Minneapolis a few months before and not having friends outside of Nick and work, knew absolutely no one. It didn't matter. We were only interested in talking to each other.

"What do you think about leaving here and going to a late-night nachos place called Little Tijuana?" I smiled.

"Sure!" We ate nachos late into the early morning, talked continuously, and finally, left for the short drive back to her car. As we arrived I asked, "Can I have your phone number?" She refused. Yes, she refused.

"But," she offered, "if you give me your number, I'll call you." It was a move Theresa had learned from her older sister. I quickly jotted down my number and we hugged goodbye.

I drove home feeling excited, but also despondent. I had never met anyone like Theresa. She was magical. I wanted to see her again. But she wouldn't give me her number. I figured it was a brushoff. But sometime late the next morning, Theresa called. It hadn't been a brushoff ... she had just learned from her sister that it was better to be safe. I wondered why it felt safer to ride in my car than to give out her phone number. I didn't ask. I just reveled in our conversation, which picked up just where it had left off earlier that morning. I asked her on our first date: "Would you like to go for a walk around a lake and come over for dinner? We can stop at the store to buy food," I asked expectantly.

"That sounds great," she warmly replied.

We saw each other almost every day over the next few months. I had an opportunity to go to New York City to stay with my aunt. I asked Theresa if she wanted to come with me. Much to my surprise—and much to the shocked chagrin of her sister—she said yes. That trip was the first of many in our first two years together. We traveled to her childhood home in Wisconsin, we joined my family in Florida, and we made plans to go to Greece. *We moved in together.* It was clear to both of us that we had found our soulmate. But I had rushed into a marriage earlier in life, and I didn't want to make the same mistake.

I wanted to make this engagement momentous. So, I waited.

I bought a ring and put it in a safe. And I waited.

We had many romantic talks about the future. And I waited.

We both knew how well we fit together, in so many ways. And I waited.

Then, finally, after a year of waiting, and a trip to the Greek island of Paros, I got down on my knee, took a deep breath, and asked the love of my life—the future mother of our children, my life partner—to marry me.

But Theresa is so much more than my life partner, and the mother of our children. She is an accomplished artist, a brilliant storyteller, a dynamic teacher, and a loving friend and sister. I have been admiring her for almost 25 years. While I have some tough moments with our children, she seems to breeze through her relationship with them. Maybe that's because she reads their emotions and anticipates their needs so well, often bringing them a dessert at just the right moment. They let her sing along with them in the car and rub their feet after a tough day. While I may be their rock, she is their pillow, with her shoulder always there for them. They are truly lucky, and so am I.

It's humbling to think about where I would be without golf, but it's unimaginable to think where'd I'd be without Theresa. These stories, and this life, would not be possible without her.

Now, however, it's time to return to the second half of my round of fatherhood and the impending teenage years.

Freedom

(2011-12)

One of my foundational commitments as a father is to help my boys grow into outstanding men. In my mind, that means they will be men who are responsible, to themselves, to their families, and to the world at large. That they will have integrity, doing the right thing when no one else is watching. That they will be kind, concerned about the well-being of others. And it means that they will be mature, able to envision a life for themselves that marries the important values of independence and mutual support. If I achieve nothing other than being able to witness my boys as grown men who I really like and admire, I think my role as a father will have been successful.

Oddly, the way I parent on the ski slopes shows how I try to instill these values in my boys. When we ski, I give my boys enormous amounts of freedom. Accused by some other parents of being neglectful, I don't ski behind my sons, watching their every move. At times, I ski past them, screaming "meet you at the bottom!" as I blow snow in their faces. There have been more than a few times when my wait at the bottom was quite long, and once or twice when I became genuinely worried. In fact, I've been waiting at the bottom when I was encountered with a teary-eyed child wondering why I wasn't there when he fell. This is not to say that I was never there when my sons fell—and they fell plenty. Just that my strategy as a father was to try to give them as much confidence in their own independence as possible.

Aidan and Elliott started skiing from a very young age. Theresa is an only-if-I-have-to skier, so she was happy to stay home and see me take the boys out of the house. They never took lessons, instead relying on me to teach them. Teaching someone how to ski is tricky. First, you must teach how to stop. Learning how to stop on a dime—which I taught them primarily by stopping ahead of them and challenging them to try to blow snow in my face with a hockey stop—that was the only true skill that I directly taught them. Of course, they asked some questions about how to use their knees and hips, how to initiate turns, how to use poles, and so on. Although I did provide some answers, I encouraged them to learn how to ski by watching and feeling. I'm sure the ski instructors who are reading this are mortified by how I taught my boys. But in my view, other than learning how to stop, the most important thing on the slopes is to learn confidence. I spent a lot of energy taking my sons on progressively harder slopes, putting them in progressively more difficult situations, and pointing out how well they did. In all honesty, I don't really know how well they did—I was usually skiing in front of them. And sure, many times they fell. But they learned how to get up, they learned how to turn, and they learned how to stay out of danger. In fact, they are now both excellent skiers who are more than willing to take on any slope in front of them. They don't have ambitions to be ski racers or anything like that. I'm just glad they are both very confident on skis.

Some parents have accused me of neglecting my sons on the slopes. In their view, the only way to properly take care of kids is to monitor them and constantly be there when they fall. They worry that any serious fall could put their children in jeopardy, and that my approach was simply too risky. I have to admit: it's hard to see your children take a fall and not help them. But as much as I might have wanted to be there to catch them slipping, I also know that learning how to fall—and more importantly, learning how to get up on their own—is far more important. I risked that my sons would be injured … I acknowledge that. But that can happen in any sport at any time. And they had helmets on, I reasoned, so what's the worst that could happen? I suppose a torn-up knee or broken arm could have occurred, but I think they were young enough that their falls were almost always benign, and the confidence they built with their freedom more than made up for the risks.

This philosophy of athletic freedom was put to the test when I was asked to coach Elliott's 10AA baseball team. Although I was an accomplished athlete and had coached at a variety of levels, all of my coaching experience was in soccer. I knew soccer inside and out—I knew when to instruct and when to let go. Not so much in baseball. While Aidan had been playing baseball for years, and while I served as an assistant coach for his teams, I mostly just learned from a fellow parent who had been a college baseball player and was an accomplished baseball coach. I didn't have the background for coaching baseball, but as an experienced coach of another sport, I was asked to step up.

I knew Elliott needed freedom to be successful. He had hung around his older brother's team for years, and he had enormous talent that he had picked up from being the little kid at a variety of baseball camps. But I had played no role other than to admire and encourage him, knowing the rules of baseball, but with virtually no understanding of how to teach kids how to play. I had watched and listened to other coaches, and I would be able to mimic them, but I realized that I would have to fake it. This made me uncomfortable. *Didn't my son and the other kids deserve a true baseball coach? Was it really enough for me to bring enthusiasm for coaching? Shouldn't a coach bring some deeper knowledge of the game?*

Most importantly, I had to figure out how best to relate to Elliott. For years I was the dad at baseball games who cheered on my sons and their teams. And Elliott was used to high fives from me, whether he struck out or hit a home run. He was used to me applauding him from the dugout as I watched him with a wide smile on my face, amazed at what such a young player could do. He was also used to us talking through the highs and lows of the games, and also bonding over our shared love of the sport. What Elliott wasn't used to was me being his coach, necessarily putting him in positions he might not want, taking him out when he wanted to play, adjusting his approach when the team needed him to do something different.

So with the advice of Aidan's coach, whose son played for him, we developed a two-hat strategy. This was metaphorical, with the teaching aid of the literal. At most normal times, you could find me wearing a golf hat, perhaps one from Torrey Pines, Whistling Straits, or Bandon Dunes. We'll call that my *dad hat*. But as the head coach, I was expected to wear the team hat, at both practices and games. So, Elliott and I talked about the plan: "I'll wear my dad hat before and after practices and games. When I'm wearing that hat, I will do everything I normally do as your dad. I'll help you get your gear together, help with your food, and give you hugs. I won't tell you what to do with baseball. I'll treat you extra special. You'll get my full attention."

Elliott smiled. We were well bonded.

"However, when I put on my *coach hat,* at baseball practice and games, I'll treat you like any other player. If you need water, you will have to go get it with your teammates. If I need you to play left field, even though you want to play second base, I'll send you out there. If I need you to pitch, you'll do that. If I need you to sit on the bench, you'll do that. I won't give you any special attention, and you can't ask me to do something that the other players wouldn't ask."

Elliott's smile was gone. This was serious. He wasn't liking the sound of it, not liking it at all.

"Like what?" he asked, about the things I wasn't going to do for him.

I thought for a minute: "I'm not going to tie everyone's shoes, so if your shoes come untied, I can't help you."

"Why not?" he objected.

"Because you'll be one of 12 players, and I have to treat all of you the same." This was not going to be easy, but Elliott knew he didn't have a choice. This was our deal, and while Elliott was apprehensive about what he would lose, I think we both liked the hat ritual. While I would be taking a brief break from dad duty on the diamond, it would only be temporary.

It was a glorious season, one of the most fun seasons I've ever had. The dozen 10-year-olds—11 boys and yes, one girl—were great. They could hit, they could field grounders, they could catch a fly ball. I had learned a few mantras from Aidan's coach Joe that I employed throughout the season:

1. *Just play catch.* "If you're a pitcher, play catch with the catcher. If you're playing second base, play catch with the first baseman. If you're in the outfield, play catch with the shortstop." Rather than trying to make the game complicated, trying to get 10-year-olds to cover a base by running to the correct spot on the field, I chose instead to keep it simple: "just play catch with your friends." I told them over and over that "the team that plays catch the best almost always wins."

2. *Shake it off.* I even played some Taylor Swift for them. "Everyone makes errors," I told them. "Everyone strikes out. If you fail two out of every three times you are at bat, you're a hall-of-famer." When a kid made a mistake—and they made a ton—I coached all of them to yell, "shake it off!" I got them excited about how to overcome obstacles. Rather than getting upset with a pitcher for walking three straight batters, I told the team, "let's stop them from scoring with the bases loaded!" I would set up practice situations that only occur after mistakes, like an error that puts a kid on first and then a walk. "Okay, let's stop the runner on second from advancing to third."

3. *Celebrate.* I made everything a celebration. A kid who was struggling at the plate fouled off a good pitch—I'd yell, "great job!" A kid who had made an error at third caught a routine popup—"whoop, whoop!" I found great plays in the most minor moments and called

attention to them. I gave a game ball for every game and made sure that I could find something to celebrate with every kid's play.

We won the league that year, winning almost every game, and I'm convinced it was because we were having so much fun. The kids loved to come to practice: we laughed even when we were working hard, and they couldn't help but play well in the games. And we had talent: we could hit, we could field, we could pitch, we could catch. The girl on the team could throw harder than the boys. She wasn't the most accurate, but I didn't tell the other coaches that ... I just let them be intimidated.

And through it all, I got to know Elliott better. This was the first time that he had success on a travelling team. While he had been on travelling soccer and baseball teams the previous two years, those teams were pretty bad. Although they always enjoyed playing, there was never any interest in or expectation of winning. This was different. Elliott knew we were good, he knew that he was one of the best players on the team, and he wanted to win.

One tournament stands out: Elliott was playing second base in a close game against a very good team. They had runners at the corners with only one out. The batter hit the ball hard, right at Elliott. He fielded the grounder right in front of the runner taking off from first. Elliott was so smooth. He tagged the runner and then calmly threw to first. Double play! That 10-year-old knows how to play! Elliott was ecstatic as his teammates mobbed him while they ran back to the dugout. I gave high-fives to all the players, not giving Elliott any special attention. But inside, oh was I proud of him. I was beaming.

Blackwolf Run—River (Kohler, WI)

I was thinking about how much I loved that experience with Elliott as I drove to Kohler, Wisconsin from my home in Minneapolis. The five-hour drive is uneventful, with few radio stations and plenty of dairy farms. A perfect opportunity to think about my sons. I thought about what it was like to watch Elliott play, when he wasn't thinking about mistakes he might make; he was just playing freely. I knew it wouldn't last—that's the great tragedy of becoming a teenager. Too many kids forget what it's like to be free of worry about the future. I would try to embody that mindset on the golf course later today. *Stay in the moment. Be a kid again. Swing freely.*

It's hard to warm up in a hailstorm. Not giant pieces of hail: it was bigger than a grain of sand, but smaller than a pebble. The layers I had on made me feel like I was swinging a club in a parka, but I managed to take some good swings at the Blackwolf Run practice area. The hail didn't hurt, and it most certainly didn't dampen my spirits—just my pants. As I stood on the range, I overheard others: "You're playing the River?" "That's my favorite!" "It's soooo hard." Pete Dye's reputation should have been enough to warm up my increasingly freezing hands.

It was about 1:30 in the afternoon as I stood on the practice tee. It had already been a long day. I had woken up at 5:30, fed and took the dogs out, said goodbye to Theresa, and set off. Before I left, I looked at the weather report: mid-40s, with rain showers expected in the afternoon. Damn. I had planned the trip for months and hoped that it would be warm enough in early May. I was wrong. No matter. I had an hour before my tee time, so I set off to the practice green to see if I could get a handle on the Dye greens on the River course.

There's a game I like to play warming up. 18 holes on the practice green, with two balls. I putt around the perimeter of the green, from one pin to another, until I reach nine holes. I allow myself four total putts per hole—two per ball—for par. I find that this game makes practicing fun and keeps me focused. If you make the first putt it counts as a birdie; and two putts is a par; and every three-putt is a bogey. I was 13-over after nine holes—that means that I three-putted 13 of 18 holes on the practice green! Diabolical greens were clearly ahead.

As I was finishing my round on the practice green, one of the staff came up to me. "Mr. Filner, we have an opening in a group going off in about five minutes. Would you like to join?" As a single, I was flexible and preferred to join another group. I hopped in my golf cart, drove to the 1st tee, and met my companions for the next four hours: Kevin, Kevin, and Brandon. These 20-somethings were there to golf, and to drink … a lot. I learned quickly that they embraced their good shots and shook off their poor ones—no club throwers here. They also were warm and inviting, demonstrating none of the dismissiveness of too many 20-somethings.

I don't know if I could've scripted the first 10 shots any better. Except for the sheets of rain. What had been hail transitioned to the heaviest rain of the day, just as we were preparing to tee off. But we were at one of the premier golf courses in the country, eagerly awaiting what was ahead. No measly rain would slow us down. After the three men put their balls in play—in widely divergent directions—I calmly piped my drive down the left side of the fairway. We all have to find our own way in golf.

I was so happy with my first drive. *Where did my sudden inner calm come from?* I huddled in my golf cart, helped one of the Kevins find his ball, and drove to mine. The namesake of the course—the Sheboygan River—was running strong along the left side of the 1st hole. The river was a milk-chocolate brown, being pelted by the rain. I scrambled to keep my clubs and towels dry and quickly donned my rain jacket.

Even though I had a strong drive, the driving rain and cold temperatures kept my drive to about 250 yards, leaving me a solid 275 to the pin. Look, I know when the risks outweigh the possible reward. I decided to lay up and played a comfortable 4-iron to the left side of the fairway. As I made my way down the fairway, I took in this truly stunning 1st hole. The hole was relatively straight, with mounds on the right down its entire length. But the star of the hole—and the star of the entire course—was the river. So, I absorbed the sounds and smells of the river as best I could, while I waited for my playing partners. Although my third shot was only 125 yards out, we were playing into the wind and the rain, and so I decided to club up to 9-iron. I struck it as well as I have ever struck an iron, flying high, with a baby draw, heading right toward the hole. From my sightline, I thought I was tight to the pin. But no, it was a tricky 15-footer; Mr. Dye would have a piece of me after all. I surveyed the first birdie putt of the round and sent it tentatively down the hill, curling toward, and then away from the cup. A foot to the right, and I settled for par.

We turned back to the 2nd hole, running parallel to the first. The mounds seemed higher going back toward the clubhouse—maybe they were steeper on this side. But no matter, I pulled my 3-wood for this short par four. Again, piped right down the middle. Six great shots in a row. I was starting to get nervous. As I made my way to the next fairway, I heard the birds above me and noticed that the rain had subsided enough to cause one of the Kevins to say that the rain was over. "No," we all yelled, "don't jinx us." He did, as we reminded him over and over during the rest of the very wet and cold round.

But that was ahead. What I was facing now was a solid 150-yard shot from the middle of the fairway. I pulled my 8-iron and surveyed the large bunker in front of the green (behind which the course superintendent had devilishly cut the cup). I would not fall for his trick, at least not on this day. I aimed at the middle of the green and hit another outstanding iron, which turned over a bit too much and left me on the far left of the green—some 40 feet to the pin. I took even longer surveying the putt, listened to Kevin playfully tease me about knocking in the impossible putt, and managed to send the putt to within three feet. Not bad at all. A second putt on the second green, and I was two-for-two in my quest to shoot even par.

The 3rd hole began a rough patch of four holes, which I played in 5-over. I didn't hit any awful shots, except if you count the drive on the par-three 4th, which faded about a foot too far to the right and bounced off the rocks into the lake. It was mainly just ... off. I got it back for four straight holes, from 7 through 10, where I hit solid drives, great irons, and left myself with birdie putts or very short par putts. I thought to myself, *stay patient and just keep swinging. You don't need every shot to be great, just need a few.*

I arrived at the 11th tee still 5-over par, playing great for the most part, and the golfing gods were ready. I don't know which hole Pete Dye would've named as his signature hole on the River course, but I would certainly nominate the 11th. The river remained on the right side of the hole for its entire, meandering length. Any golfer whose shot landed anywhere but the farthest left side of the fairway would face a dilemma: stay left of the river with a short wedge (because a longer shot would miss the fairway to the left), or cut across the river (the farther right, the longer the shot can go, but the more the river is in play). It's a truly stunning hole. As I stood on the tee box assessing my options, I spent too much time thinking of my second shot and nowhere near enough time focusing on my drive. So naturally—with the gods in a greedy mood—I hit my worst slice of the round. For reasons I can't quite explain, I had set up so far left that my drive banana-ed from the far-left rough all the way across the fairway and landed in the right rough, only to bounce toward the river. I didn't see a splash, so I retained hope that the ball had held up just shy of the river. *Shake it off.*

Lo and behold, I found my ball, perched on what can only be called a shelf, below the fairway level by a few feet but most definitely not wet. As it turned out, however, it didn't matter—the shelf was about two feet wide, and while I could reach down and grab my ball, there was absolutely no hope of a stance that wouldn't put me in serious danger of dropping down 10 feet into the freezing cold water. I didn't give it a second thought: I grabbed my ball, took the medicine of a drop, and looked at my options. With a dropped ball in the rough, I knew that the best club for me was my hybrid. But there were also three trees straight in my line. Go too far left of the trees, and I would cross the fairway and bring the left trees into play. Go too far right, and I might not clear the river. Go straight at the trees, and I could easily hit one of them, bouncing anywhere. There wasn't a good play here, so I did the sensible thing: I aimed straight at the trees, assuming that if I tried to hit one, I would certainly miss. And miss I did, making the oft-repeated phrase, "trees are mostly air," true for once. I don't think I could have hit my ball more directly at the trees, and somehow it miraculously missed all three. My ball landed on the fairway, giving me a perfect 175 yards to the pin. "Nice shot," Kevin said, clearly caught between genuine admiration and competitiveness. I took a calculated risk and avoided too much danger. I had to celebrate it.

The approach on the 11th presenting an eerily similar iron shot to the 9th and 10th holes. With the river below and to the right, and bunkers and mounds surrounding the green, I knew I had to put the ball on the green (or nearly so) to have a realistic chance at par. After scrambling the past two holes, my 6-iron had to be true. Kevin challenged, "closest to the pin?" I readily agreed, and hit a high draw (I can't imagine a better visual than the ball flying toward the green with the Sheboygan River in the background). The ball landed about eight feet short of the pin, with a tough up-and-down putt. Kevin missed the green to the left. I smiled at him; he wasn't so pleased. It was now clear to me why Dye had named this hole Rise and Fall—this part of the green was like a rollercoaster. I knew this was not the putt to be too aggressive, so I hit it solidly, aiming to be within two feet for the bogey putt. It was true, and I settled for a comfortable bogey after the terrible drive. There are good bogeys and bad ones, and I had to admit that I was happy with this one. It's all in how you see things.

Although I was pleased that I had saved bogey, my great play earlier in the round had dissipated. I was able to grind out four more pars on the back nine. Closing with a sloppy and unfocused double bogey, I came in with a 41. My round had meandered through good and poor play much like the river, along which I had spent a truly fun—if a bit rainy—day.

Discipline

(2012-13)

I worked hard as a dad to create a confident sense of freedom for my sons. That might sound like an oxymoron: if it were so free, why did I have to work so *hard* at it? When I think about what it took to create that sense of freedom, I realize that it took a tremendous amount of discipline on my part. It's so easy to do things for our kids, to correct their mistakes, to coach them throughout their lives. But I knew they needed to feel free, so I would have to remain disciplined. But I also wanted them to *learn* discipline. I had learned it from hard work: to succeed in soccer, to finish my degrees, to flourish in my profession. Discipline doesn't come magically. So I had to find a way for my boys to learn discipline, without taking away their freedom. We found it in the martial arts.

"Kihap!," they all yelled in unison. They shouted it when they entered the dojang, when they bowed to the Grand Master, before they performed, and often when they finished. Literally translated, kihap means "to gather and focus one's spiritual energy." Colloquially, *kihap* means "fired up and ready to go." But my seven-year-old son Elliott had no idea what *kihap* meant literally, and no connection to feeling ready to learn taekwondo. He yelled "kihap!" because the Grand Master told him to, because everyone else in the dojang yelled it, and—most importantly—because his older brother yelled it.

My boys were not the disciplined type. At home, we parented with a lot of freedom. While we expected them to put away their electronics at the dinner table, and clear their plates when they finished, we were hardly drill sergeants. We allowed a lot of banter, teasing, and generally just being a kid. While we expected them to do some cleaning in their rooms, we didn't strongly enforce it, so their rooms tended to appear more like a pigsty than a dojang. Clean, orderly, and disciplined my boys were most certainly not. Getting them to pack their gear for soccer or baseball practices was an exercise in parental exhaustion. I lost count of the number of times we went to a practice only to find out that a glove, or shin guard, or water bottle was missing. While in later years I resorted to a carefully constructed check-off list, at this time I was still in the did-you-remember-your stage.

So, it was even more surprising that when they arrived at taekwondo practice, they always immediately sprang into orderly discipline. They kept track of their shoes and socks, which had to be placed in a precise area of the studio, or face a clear and unmistakable talking-to from the Grand Master. Grand Master Ro is a diminutive yet powerful South Korean taekwondo teacher who commands the room. While Grand Master Ro never yelled at the students, he also never let any mistake go without comment. He garnered their immediate and total respect, and our boys soaked it up. They didn't make jokes on the dojang floor, they didn't goof around, they didn't forget what they were learning. They simply did what they were told and threw in frequent "kihaps!" for good measure.

Both of my sons had been studying taekwondo for several months. They were progressing well, learning each of the moves and earning belts. Elliott seemed particularly excited, with terrific balance and energy. Three days a week, we arrived for the one-hour session with the Grand Master (sometimes the class was led by one of his disciples). Students lined up according to their belts, with the black belts up front, and the lower ranked belts filling in behind. Now, my sons were in the middle, even with some adults behind them. As a dad, I didn't much care what my sons pursued, as long as they did it with passion. This day, as all the days before, my sons brought passion to taekwondo.

The day started out as usual. "Do you have everything for class?" They answered in monotone unison, annoyed at the daily reminder. When we arrived, the boys placed their shoes and socks carefully in the downstairs shelves, and they changed into their robes with their belts (mostly) in the right place. One of the disciples fixed their belts, checked their overall appearance, and gave them a ritual kihap to indicate that they could enter the dojang floor. They did with aplomb. They took their place in the lineup and went through the warmups. I was only vaguely watching, instead striking up a conversation with some of the other parents whose kids were at various levels. I noticed their warmups transitioning toward more intense running, across the dojang, perpendicular to where I was sitting. I could see them straight ahead as they ran to the south end of the mat, and they would disappear around the corner as they ran straight across to the north end.

This continued for several minutes, my attention waning away from the floor. Then, we heard a loud "thump," followed by Elliott's unmistakable scream. I had become very adept at distinguishing between various types of cries from my sons. There was the "I need some attention" cry, the "I hurt myself, but not very badly but still want you now" cry, the "my brother is annoying me" cry, and the "I'm hurt but I don't know how serious" cry. This cry was different—it was louder, more intense, more insistent, and more terrified. It was a cry that I hadn't heard before, and I took off running. Ten seconds later, I found Elliott, laying on the ground, with Grandmaster Ro holding two parts of his forehead together. There was blood everywhere—on the floor, covering the Grand Master's hands, all over my son's forehead, all over their robes. Everyone, including Aidan, was gawking, except Grand Master Ro. He quickly explained what happened in broken English—Elliott had slipped at the north side of the building and fell forehead-first into a small bookshelf. He sliced open his forehead, right at the hairline. Grand Master Ro signaled with his hands: he didn't want to let go; he was holding my son's head together. So, we walked quickly to the bathroom, where one of the assistants grabbed some cotton balls, gauze pads, band-aids, and tape. I thanked Grand Master Ro, replaced his hands with mine to stem the bleeding, and tended to my son in the bathroom. "Elliott!," I enthused, "Do you know that you're going to have a really cool scar to show your friends?" Although he looked at me skeptically, it did help to settle him down. "You're going to be okay," I assured him. "We'll go to the hospital, and they'll sew you right up."

"Will it hurt?" he managed to ask through his tears.

"You're going to be fine." I got the wound temporarily bandaged up, and we left the bathroom.

My mind raced—Aidan, Theresa, the emergency room, the Grand Master. I have many faults as a dad, but one of my strengths is handling a crisis. I knew that I needed a specific plan, and I'd have to clearly communicate what I needed. First, Aidan: "your brother needs stitches right away. Please finish the class and your mom will pick you up when it ends."

"Is he going to be okay?"

"Yes. I love you and will see you later tonight."

Second, I called Theresa (I don't know how parents did it before cell phones): "I need you to come pick up A in 30 minutes at taekwondo. E needs to go to the hospital to get stitches. He fell, and his head is cut open pretty badly. But he'll be okay. We just need to go now."

"Shit. Of course, I'll be right there. Is there anything else you need?"

"No, I'll call from the hospital."

Third, I spoke quickly to Grand Master Ro: "Thank you for helping my son. We're going to the hospital." His spoken English was poor, but his understanding was strong. I could tell that he was apologizing—nothing like this had ever happened before. "It's okay," I assured him.

Fourth, get to the emergency room. Through it all, I had been holding Elliott's hand. He was scared, and in a lot of pain. We went downstairs to grab his shoes and socks, and we quickly got into the car. In 10 minutes, we arrived in the emergency room.

I shouldn't be surprised given their jobs, but I found it remarkable how warm and professional the emergency staff was at Children's Hospital. They sprang into action upon our arrival, making Elliott feel comforted and making me feel confident in their abilities. We didn't have to wait long—maybe 10 minutes—before we were brought back to one of the emergency care rooms. The nurse came in and asked what happened, and before long Elliott got some numbing cream put on his forehead. As it started to work, the pain dissipated, and he began to return to his normal self. He even smiled. I kept reassuring him. "Wesley is going to think those stitches are so cool." Anything to get Elliott's best friend in the conversation. Even to this day, the part of the entire episode that he remembers most is showing the stitches to his friends in second grade.

But for me as a dad, this was the first of several trips to the emergency room for stitches. As a kid, falling and needing stitches was a common occurrence. There are stories about me involving a hobby horse, slipping while racing on a wet floor in the kitchen, and jumping on the bed, not to mention dozens of soccer injuries. But as a dad, in the accident realm, this was a first. You're never prepared for an accident and a trip to the emergency room. But here we were, and I was going to handle it.

"Yes, he needs stitches," the doctor had just arrived. "He should dive into water, not bookshelves." Elliott laughed, which is always a good sign. Cleaning the wound and applying the stitches took about an hour, all told. In the end, Elliott's forehead was reattached. He didn't have many questions—just needed to be reassured throughout that all would be okay. And, lucky for us, it was.

Despite loving taekwondo for the months leading up to the injury, Elliott announced in no uncertain terms: "I don't want to go back!" He had been simply running back and forth across the dojang, slipped on the mats, and fell into a bookshelf. Maybe he worried about what else could happen to him, especially when sparring began.

"It's okay. You didn't do anything wrong. It was just an accident. Everyone else will be very excited to see you again." It didn't matter. Whether it was because he was scared to return, or didn't want to have to face the people who had witnessed his accident, he was adamant against returning. On the one hand, we want to teach our boys to persist and overcome fears—to get right back on that horse, as it were. On the other hand, forcing them into something is a guarantee that they will hate it. I wanted the drive to learn taekwondo to be internal, to come from that place of passion and commitment, not simply doing what he was told. At the same time, I knew that letting him quit was, in a sense, accepting defeat. In the end, taekwondo just wasn't enough of a priority to force him to overcome his fears. There would be other injuries, we were sure of that. And so we decided that we wouldn't fight him on this. His last taekwondo experience would be his worst one, and we'd support his decision.

Yet the lessons he'd learned from Grand Master Ro, his disciples, and his time in taekwondo seemed to stick with him, even if he was no longer practicing. He seemed to stick with his schoolwork just a little bit longer, he took off his shoes and placed them just a little bit more neatly, he kept his room just a little bit cleaner, and he took on new challenges with just a little bit more discipline. And that made it all worthwhile.

Blackwolf Run—Meadow Valleys (Kohler, WI)

I usually play golf with either with my friends and family, or I get paired up with strangers. I also almost never take a golf cart, choosing instead to get the exercise and the mental freedom of walking. So, it's a rare circumstance when I play golf alone with a cart. I usually only do it when the course is particularly difficult to walk, or I'm in a rush. My round on the Meadow Valleys course at Blackwolf Run was neither difficult to walk, nor was I in a rush. The only reason I took a cart is that they told me it was a very long walk to the 1st tee. Not having played the course before, and not wanting to upset the apple cart, I hopped in a cart and set off on my way.

The Meadow Valleys course is not short by any means, tipping out at over 7,200 yards. I wasn't going to play Dye's least famous course at Whistling Straits/Blackwolf Run from the tips, so I settled for the more reasonable 6,450 green tees. The front nine of the Meadow Valleys was added in 1990 (the back nine, plus nine of the holes of the River Course, were the original 18 at Blackwolf Run). I was excited to see Pete Dye's 1990 add-on, in addition to the original nine on the back.

I played the first two holes rather indifferently and was dragging at 2-over as I arrived at the 3rd tee. I realized that if I had any hope of playing well, I'd have to engage in some serious mental discipline to stay focused. The tee box sits among the trees, with a beautiful green complex only 160 yards to the pin. Having switched directions to downwind, and—seeing two apparent newlyweds coming up to the 2nd tee behind me—I decided to swing easy with one-less club. I realized that this was the first time I had made a conscious choice about anything since I drove off in the cart. The 8-iron was the perfect choice, as I sent a high draw into the air, coming to rest pin high only 18 feet from the hole. My first legitimate chance at birdie. One of the reasons, among many, that I dislike taking a cart is that the time I have to enjoy my good shots is so limited (as is the time to shake off bad shots). So, while I couldn't really drive slowly, as carts only seem to have one speed, I did take the time to have a snack, a drink of water, and take in the expanse of the meadow in front of me. It was a beautiful, wide-open view of the front nine. I walked over to my ball and saw a great look at birdie, with a subtle but unmistakable left-to-right break. I took my sweet time reading the putt from every angle, imagined myself with a crowd watching greenside and ready to erupt, and sent the putt along its way. *Could it be? Maybe? Yes, Sir?* I don't think I could have struck it better, as it went perfectly on the line I chose, headed for the left side of the cup. As it lost speed, it dipped right and caught the right edge of the hole, incredulously spinning an entire revolution around the hole. It came to rest an inch from the cup. I looked around to see if anyone had witnessed the crime that had just occurred here on the 3rd green. No way! And yet, I settled for a first par of the day.

I walked off the 3rd green with a wry smile on my face: wishing someone had witnessed the robbery, but pleased with the 8-iron swing and the solid putt, and mostly the conscious focus that I had re-discovered. So, I was ready for the par-five, 516-yard 4th hole. Called Gamble, I presumed that the name was referring to the risk-reward temptation that this hole would present, but given my lack of distance off the tee, wasn't expecting to have to put much money on the table. Straight in front of the tee box, the hole is fairly straightforward: hit a drive down the fairway, layup with the second shot to 80 yards or so, and a wedge in. The further right you place your drive, however, the easier it is to go for it, and the more challenging the second shot. Although I was tempted to take on the right side, I decided to play it left to stay safe. I took a few practice swings and sent my ball in the air. As I watched my ball fly, I noticed something that incredulously had escaped my attention: right in between the main fairway on the left and a neck of fairway on the right is one of the most massive centerline bunkers on the planet. I didn't measure it, but I would guess it was 50 yards from front to back, and at least 10 yards wide. So, of course, I hit what began as a great drive headed for the left fairway, but it faded just enough to catch the very front of the bunker. No money to risk here.

As I quickly arrived at the bunker, I found a perfect lie in the sand and decided that with no lip to contend with, I would pull 5-iron and work the ball back to the fairway. A good sand shot later, I was 125 yards from the pin in a valley on the right side of the fairway. From the photos, it looks like a wide-open shot to the green. From the fairway, however, the shot is completely blind. I walked to the left and located the pin in the front of the green. I was stuck: should I hit pitching wedge or 9-iron? I decided to opt for the latter, and moved to the ball.

Anyone who has played in Ireland or Scotland (I haven't) surely is accustomed to playing a blind shot to an elevated green. It isn't the type of shot we face very often in the US, so I wasn't at all comfortable. Yet at the same time, because I couldn't see the green, I was freed from the desire to watch. The result was a calm, confident, and head-down swing that had about the best trajectory I've ever seen coming off my club. It was as if I had been momentarily replaced with a scratch golfer who really knew how to compress the ball. As it flew, I couldn't tell if the distance was right, but the direction seemed to be perfect. I would soon find out. I got back in the cart and drove to the path and up the hill to the green. Based on the ball mark, the ball had almost flown directly into the hole, took a bounce, and promptly stopped, less than three feet from the pin. As probably happens to most golfers whose shot produces a tap-in birdie, I was pumped. *Yes, yes, yes!* I yelled to no one. I tapped it in, took a bow, laughed at myself, and walked back to the cart with some extra spring in my step.

After the birdie and three successful drives—including the well-struck drive that was beached on the last hole—I came to the 4th tee riding high. My back felt loose, I had no one to wait for or to push me to play faster, and it was a stunning day. I just took it in, attempted a flowing practice swing, and promptly hooked my drive. For the next three holes, I battled poor drives, indifferent irons, and limped my way through three successive bogeys. The focus I had found on the 3rd tee seemed to be lost in the meadow—I had to get it back.

Turning back into the wind, over a mound with the lake looming to the left, I faced a very difficult par three called Wet and Wild. While it was definitely wild, I hoped it wouldn't be wet. With the wind, I decided that I needed more on this 176-yard tee shot and pulled a 5-iron. It turned out that I needed *much* more. I hit a good shot right over the mound, heading straight for the green. I figured I landed in the middle of the impossibly long green. But I hadn't realized just how strong the wind was, and I found my ball at the very front of the green.

In the yardage book, the course noted that this green is almost 40 yards long. Could that really be? With the couple of golfers long behind me, and no one in sight in front, I decided to step off this putt carefully. By my non-laser feet, I faced a 114-foot putt, without question the longest one I've ever faced in my life.

It's difficult to know how to handle such a long putt. I've seen golfers mimic an underhand toss to get a feel for how hard they would have to hit a putt to cover a long distance. I also walked it over twice more to get a sense of the length. But, basically, I would just have to guess. So, after assessing it a few more minutes, I lined it up, took more-than-a-few practice swings, and sent the putt off into a fog. It rolled, and rolled, and rolled some more, coming to rest, four feet from the hole. I couldn't believe that I had putted it this close. I was tempted to try 10 more and see if I could get any of them inside the putt. I didn't, choosing instead to focus on the still-substantial second putt, which I thankfully made. A 114-foot two-putt.

I framed the turn with two poorly played holes, a double and a bogey, and arrived at the 11th tee 7-over. I would have to play the final eight holes at even par in order to break 80. I took a deep breath, looked at the wide expanse of meadow, and committed myself. This would take self-discipline. I hit a fantastic drive, long and far up the right side of the fairway. Although there was nothing on the hole that was particularly notable—no water hazards, no snaking creek, no bizarre green complex—I found the 11th hole to be a highlight of the round. It was just so beautiful: a picture-perfect valley of a par four set in a meadow. From the right side, I hit a solid 4-iron to about 150 yards. As I arrived at my ball, two things were clear: the wind had picked up and the green was elevated. I therefore decided that I needed an extra club and hit a high fade with my 7-iron. Unfortunately, the great shot came up just short, leaving me with a 10-yard chip to a left pin placement. I arrived at the green site, took in the majesty of this inland course, and knocked my chip to a few inches. A patient par.

Although my final seven holes did not produce that sub-80 round that I craved, I played much better than on the front, closing with a solid 39. Highlights include the par-four 14th, a reintroduction to the Sheboygan River, which makes a brief pass along the right side before disappearing until the 18th hole. With a severe downward sloping fairway, and the river along the right side, I decided that driver was too much for this 384-yard hole. I hit a strong 3-wood straight down the fairway, actually catching the right-hand turn to put me in perfect position for the peninsula green. The second shot is nothing short of picturesque. With the river on the right, and the creek framing the green on the left, behind, and near right, finding the putting surface is no mean feat. Fortunately, I had been hitting my 4-iron well, and the 14th was no exception. With the ball in the air, I legitimately thought it would be in there tight. However, it came up about 20 feet short. With a makable birdie putt, I took the time to look down the embankment to the creek and take in the river's flow. With no one around, it was one of the most serene moments I've had on a golf course. Two putts later, I was in with my fourth par in a row. I traded bogeys and pars over the final four holes and walked off with an 81. Breathing in river air is not the same as the oceanic elixir, but it sure felt good that day on a well-designed course. But my up-and-down round also demonstrated just how easy it is to lose focus, and the self-discipline needed to get it back. It's a lesson of a lifetime.

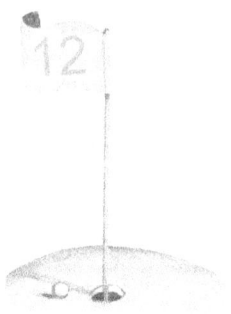

Fun

(2013-14)

O ne of my dreams as a parent was to play in a father-son golf tournament with one of my sons. It didn't matter to me where it was, or how well we played. I just dreamed of the opportunity to put ourselves, in partnership, to the test. I dreamed of playing a practice round together, where we would strategize how best to play each hole. We would figure out together where we would try to put our drives, where the best miss on our approach shots was. We would learn together about the nuances of the greens. We would coach each other, with shared disappointments and many high fives.

When Aidan was almost 12, I saw an advertisement to play a parent-child tournament at Madden's in northern Minnesota over the Memorial Day weekend—his birthday weekend. "Aidan," I asked timidly, like a teenager asking someone on a first date, "would you like to spend your birthday weekend with me? We would drive the two hours, play golf for a few days, and we could go fishing or play shuffleboard as well." I did my best to sell it, but I still had my ace in the hole. "The food is all-you-can-eat."

His eyes opened wide and, to my excitement and surprise, he said, "yes, I would love to." I was looking forward to realizing one of my dreams of fatherhood.

I remembered what it was like to be 11. I loved playing with any round ball or ball-like object, whether it was a soccer or basketball, a frisbee, or even shuffleboard. I just wanted to move. My mother has said that when I turned 11, I levitated off the ground and spent a year in constant motion. So, what did she do? She shipped me off to Seattle to stay with her brother and sister-in-law for three weeks.

With cautious, suburban parents, I hadn't roughed it very often. So, to visit my hippie aunt and uncle who were not yet parents was an eye-opening experience, to say the least. I arrived, wide-eyed, nervous, and ready for anything. The first day, my uncle pulled out something called *tortillas*—corn, it turned out—some cheese, oil, and a fry pan and announced: "we're going to make quesadillas." I had no idea what he was talking about, and it probably showed on my face. But I said "sure," and we launched together into cooking. I don't think I had any idea what that meant, since my usual experience had been to show up at a table with food already on it that had apparently been produced out of the ether. But I loved the experience of it, the splattering of the oil only matched by the splattering of our laughs.

It was the summer of 1980 in Seattle. In March of that year in southern Washington, Mount St. Helens had begun a series of minor explosions which culminated in the May 18th eruption, one of the most disastrous volcanic eruptions in US history. The eruption sent an estimated 540 million tons of ash into the atmosphere, with inches of ash falling and piling up in cities around Washington and travelling around the world in less than two weeks. My aunt and uncle, eager to get as close as possible to the blast site, had planned a camping trip for us. "We're going to be near Mount St. Helens," my aunt announced. "We won't be allowed to get really close," she assured, "but we'll be able to see a lot of what happened." As we drove south, the devastation was clear. Felled trees, burned out landscapes, and several inches of ash covered everything we saw. They knew immediately that we would have to stay as far away as possible.

For me, though, it was simply an adventure, seeing this desolate moonscape, touching the sea of ash, and readying for camping for the first time. When we finally arrived—I have no idea how long we had to drive to get out of the severe ash zone, but it felt interminable—my aunt and uncle asked me to take the dogs for a walk while they set up camp. Their dogs George (a large lab mix) and Maxine (a small terrier mix) were fun and playful. Uncle Kenny pointed me in the direction of a small river in the woods and I took off. I walked for 15 minutes or so, exploring the woods and the river and then thought to look up. George was right there with me, supervising my exploration. Maxine was nowhere to be seen. At first, I simply called for her, assuming that she was right around a bend or behind a tree. No Maxine. I called a bit louder. Still no Maxine. George looked at me, wondering who I was and why I was calling Maxine incessantly. I began to panic, convinced that somehow she had fallen into the river and drowned. I looked everywhere I could think of, convinced that I was going to be sent home by my aunt and uncle for killing their dog.

I went back to the campsite, hid behind a tree, and looked for Maxine. No sight of her. I went back into the woods, now more than ever convinced that Maxine had met some untimely death. I don't remember what words I used under my breath, but everything was certainly on the table. I had really screwed up. The second day on the trip and I had already lost their dog or worse. George seemed unperturbed. I was apoplectic. But I knew at some level that I needed help. Maybe with a team of three in our search party, we would have more success locating the missing pup. I took a very deep breath and resolved to tell them. As I arrived back at camp, I called out to my uncle and aunt. "Yes," they said in unison.

"Um, I need to tell you something." I was getting up the courage to tell them that I had lost or killed their dog. I was getting up the courage to admit my unforgivable mistake. The lump in my throat was unbearable. But I knew I had to tell them.

And then, sitting right next to my aunt, taking in the pine smells half asleep, was Maxine. Apparently, she had gotten bored of my jaunt into the woods, or maybe simply missed them and returned unscathed. I hesitated.

"What is it?," they asked, clearly aware that something was wrong. "Oh, I just wanted you to know that I had a good walk in the woods." They looked at each other and wondered what possibly could have happened. It's amazing how as a kid, you're fairly oblivious to how obvious your lies are. Thankfully for parents, their kids develop a poker face much later on.

This story was in my mind as Aidan and I arrived at Madden's, a northern Minnesota family resort. No matter how old he seemed, he was just a little kid. The experiences we had up north were all new to him, and he would remember the details. Although ostensibly we were there to play golf, we were really there to experience something new. We would have to try everything—from shuffleboard and bocce ball, to nature walks and fishing, to cafeteria-style meals and ice cream cone walks along the lake. I would exhaust him, whatever it took.

When we teed it up on Pine Beach East, a 1926 design by Scotsman James Dalgleish, I was excited and optimistic. There were several dozen parent-child pairs, and Aidan seemed genuinely interested in competing. He had taken lessons at the First Tee camps and seemed to like golf—at least as long as he did well. We were sent off on the par-three 10th hole on this hidden gem in the Brainerd Lakes area. At only 6,100 yards from the tips, I felt confident that we could be competitive, if we could keep the right mindset together. While I continued to encourage Aidan and keep things as light as possible, ironically, the better I played, the worse he seemed to feel. I started out with three straight pars, and while I bogeyed the par-three 13th, I got it right back with a great birdie on the par-five 14th. The only moment he seemed the least bit excited to be on the course was when I pulled my drive left and out of bounds on the par-five 15th and stumbled to a double bogey 7. He liked that.

With another birdie on the par-five 17th and a bogey on the par-three 18th, we made the turn at 2-over par. I had no idea what the competition was like from other parents and children, but I felt like if we could get back to even par, we'd have a chance. Aidan was not interested. He wasn't interested in the competition of the moment, nor in the golf; he wasn't interested in being there at all. He was eager to get off the course, get an ice cream, and play some shuffleboard. But I was playing well—we were in the middle of the tournament, and I insisted that we wouldn't quit. He wasn't happy.

With two more birdies and two bogeys on our back nine, we finished the round with a respectable 2-over par. We drove back to the clubhouse, and I tried to lighten the mood: "as soon as we're done here, we can go get an ice cream and check out the shuffleboard court!" I tried to get his mind in a better place. Ironically, now that we were finished, he only had one question: "Did we win?" I suspected that over par wouldn't get it done, and I was right. So, I was in the unenviable, fatherly position of having played too well to keep my son's poor play in perspective, and too poorly to win the tournament for us. It would be years before he would come to appreciate golf, no matter how many good or bad shots. But when those later years came, the first foray into competitive golf was all worth it.

But more important than the golf, Aidan and I had that weekend together that many dads dream of. He was at an age where he still would play games with me, and we played a ton of them aside from the golf: the aforementioned shuffleboard, bocce ball, frisbee golf, fishing, and badminton. We were regulars in visiting the equipment room. Aidan also was excited to try the foods, eat the ice cream, and generally just be together. It was totally fine that he didn't love the golf. I knew better than to push it, but more importantly, I resisted the urge to push it anyway. Most of the ride home was spent in silence as Aidan slept next to me. I wondered how many more of these types of trips we would have. Becoming a teenager was right around the corner, and then first loves, puberty, driving, college … the rest of his life. I stopped myself. I was getting lost in the future and not experiencing the present. When he woke up, I said to him: "Aidan, I had a lot of fun with you this weekend. Thanks for coming."

"I did, too, dad." It's amazing how just a few words can mean the world to a father.

I don't need much from my sons, but the feeling of actually having fun together caught me hook, line, and sinker. Whatever problems I had with my own father—and there were many—the most tragic part of our relationship, such as it was, was that we never had fun together. We didn't like to be together. It was just one struggle after another, my father using words like swords to cut me down.

As a father now, I know how much my words mean, and I choose them carefully. I rubbed Aidan's head and said, "I had fun, too."

Erin Hills (Erin, WI)

Have fun would be my manta as I visited the young and brilliant course in eastern Wisconsin: Erin Hills. The arrival offers a quintessential understatement. With a small sign along a minor Wisconsin road, non-golfers would never know that they were entering the property of a top golf course in the US. The farmland extends in all directions, with only the welcome hut to focus your attention. I lowered my window as the older man leaned out and asked me for my name. "Yes, you're in the final group of the season. Did you know that?" I did in fact. It was mid-October, and not only was Erin Hills closing to the public this day, but the 1:00pm tee time was the final public tee time of the season (the caddies would get to play the course the next day). Although far from a celebrity, I felt a tiny bit of special status to be able to close out the season. I wouldn't be afraid to take a few extra divots.

I drove along the meandering road through the farmland until I could see a large barn and a stately clubhouse. I took a deep breath and wondered what the day would bring on this course that I had dreamed about since first learning about it. I didn't know much about the story of how it came to be built. But I did know that the owner had hired three lesser-known architects: Michael Hurdzan, Dana Fry, and Ron Whitten. Hurdzan and Fry had worked with the likes of Jack Nicklaus and Tom Fazio. Whitten was the head architecture editor for *Golf Digest* for many decades and is the author of five books on golf course architecture. But the three had never designed a course together, and the property in southeastern Wisconsin was truly a one-in-a-lifetime opportunity.

The course that Hurdzan, Fry, and Whitten created has received numerous accolades and a treasured US Open in 2017, won convincingly by Brooks Koepka. But I needed to see the property for myself before I would be won over. I needed to get a sense of the scale of the property and feel the undulations under my feet. I needed to know firsthand what the "Hills" was all about. So, I ventured 90 miles east of Madison in mid-October, hoping for some favorable weather. When I arrived 90 minutes before my early afternoon tee time, I knew that I would have plenty of time to warm up. I walked to the barn—as it turns out, the Caddie Barn—dropped off my clubs, and the welcome staff pointed me toward the clubhouse to pay my hefty greens fee. I bought my requisite ball marker—now, unnecessarily, sold in a ball-marker magnet—and headed off to the practice area. The caddies had brought my clubs over to the range where I had a leisurely warmup, moving slowly and deliberately through my bag.

"Are you Matt?," I heard from behind me. I looked up and saw a shorter person in a full-body white jumpsuit who looked to be well-aged but eager. He had to be my caddie. "Tim," he announced. "Let's head over to the practice green soon, okay."

"Roger that." We didn't say much on that short walk, as I was more focused on the temple that was building in front of me. Tim had a brief chat with the starter. "We're about 10 minutes delayed," he announced.

"No worries," I replied. I could use more time on the practice green. While we were there, I met my three playing partners: two college students from Chicago and a man roughly my age who was coincidentally from Minneapolis.

The four of us, plus the two caddies, were in for an amazing day on the course. It was 55 degrees with a strong, sustained wind—25 miles per hour, according to the Tim—coming in straight toward the 1st tee. Tim was practical and direct: "the first four holes will be straight into the wind, and then we'll have to battle it for a few more holes later in the round." There would be no cheerleading … just the facts.

So, while I had a spectacular warmup, I was more than a bit nervous as we made our way down to the 1st tee. Although one of my younger playing partners announced, somewhat arrogantly, that he would going to play it from the green tees (stretching a get-your-attention 6,700 yards), I was going to stick to my plan and play the green/white combo—which measured a still substantial 6,465 yards. The other two golfers joined me. As we walked down the hill, we passed the Black tees (the tips) which challenged Koepka, DJ, and, memorably, Justin Thomas from an astounding 7,731 yards. I could hardly believe the sightlines. And even from the "one-ups," at 7,147, I was still amazed. As we arrived at the eminently more reasonable green tee box, playing from 512 yards on the opening hole, I felt much more comfortable.

Unlike many rounds in which my nerves continued for much of the first few holes, I seemed to settle down right away as we reached the tee. Having seen the young gunslinger hit an incredibly long draw into what the caddies call the wetlands, his friend hit a slice into the right rough, and my compatriot hit a solid pull into the left rough, I was in a mood to swing freely. I hit a great drive, if not the longest, certainly the straightest. *Okay, solid start*, I thought to myself.

We set off. While the caddies looked for and successfully found two of the three balls, and the gunslinger dropped to hit his third, I waited next to my perfectly placed drive and took in the scene. Tim announced his presence, a continuation of the style I had discovered on the practice green. "Two hundred yards is a solid distance. Anything right would be fine; anything left would bring in the wetlands."

"Okay, I'll hit a 4-iron."

"Love it," Tim replied. So, maybe there would be some psychological coaching. I aimed right with my 4-iron and hit one of the worst shots of the day: a low runner. Fortunately, it ran right up the hill, between the bunkers and the wetlands, and left me with only 150 yards to the pin from a flat lie on top of the hill. "It's fine," Tim encouraged. "The wind will be coming in from the right for the third shot, a bit helping. And the green slopes right to left. Aim for the front of the green and the ball should funnel down toward the pin." I was learning quickly that the best thing to do was follow Tim's directions. He knew what I should do, and he'd keep me focused on each shot and nothing more. I hit a stunning pitching wedge with a perfect draw headed straight for the pin. It missed the pin by only a foot or so, but the extra-firm green and the lack of spin off my wedge meant that the ball continued to roll down the hill and onto the fringe. I faced a tough uphill left-to-right putt off the fringe, which I managed to get down to three feet and made the putt for par. A great start.

The 2nd hole, only 316 yards from the green tees, is considered by many players to be easy, and it ranks 13th on the handicap list. For me, it was brutal. I hit a high fade off the tee, worsened by the brisk wind coming straight at us. While it was still very much on the highly sloping fairway, I had 150 yards, over a large mound to a blind pin. "With the hurting win, I think you'll need at least 175 yards." I pulled a 6-iron, following Tim's advice. But with the ball above my feet, I didn't get a clean strike and left my ball at least 30 yards short of the turtle-back green. As we arrived at my ball, Tim entered into his most strategic mind: "you have so many options. You could play it high and try to stop it on the green. You could play it low, and try to hit the upslope, which will knock your ball down. Or you could run it on the ground, up the hill, and then let it roll toward the back pin." I'm sure talking through a shot is very helpful for the seasoned pro who has all of those shots in his bag. But I'm neither seasoned, nor particularly experienced in dealing with firm, elevated greens. I didn't have any confidence with the high flop, and putting along the ground seemed impossible. So I decided to try hitting a low runner with my gap wedge. Somewhere in the vestiges of my memory, I remember Tim saying something like, "don't go long." It's one of those comments that caddies probably wrestle over every day. *Should I point out the danger, and thereby call attention to it? Or should I keep quiet and risk failing to tell my player about what lay ahead?* Tim was clearly unsure, so he gave me those instructions a bit too late. Now, I'm not blaming him for what happened—I have the same questions for myself every time I play golf. But as I watched my well-struck pitch land on the green and began to roll, I became increasingly aware of the false back. My ball was slowing down as it reached the back of the green, but not enough—it rolled straight off the back.

I was then faced with a truly daunting shot. I had to get my ball up a steep slope from a very tight lie, and I didn't have much green to work with. And, I had already completed three shots. I was thinking bogey as I putted the ball, not nearly hard enough, and watched it nearly reach the top of the embankment ... and then rolled straight back down to my feet. Now, I was thinking double bogey. And I did it again. Seven? I did it again. Three putts, three balls up and straight back down the hill. I realized—*what took me so long?*—that I had to hit the ball *harder.* I putted it much too hard, and lo and behold the ball cleared the top of the hill with a perfect speed and stopped a foot from the cup. I made an 8. Not fun. I was boiling inside.

Little did I know that most of the bad shots of the round were now in my rearview mirror. I played the next three holes with aplomb, hitting three fairways, three greens, and making three solid putts. While there were no birdies on the card, I had played 4 of the first 5 holes about as well as possible. The 6th hole was playing almost 180 yards, slightly uphill and with a steep false front. "The pin is only a few paces from the front, and you don't want to go too far—that would leave a treacherous downhill putt. What do you think about playing your 165-yard club? I think the wind will be enough to get your ball over the false front."

"Sounds like a plan," I responded and asked for my 7-iron. Tim was convinced that it was enough club, and he convinced me. It's one of the great things about a caddie—you're freed from the weight of a bad decision. I just ignored the false front and the deep bunker just right of the green, and put my 7-iron to the test. I don't think I've hit a 7-iron better, with a perfect draw off the bunker. The only question was distance. From my vantage point, when my Chrome Soft—the green soccer-ball pattern kind, to celebrate Erin Hills' Irish theme—landed, it looked like it could roll right back down the false front. But it held its spot, and I had a 10-footer for birdie. Tim gave me a great read, and I buried the uphill putt. One under over the past four holes. Magical.

After a sloppy bogey on the long (but not longest!) par-five 7th hole, I countered with a solid par on the 8th, bringing me to what the caddies call the shortest par five on the course. I looked up and saw the green about 150 yards away, straight downhill. While the wind was hurting from the right, it just didn't seem that impossible. And then they started to explain: the green was long but narrow, a bit of a turtleback with a massive depression on the right side, and a set of bunkers that would make even Seve squirm.

I was the first to play. Tim gave me his lowdown: "keep the ball short of the back pin, which is 150 yards. The wind is hurting from the right. I think you should pull your 135-yard club." I agreed quickly and unquestioningly pulled a 9-iron. After a few comfortable practice swings, I hit a great shot, drawing off the right side of the green right to the middle about 45 feet from the pin. I had managed to avoid all the bunkers and the valley, and would be putting for birdie on this treacherous hole. My playing partners were less fortunate, as their shots went left and right, finding sand and devilish lies all around. I watched them ping pong across the green a few times and got a full appreciation of just how hard this hole was—these were not bad golfers, and the 9th was making them look pretty bad.

Yet here I was with a birdie putt. It wasn't at all makable—I was simply trying to putt to within a few feet. But the putt had to stay left of the gulley, or I could easily putt it off the green. I didn't want to putt it too lightly and have it lose its line and end up right where my partners were. So I putted it too hard down the hill, and watched it stay left, sniff the hole, and roll seven feet past to the very back of the green. I heard words of encouragement such as "that's a great par putt on this hole," but I was disappointed that I wouldn't be tapping it in for par. I hit the comebacker well, but missed it on the low side and tapped in for bogey. I was having so much fun on this course, that even the disappointment of a three-putt bogey didn't weaken my ear-to-ear smile.

We walked off the green and I bought our caddies food and drinks and took in the front nine: five pars and a birdie, six of the first nine holes played really well; the remaining third a combination of an unforced error, a tough bogey, and a regrettable snowman. While my nine totaled 41, Equitable Stroke Control would keep me under 40 for handicap purposes, which is outstanding given this was my first time around this massive course. After replenishing our tanks, we hiked up the hill toward the 10th tee. I was a bit off for the first three holes of the back nine, playing the three par fours in 2-over. I would need something to get my round back on track. I found it on the par-three 13th. A downhill shot to a long green with a swale on the left side, it was listed on the card at 170 yards. Tim kept up the enthusiasm: "we want to play it no more than 165. Short isn't great, but long is very bad." I pulled my 7-iron. I hit a decent shot, but it was also just a touch too far left, and the ball landed about three quarters of the way up the false front. I looked helplessly as my ball trundled back down the hill. Although I would have liked to putt my ball from the bottom of the false front, it had rolled off the closely mown grass and into the thicker fescue. That left me with no choice but to try to get a wedge on the ball and take my medicine. So I aimed toward the fat part of the green and hit my lob wedge just over the false front and watched it roll out to 45 feet, just barely holding on the green. Tim and I took the putt seriously, although it was mostly just an exercise of him doing his job and me pretending. We settled on two cups to the right, I took my putter back, and struck the putt at the perfect speed.

You know the feeling when you strike a long putt perfectly? It feels like time stands still. The audience of the six of us all watched the ball slowly move across the green, seemingly magnetically pulled straight toward the cup. I did not dare make a move to celebrate too early, as I had seen many putts look good from 30 feet, only to miss. But this one was true. As I reached in the hole to gather my ball, I heard phrases like: "best par I've ever seen on this hole," "fantastic save," "amazing putt," and "wow!" It was a great feeling, and I was having fun playing well. Thank you, Tim.

I played the next four holes well, with three pars and a bogey at the tough 17th. That brought us to the hole we had been talking about all day. From the tips, the gargantuan 18th hole measures 663 yards. I couldn't even believe it as we made a quick stop at that tee box and marveled at what the pros dealt with. We all said our requisite version of "they play another game," and moved to the more reasonable 542-yard tee box. I was third to play, and unleashed my best drive of the day, maybe one of the best drives of my life. The ball came off like a rocket: high, far, and right on the wind. And yet, when we arrived at the ball, Tim turned my attention to the Justin Thomas plaque in the fairway. Although I had a 120-yard advantage playing up tees, I had just barely outdriven him. And then we looked at where he hit his brilliant 3-wood from in the 2017 US Open. Not only was it 290 yards from the green, but the green was elevated with nothing but deep rough in front. There was simply no way I would try it, even if I was 100 yards closer. Instead, I pulled hybrid and aimed much farther to the right. I hit what I thought was an excellent shot: well to the right of the green, and elevated from where I was standing. My ball hit just below the crest of the hill, however, and tumbled back down. I had probably missed my spot by a few feet. I found my ball at the side of the hill, with about 70 yards remaining to the elevated green. From the rough, I figured I needed to take a bit off the lob wedge, and I was probably right. But the actual swing was more complete than I intended, and the wind took my ball straight to the back of the green, where it sadly went off the false back, 30 feet below the hole. Using that exact same club, I chipped up to pin high, and needed two putts from 20 feet to end with a closing bogey. Although I had failed to break 80—missing by two—I had made *have fun* my mantra on a highly challenging, championship-caliber golf course, and I had a lot of it. I had played an overall outstanding round at Erin Hills, one I would remember for a long time.

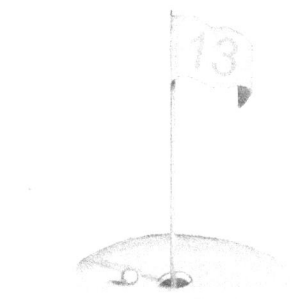

Dreams

(2014-15)

Aidan was born at the end of May, late in the academic year, so he was always one of the youngest in his class. Since he was capable in elementary school, being young wasn't a problem, at least not academically. In sports, however, being young meant being small, and so for the first few years of baseball, he was always one of the smallest on the team. He was fast and a good athlete, so he was still able to compete. But we could tell—he felt second-class. So when the opportunity arrived that allowed him to switch teams from the group aligned with his grade to the one aligned with his age, we jumped at the opportunity. He would still have to play well to make the team, but instead of being one of the youngest, he immediately became one of the oldest.

And he thrived. He had a new coach and team, and we had a new group of parents, but everyone welcomed Aidan and our family with open arms. This group was serious about their baseball. They had all the gear and competed at the AAA level (rather than AA or A).

These were the best players at his age group in the area. But instead of being intimidated by the level, Aidan was comforted by the age. He was consistently one of the best hitters on the team, not hitting home runs, but rather singles and the occasional double. He also had a great eye, and lots of speed, so he was able to get on base and steal when the opportunity was there. He enjoyed his confounding place as one of the few lefties and exuded a quiet confidence throughout the season.

Everyone knew from the beginning of the season that this was the "Cooperstown Team." The traveling club that our sons played for could only afford to send one team (out of 15 or so) on an out-of-state trip each year. This year, the anointed team was the 12AAA group, the parents of whom had the distinct opportunity (or burden) of raising money to fund their team's trip to upstate New York to compete at Cooperstown Dreams Park. It isn't the Little League World Series—that's reserved to a different scale of traveling players—but for our league, where kids travelled throughout our metro area to play, this trip to New York would be magical.

The kids were excited throughout the season. They were very talented, with the collective ability to make plays that I had rarely seen among a group of kids. And every disappointing loss was immediately followed by someone remarking, "but we get to go to Cooperstown." My son loved every minute of it. And during the season, the families bonded well. We had many between-game picnics, shared rides and snacks, while each family did its part to support the team. It was clear that the families bonded just as the players did.

But despite out clear fondness for each other, all of the players' parents were clearly overwhelmed by the talks we had to have, the consensus we had to reach, and the tasks we had complete to prepare for the trip. We needed to reserve a home or other property—or several—for 12 families. Luckily we found a farmhouse with adjoining motel that could accommodate all of us. We had to arrange flights. Our family would be flying to Washington, DC to stay with my mother and renting a car for the drive north to Cooperstown. We had to help the boys pack—we would be able to attend games, but otherwise could not see them during the week unless they were "checked out" of the facility.

As we drove from DC to Cooperstown, neither Aidan nor his younger brother Elliott said very much. Aidan seemed nervous, but most definitely didn't want to talk about it. "Are you okay?," I asked several times. "Fine," he dismissed. Elliott was happy to be along for the ride. Over the many miles, we saw fellow ballplayers and their families, more than a few of whom had "Cooperstown Bound" written over their car windows. Our excitement—and Aidan's anxiety—grew. When we arrived at Dreams Park, we saw the fields spread far and wide. Each field has a short porch of 200 feet, giving these 12-year-olds a legitimate chance to hit a home run. It would be their quest. There was a designated drop off time, which meant a long line of cars. This would be my first and only opportunity to see the bunks, which were basically small but permanent tents with six bunkbeds (12 kids per team) and two slightly larger beds for coaches. Kids would have to stay with their team at all times: for meals, practices, and games. The rest of us parents and siblings were consigned to our off-site property. The kids would have a week-long whiffle ball game while we parents would cook meals and drink from the well-stocked fridge.

As we arrived for our opening ceremonies, it was clear that the owner and founder of Cooperstown Dreams Park, "Coach" Lou Presutti, had created a highly lucrative business. Over the course of the summer, during the 16 weeks from late May to late August, approximately 105 teams make the trek to Cooperstown for a tournament *each* week. Stop and think about that for a moment. If there are 105 teams per week, that means there are 1,680 teams over the course of each summer. If there are 12 families per team, that means that each summer approximately 20,160 families travel to Cooperstown Dreams Park and open up their wallets. Conservatively estimating that each family spends about $1,000 to make this trip, much of which is spent on the registration fee and the countless "opportunities" to buy memorabilia, Cooperstown Dreams Park costs this large group of families approximately $20 million per year. It's a stunning amount of money for youth baseball. It's Disney World for baseball.

And there are opportunities to spend money at every turn. When we were on site for games, we would see Coach Lou patrolling the grounds in his signature golf cart, ensuring that every kid's uniform was properly tucked in—he had to keep the right image. We were shuffled to the concessions booths before, during, and after every game to buy an obscene amount of hot dogs, popcorn, chips, and countless other items. We were encouraged to buy photos of the kids, taken by the army of photographers that the tournament hires every summer to maximize family spending. We were encouraged to buy the ball that each kid hit over the short fence, often collected by the tournament staff to ensure that it could be authentically sold. Everywhere we went, dollars were flying out of my pocket.

When the kids weren't playing baseball or eating, they were trading pins—yes, pins. Each team had been expected to buy team pins, which the kids would bring to give to other teams. At worst, the kids would have a pin from every team they played. At best, some kids devoted much of their free time to amassing dozens of pins from teams all over the country. Elliott was all in. Not old enough to play in games, Elliott focused instead on trying to collect pins from all 105 teams. He would collect duplicates and then trade them for pins he didn't yet have. He was learning the high art of horse trading and loved every minute of it.

Several of Aidan's teammates had the immaculate joy of hitting home runs over the 200-foot fence. Built with the expressed purpose of ensuring that some 12-year-olds would hit homers, the kids loved the opportunity. Any ball hit high and far enough would clear the fences. After just a few games, all of his larger teammates had hit home runs. But Aidan hadn't yet done it; along with the majority of his teammates who hadn't experienced this particular glory. In the fourth game, Aidan was at bat with a hungry look on his face. The pitcher was clearly gettable, and Aidan was swinging like he was ready. He saw a slow curve that didn't break and cracked the ball, pulling it straight for the right field fence (he's a lefty). My fellow parents and I all inhaled at the same time and watched the ball.

Please let it go over the fence, I whispered to myself. I'm not sure who I was asking, and I'm sure no one was listening. But I sure wanted it for him. It wasn't meant to be, as the ball bounded off the top of the fence for a double. Two games later, in a similar situation, the same thing happened. *So close.* But Aidan was happy.

Having Elliott there was also so much fun. He eagerly watched every play of his older brothers' team, cheering and learning the game. After and between games, he was a gamer. He played catch with other kids, joined the perpetual whiffle ball games, threw frisbees, and traded pins. He was completely engaged, even though he didn't get to play, officially, in the games. And I loved watching him embrace the time he spent at Dreams Park, as if he were one of the boys. I'm not sure his brother noticed him—Aidan was too busy with his own team. But watching Elliott and the other little brothers made the trip complete.

As a parent, you know full-well that you can spend a lot of money doing just about anything, regardless of whether your kids actually enjoy it. So having our boys have so much fun really helped make it all worth it.

We also loved visiting the Hall of Fame, which we did on our penultimate full day in Cooperstown. A quintessential New York small town, there were more candy stores and gifts shops than anything else. If you wanted to buy something to commemorate the visit, there were endless choices. But we weren't there really to buy novelties, we were there to see the history of the game. After waiting in line for a painful 30 minutes, our team was welcomed in. I would imagine that the boys mostly remember being with each other, and maybe some of the videos of the great players. For me, I was in adult baseball heaven. I read about Babe Ruth and Hank Aaron, Lou Gehrig, Willie Mays, my childhood idol Cal Ripken, Jr., and even a tribute to the great Barry Bonds (who hasn't been voted into the Hall despite his home run record). I reveled in seeing the original gloves and how they had transformed through the years. I tried to get my sons to be as excited about baseball history. They were more interested in their friends.

And so, it began.

Bandon Dunes (Bandon, OR)

Dreams Park was not the only dream in my mind. In fact, I had been dreaming about Bandon Dunes since it opened in 1999. I read about the course in *Golf Digest*'s annual summary of America's Greatest, and every few years as Mike Keiser added Pacific Dunes, and then Bandon Trails, and then Old Mac. Bandon is a golfer's paradise, especially those of us who covet links golf. Keiser had famously looked for many years for available dunes-land, perfect for golf. With Royal Dornoch and Lahinch as his stated models, he searched for a plot of oceanside land, built on sand, with the potential for dunes golf. His good friend actually found it in southwestern Oregon, and he found his slogan: Dream Golf. Thanks to his vision and risk-taking, Keiser has singlehandedly made this remote part of the country the golf destination in the United States.

But it took me 20 years to get there, along the way earning my "piled high and deeper" degree, marrying, taking several jobs, and becoming a father. Finally, with my 50th birthday came the ultimate gift: a trip to Bandon. I knew about the gift for almost a year. I had watched every video on YouTube and elsewhere that I could find. I read the scorecard, over and over again. I watched the hole-by-hole animated course-flyover. I was so ready.

Then, when I finally stood on the 1st tee of Bandon Dunes, after decades of anticipation, I realized something unwelcome, and unplanned: my neck was locked up. Yes, I had spent the day traveling across the country: waking early (no problem!); flying to Denver; waiting in the airport for the small plane to take us to Southwest Oregon Regional Airport; taking a shuttle 35 minutes to the resort. Although I had smartly sent my clubs ahead, I still had to lug a carry bag full of golf clothes. Finally, when we arrived at the resort and I managed (with Shoe's help!) to find my golf clubs, I spent 30 minutes lightening the load of my golf bag so our caddie would be less burdened.

Throughout the entire travel day, I thought of nothing other than golf. The swing, the ocean air, the feel of the fescue, the bounce of the ball. With no time to warm up, I took my first few swings on the 1st tee. *Ouch!* Yes, my neck was locked up. If you've had any cervical spine problems, you know how this feels. I've had many such neck problems—spending over 30 years chasing a soccer ball across the pitch, being on the receiving end of elbows, knees, and other body parts on several concussions, and being thrown to the ground my fair share. I competed hard my entire career, and had a blast, but my body didn't forget. My cervical and lumbar discs had been flattened to near paper width, and I was going to have to deal with significant flareups from time to time. *But why this time? Why now?* I had prepared my mind and body for Bandon, working on my swing, my mental attitude, my putting, even my woeful bunker game. And now, on the 1st tee, I couldn't turn my head more than an inch to the left or right. Nothing prepares you for many aspects of fatherhood, but also nothing prepares you for this.

With no option of cancelling our tee time, I played. The opening two holes at Bandon Dunes are a bit of a teaser, and I played them as if I were teased. While beautiful and challenging, they pull your attention away from what you know is just west: the mighty Pacific. But unless you take a walk to the top of a dune, the Pacific is out of sight. The 1st hole plays north, and then slightly northeast, and the 2nd plays due east. It's as if David McLay Kidd—the precocious designer of Bandon Dunes who began work on the course when he was just 27—wanted to distract golfers while hitting us in the mouth. Though the first two holes are not difficult, per se—the 1st plays 386 yards from the tips, while the 2nd is an uphill 189-yard par three—they're the type where the slightest inattention can put you in a terrible spot. Your attention is focused to the west, to the vast Pacific Ocean that largely can't yet be seen, but can be slightly heard, likely smelled, and surely felt. And while we're being pulled to the west, the opening holes require attention and focus to the north and east. Well, the combination of a mind on the Pacific, and a neck that literally couldn't turn, my first drive—actually, more like a putt—lopped a few mushrooms on the way down the fairway. At least I would find my ball!

One of the great truisms of golf is we've all had truly terrible first drives. And on perhaps my most anticipated opening tee shot in many years, it happened to me. While I wasn't pretentious enough to be playing from the tips, I did choose the green tees, covering over 6,200 yards at Bandon Dunes. Now, the pain, distraction, and a hefty sense of embarrassment carried me down the fairway to my ball. But I didn't want to be *that* guy ... I didn't want to fill my compatriots with an ear full of excuses that, frankly, they didn't want to hear. They were just as gobsmacked with Bandon as I was, and no one cares about anyone else's shots. The "good shot" commentary, along with silence after a bad shot, is just the golfer's way of being neighborly—a polite hello over a tall fence. And nothing I could say would help to bring the fence down. I wish my friends had been there, so we could've engaged in some friendly banter. No matter, I had to play it—even if it lay only 50 yards from the tee box. Solid iron down the fairway, wedge over the green, another wedge on and then two putts: an opening double bogey ossified my first-drive embarrassment.

And then on the 2nd tee, David McLay Kidd seemingly did the unthinkable: he turned our backs to the Pacific. As the caddie walked us to the tee box and faced us east, I thought that maybe he was new, maybe he was mistaken. "We are going to the Pacific, right?," I asked Luis. I had perused the scorecard, read the articles, seen the photos, watched every video, and no one said anything about turning my back to the Pacific. "Yes," Luis insisted, "the green is over the gully, right there." And he pointed, straight behind me, as I strained to get an ocean-sighting. I didn't want to look away from it, and when I turned my back for the second tee shot, I had the feeling like someone was right behind me. I kept looking back, convinced that someone was sneaking up behind me and then did what, apparently, many golfers do: I hit a solid iron that propelled my ball straight to the middle of the green ... and then was promptly rejected by the slope and the wind, blown just right enough to trundle down to the right-side collection area.

And then, Mr. Kidd begins to laugh, as we novice-links golfers try to figure out whether to chip from the tightest of lies (don't do it!) or judge the weight of a hybrid or putter (yes!). Inevitably, the ball comes up short or overshoots the hole. I committed the latter, ended up across the green, and then faced a downhill putt which I mercifully completed in two strokes. Three-over-par after two holes and no real sighting of the Pacific. And, I still couldn't turn my neck.

As you walk up the hill to the 3rd tee, you get yet another playful smack from the architect. The tee area (there aren't really tee boxes at Bandon) sits high on a dune, overlooking a truly stunning par five. While the pin is straight way, the eyelines are hardly straight. The hole appears to snake to the left, then to the right before straightening up at the end. But it isn't a dogleg. Two—or three—straight shots will get you right to the green, and shots hit well but slightly left or right will funnel in the opposite direction. It's a welcoming tee shot, but there in the distance is the mighty Pacific. My eyes were pulled up. Luis could see my distraction—a look he probably had come to know well. "The hole is right in front of you. Don't get distracted," Luis encouraged, not naming the 20 visible miles of ocean in the distance. What I failed to see as I vacillated between the beautiful expanse of wide fairway meandering between the gorse to a reachable green was the fact that for the first 100 yards or so was a waste area. And somehow, mimicking my opening drive, I managed to swing too fast, and too tight, and too stuck, and hit it right in the waste. But there was no stopping, no sulking, no mulligans. My ball was partially under a gorse bush, enough to see but not enough to advance more than 20 yards. I played my ball and dealt with it. A chip forward onto the fairway, then two solid irons to the green. Mercifully, Luis just kept handing me clubs. My solid putting, always a strength, continued with another two-putt. Double, bogey, double. Five-over after three holes. And this is Dream Golf? So far, it felt like a nightmare.

They say that stress is the gap between expectations and reality. My expectations were sky high. I expected a beautiful course—indeed, it was! But I also imagined my A game, and what I brought, it appeared, was a failing grade. I was so stressed heading down the path to the 4th tee that I barely heard: "Are you *ready* for this hole?," Luis asked. I really didn't know what he meant. Was he sending me a message about my poor play? It must be so difficult for caddies to judge whether to say something to their player who is clearly struggling. *Slow down*, I imagined him saying. He erred on the stay-silent-when-seeing-a-terrible-shot side of things, so I concluded that *ready* had nothing to do with my play.

I looked at Luis, hoping that a simple look would expose my faults and transform me into the golfer I wanted to be. No such luck. I would have to fix it myself. I realized that if I were going to get any enjoyment about of this brilliant first day at Bandon, I would have to shorten my swing and probably abandon my driver. So, I pulled a three-metal at the fourth. Luis pointed to the gorse: "Hit it right over there."

I started laughing. "Hit it where?"

He pointed straight ahead, right into the gorse. "Just aim for the clutch of trees in the distance and don't play it more than 200 yards. Trust me." *Ah, okay,* I thought to myself, *we've known each other for three holes and now you want me to trust you.*

"I'll try," I said. I ignored the pain in my neck, put the first three holes out of my mind, and aimed straight ahead. And lo and beyond, the ball flied straight ahead. I couldn't see it land, but Luis's enthusiastic fist pump assured me that it was a good shot, the first one yet.

And then, the money moment at Bandon Dunes. I've read several accounts that described the second shot on the 4th hole as the most magnificent across the entire property. It's certainly the most breathtaking. The Pacific had been an ever-present fact looming over the first three holes and the fourth tee shot, but it hadn't really been *present*. Yes, I could see it in the distance, from the 2nd green and the 3rd tee, but it was hazy and not really *there*. That all changed as I reached my ball on the 4th fairway. As the fairway narrows around the 200-yard mark, and you turn slightly west, there it is: the massive expanse of the Pacific. At this point, I was close enough to see the beach, close enough to hear the waves, close enough to smell the ocean.

And at that moment, I knew: whatever troubles I had encountered on my journey to that moment, saying goodbye temporarily to my wife and pre-teens at home, traveling all day, suffering through poor play on three lousy holes, it was worth it all. It was worth every poor shot, every early wake up, every late return, every moment on the range. It was all worth it. That first moment seeing the ocean from the fairway—it's one of those rare golf moments when every first-time visitor audibly gasps as the Pacific comes into sharp relief. *How silly to complain about bogeys when you're at such a magical spot of the world.* And so, I promptly skulled my 8-iron to the right of the green. I wouldn't have it any other way.

I chipped onto the green and had a look for par, except I don't think I even looked at the line. Maybe there are golfers who can easily putt with the sounds of crashing waves right next to them, but I'm not one of those golfers. I made an indifferent putt from 10 feet, missed on the low side, and tapped in for a five. But my score didn't matter: it felt like a kid at Disneyland. I was living a dream.

Somehow, I recovered some semblance of a swing following my 3-wood on the 4th that preceded my mind-altering encounter with the Pacific. Although my score was a grinding 2-over through the final five holes of the front nine, I didn't feel as lost as I had on the opening three holes. And, for the first time that day, the Pacific had seeped into my bones, making everything feel better. Then, as Kidd once again turns our backs to the Pacific on the 9th hole, something clicked. After two decent-but-not-great shots, I pulled my gap wedge, choked down to accommodate the ball above my feet, and hit an excellent, high draw that landed pin high, just 15 feet from the cup. A second look at birdie. And this time, to my great excitement, I wouldn't be denied. Luis and I walked both sides of the putt and agreed on two cups to the left. I buried the left-to-right putt, with the ball dropping gently from the high side. While the front nine had taketh for most of the afternoon, it gaveth back on that closing hole. I don't think my face could have handled a broader smile.

I practically skipped to the 10th tee, which once again faces the Pacific, but from a distance where it remains out of reach. With a surprisingly light wind at the moment, I was able to hit my next two drives smoothly, if not sharply. While I missed the green on the 10th and settled for bogey, I was able to hit the green on the 11th and manage a solid par. Although I believe that the best moment on the course is the first sighting of the Pacific on the second shot of the 4th hole, it's quite possible that the tee shot on the 12th is the most photogenic (although the 16th probably vies for that title). Mostly stunned by the beauty of the 12th and not wanting to leave, Luis subtly brought me back to reality by handing me a club. "This is definitely a 7-iron," he asserted with a certainty that I hadn't yet heard. I couldn't argue. Hitting what could best be described as a lame hook, my ball started at the pot bunker and curved left, rolling up into the rough, just short of the green. Given the green contours, I knew that this would be a tough chip. So I naturally babied it and paid the price, leaving myself with a 10-foot downhill putt. I missed it, but made the tap-in and took a deep breath of ocean air.

After an indifferently played par five, seemingly distracted by the waves of fescue in the fairway, I arrived on the 14th tee. A short hole at only 332 yards, with high fescue to the left and plenty of room to the right, it didn't bother me that the green is hidden from the tee. There is also a collection of more than a half-dozen bunkers, several cut right in the middle of the fairway. Luis pulled driver, 3-wood, a hybrid, and an iron. "You can hit just about anything off this tee. How close do you want to get?" Though I'd always accept being closer, he wanted to know which club I felt most confident using. Somehow, I could see the line off my driver perfectly. The confidence standing at the tee translated to a solid fade. What a difference from the horrific drives in the opening nine. Luis confidently announced that I was "only a wedge from the green." Although my wedge was a bit right of perfect, it was a solid strike that left me 20-five feet from the pin. Luis and I took a careful look at the putt, decided that it was four cups to the right downhill, and I struck the putt. At the start, it looked like I would miss on the high side with too much pace. But as the ball slowed, it turned sharply left and dropping into the middle of the cup. Boom! What a putt.

That high carried me up and over the 15th hole, where I missed the green with my iron, then putted up and over a greenside mound onto the green, and two more putts on the green for bogey. We turned the corner to the left, saw the setting sun across the Pacific, and took in one of the most amazing holes on the planet. With the stunning red rock-face between the tee and the green, and a promised-but-not-quite-seen fairway somewhere out there, the hole is truly breathtaking. Luis volunteered to take our requisite photos, and we stepped to the teeing area. Two of my playing partners thought they could drive the green—they couldn't. I wasn't so optimistic, and Luis sensed the moment: "there's plenty of room left."

"Where?"

"Right there," he pointed to waves of dunes, fescue, and gorse. I had no choice but to trust his line and hit my drive straight over the chosen dunes. From the tee, it looked like my ball was long lost into some gorse, but Luis was confident. Sure enough, I was sitting in a great position 100 yards from the green. With some hurting wind, we thought I needed an extra club, and hit my blind shot about as well as I could. Although I couldn't see the ball land, the whoops and applause from the group put a wide smile on my face. I had hit it to five feet. Although I missed the five-footer—I still don't know how—I was thrilled to have hit such a great shot on such an iconic hole. It felt like Aidan's near homerun at Cooperstown, but like him, I was still very satisfied.

I enjoyed that high as I played the final two holes solidly, hitting both fairways, both greens, and notching two putts per hole. Whatever poor shots I had that day didn't change the fact that *I was at Bandon Dunes!* The first round was finished, and I was flying. I couldn't even feel my neck pain anymore. Bandon Dunes had punched me in the gut the first time around, yet the pain of the moment was replaced by a long embrace. I gave Bandon a metaphorical hug, and it hugged back. Two birdies and I had fallen in love with a golf course. I hoped aloud that it wasn't a long-distance relationship.

Trust

(2015-16)

It was a brilliant plan.

Theresa had spent so much time with the boys that she was going a little batty. Elliott was feeling more and more independent (even though he was only 10) and was ready for an adventure. I had to work in the morning but was free all afternoon. I would take him around one of the most interesting neighborhoods, show him the sights, and maybe buy him an ice cream and a present. All I had to do was meet him at the train station. In Akihabara. In Tokyo. Japan. Where none of us spoke the language. He was two hours away. How hard could it be?

To an American's ear, hearing about our plan—to send our 10-year-old son alone for two hours on a train ride from southern Yokohama (population 3.7M) to Akihabara, a neighborhood in Tokyo (population 14M)—no doubt seems like total lunacy. After all, we keep a close eye on our children in the United States, worried about the myriad dangers that lurk around every corner. But by the time we hatched our audacious plan, Elliott had lived in one of the safest countries in the world, had developed a remarkable sense of independence, and we were ready to give it a try.

To understand what *it* was, however, some specifics about our time in Japan are in order. I was the fortunate recipient of the Fulbright Scholar Award. I was given a unique opportunity, joined by my family, to spend a year in Japan. We would be living in Yokohama, the second largest city in Japan, and I would commute to Tokyo twice-per-week. At times, therefore, I was 40 miles north from my family. We often met in Tokyo to take our kids to explore one of the largest and most dynamic cities in the world. And, increasingly over the course of our time in Japan, our boys asked for some independence.

The kind of independence they sought could be understood as child neglect in the United States, but it was par for the course in Japan. Kids routinely travel without adults throughout the country, and in particular in the cities, from a very young age. One of the favorite reality shows on Japanese television, *My First Errand*, tracks the actions of a four-year-old who has been asked to go to the store to buy a few things. *A container of milk, a loaf of bread, a stick of butter.* Viewers watch the child as she gets distracted by a puddle, or a squirrel in a tree, or a candy in a store window, while all along she is making her way from home, often via public transportation, to the store. In my two-hour commute from Yokohama to Tokyo, it was routine to see young kids in uniform travelling alone on their way to school. Our sons wanted—no, demanded—some of that childhood independence.

The trip Elliott would have to take goes something like this: he would have to leave our small apartment in southern Yokohama by bike and ride approximately 10 minutes to a small train station on the Seaside Line. He would have to park his bike and lock it to the bike rack below the elevated line. He had to climb a flight of stairs, cross the road in a skyway, and enter the tiny station. Using a PASMO card—a touch-activated debit card that can be used on all subways and trains, as well as many convenience stores—he would have to go through the turnstile while paying for the first leg of his trip. He would then have to go up the escalator and get on the train on the correct side. Yes, he was only 10-years old.

If he managed to get on the train heading north, he would ride for about 20 minutes to Shin Sugita station, get off the train and manage the crowds, walk down the station, through another turnstile, down a flight of stairs, through a small indoor mall (past a bakery, where we often stopped for doughnuts and other treats) and into the connected Japan Rail (JR) station. He would have to enter the station, use his PASMO card to go through another turnstile, and continue walking straight ahead with the growing crowds. There, he would have to go to the left—the correct side for the northbound train—where he would go up another escalator to the platform for the Negishi Line toward downtown Yokohama. You can imagine how much we prepped him.

Assuming that he made it on the Negishi Line correctly heading north toward downtown Yokohama, he would have to take that train for about 10 minutes until he arrived at Yokohama Station. Yes, the *fifth busiest train station in the world* serving some 760 million people per year. Yes, we were sending our 10-year-old into the chaos of Yokohama Station where he had been several times a week for the past six or so months. He only had to transfer a few tracks over—from track 4 to track 7. He would simply have to exit the train, walk along the platform to the stairs, go down the stairs, turn the correct direction underground and walk with the crowd to the Tokaido Line toward Tokyo Station. Then, he would have to go up another flight of stairs, walk to the correct side of the platform and wait in line for the next train. One more train to go.

Assuming he got on the Tokaido Line correctly, he would then have a 25-minute train ride to Tokyo Station, which is only the 8th busiest station in the world. When he arrived there, he would have to exit the train, walk down the platform to the main station, and find the Yamanote Line (the line that forms a loop around Tokyo). He would then have to get on the Yamanote Line going in the correct direction (the inner loop) toward Osaki. Ten minutes later, if he had done everything correctly, he would arrive at Akihabara Station, where I would be standing on the platform waiting to meet him.

If you're a parent, you know you can't do everything for, or with, your kids forever. At some point, you have to start preparing them to do things on their own, and to learn how to navigate and problem solve themselves, while increasing their knowledge and confidence. We realized that Japan would be a safe place for our kids to gain some valuable independence. At least, that was the plan, in one of the largest cities in the world. And parents out there will know what it's like to worry about much lesser things. What could possibly go wrong?

For me, as a father, one of the most harrowing movie scenes I've ever watched is the Central Park scene in *Ransom* starring Mel Gibson. Gibson plays an airline executive whose son is kidnapped in Central Park. Gibson's son Sean has invented a helium-powered flying object—really, a 20th-century drone—and wants to enter it in the Children's Science Fair contest. However, because Sean's mother is one of the judges and because of his father's wealth and influence, Sean is flying the "drone" alone, just for fun.

The Central Park location—the Bethesda Terrace—was filled with parents and children, many of whom looked from a distance just like the character Sean. As kids are apt to do, Sean was engrossed in flying his drone while his parents were distracted—the Mel Gibson character chatting with some friends while the mother (played by Rene Russo) was busy judging. Sean drifted unnoticed from his parents, and seconds later Sean was grabbed and forcibly taken into a white van. In a matter of seconds, Gibson went from chatting lightly with his son and others to entering into the panicked dizziness of losing his son to extreme danger.

For much of my time as a father, I have fended off that feeling—*what if?* If you think too much about the horrors of the world, you'd become psychologically paralyzed, unable to go anywhere or do anything. And yet, the *what ifs* were the most acute of my life that day, while I was in the cavernous Akihabara station, trying to locate my son. The station was largely empty between trains, then jam packed when trains arrived and departed at regular intervals. I was using Hyperdia, a great Japan train app that indicates the precise arrival time. And, if you know anything about the Japan rail system, you know that precise means exactly that. If the train was supposed to arrive at 12:02, it would arrive exactly at 12:02.

So, at exactly 12 noon, I made my way to the train platform. Some Japanese train stations are built wide and open, so that it's possible to see easily from one end of the train to the other. This was not one of those stations. At roughly 50-foot intervals, there were large concrete columns in most cases connected to escalators going down to the main station. It was impossible to see more than one car in either direction. So, I readied my phone to call Theresa, thinking maybe Elliott hadn't left as planned. I continued to hope that he would be getting off the first car as we had planned, and waited. The train arrived, right on time. And as the doors opened, the throngs of passengers eager to get to their destination in Akihabara poured out of the train. I looked at, between, beyond, and below all of the passengers for a 10-year-old boy with light-brown hair. He was nowhere to be seen. I walked down the platform adjacent to the track, looking among the hundreds of passengers who were busily exiting the train and heading down to the main station. Noth-

ing. I continued walking as the train chimed and the doors closed. I looked inside the train. I looked everywhere. No sign of Elliott. I pulled out my phone, looking for a text or call. I texted Theresa, and then tried to call her. Nothing. That dizzying panicky feeling started to grow. *Think*, I told myself. *He probably just missed one of the connections. He's probably fine. But what if something happened to him? Without a phone, there's no way for him to get in touch with me. What if he got lost and can't find his way? Were Theresa and I fucking crazy?*

Anything and everything seemed possible, and what had begun as a wonderful plan to help our son grow and mature was rapidly transforming to one of the most careless, idiotic, and devastating mistakes. I tried to talk myself down from the ledge. First, I called Theresa. I didn't want her to panic, too, but I needed to know if Elliott had left on time. She didn't answer. *Okay*, I breathed, *I know my son, he has a great sense of direction, he's very responsible for a 10-year-old, and he's also 10—he just got distracted. Of course!* I walked downstairs to see if maybe I had missed him getting off the train and he was downstairs looking for me. No sign of him. I checked the app—in three more minutes, another train would arrive. I rushed back. *Should I stand near the front of the train, as planned, or stand near the back so I could see the train go by and maybe catch sight of him on the train as it slowed?* I didn't know what to do. I decided to go with our original plan. I walked to the front of the tracks and reached the front—right as the train arrived. No Elliott.

Okay, now I wasn't just having a panicked moment, I was getting worried. What was initially possibly just irrational fear was now full-blown rational worry. *Could he have missed two trains? Well, yes, since they run every six minutes ... and so many connections ... If he missed just one connection ... and then another ... that's 20 extra minutes.* I just had to trust that he would be on the next train. When it arrived, as I finished my nervous pacing up and down the track, again, no Elliott. *Should I call the police?* I quickly dismissed this idea. First, I didn't know the number. I knew that Japan's emergency number is 119 (yes, the inverse of the number in the US), but I had no idea what to do after that. *Ego ga hanasemasu ka? Do you speak English?* I could call and ask the operator if they spoke English, but in my experience, the answer would inevitably be "no"—or silence. And even if they did, did I really want to bring about an international diplomatic crisis? I could see the headlines—"America's Craziest Dad Loses Son"—and knew that the locals would bring out the cavalry. I practiced breathing, avoiding the catastrophizing in my head. My son was probably just late.

And sure enough, on the next train, I see that little boy get out of the train, happy to see me. I was *thrilled* to see him. I asked him how he was. "Fine," he replied, clearly having no idea that he was late. And given what he had just done, alone, to get there, was he really that late anyway? In normal-situation time, not really. In anxious-parent time, for sure.

Elliott had circumnavigated the trip from southern Yokohama to Tokyo alone, as a 10-year-old. I was so proud of him that I quickly forgot the panic that I had worn for the past 30 minutes. What we thought was an exercise in letting our son learn some independence turned out also to be an exercise for me to let go a bit and trust. I squeezed his hand tight and said, "let's get some ice cream," knowing well I deserved a treat, too.

Pacific Dunes (Bandon, OR)

Probably my favorite afternoon on a golf course (although definitely not my best score), was my four hours spent in the fog at Pacific Dunes in Bandon, Oregon. As anyone who has been to Bandon knows, there is something magical about the place. I spent four days there, and every day—no, every few hours—brought a new feeling to the property. During the four hours I spent at Pacific Dunes, the main feeling was wonder. With visibility down to about 30 yards, the incredible vistas that I had seen in photos were obscured. Instead, the course was enveloped in an eerie mist, not raining at all but the sea air was thick with fog.

I would have to put my full trust in Luis, the 6'2" caddie with a bright smile, who would be carrying my bag again. He took my clubs and shared this moment of complete excitement. While he had walked the course (and played, I later found out) many, many times, this was my first time laying eyes on one of the premier golf courses in the world. And by laying eyes, I mostly mean the fog in front of us.

I had spent the morning with the Wizard of Bandon, Grant Rogers. Grant's main mantra was "have fun!" He repeated over and over that we were there for one reason, and one reason only: to have a blast. It truly didn't matter to anyone whether we played well or not, whether our shots were good or not. He reminded me over and over to stay in the moment, to embrace the shot before me, to *be present.* We worked on smooth tempo, a comfortable backswing, a slow (almost lazy) transition, and a full follow through. Grant builds confidence by practicing what he preaches. He's in the moment, focusing entirely on what I needed most. He has a way about him—easy, calm, understanding. He demonstrated shots to me. Some weren't very good. But his eagerness to hit the *next shot* after a bad shot was a revelation. Grant helped me manage my anxious mind: "of course, we make mistakes. Of course, we have bad swings. A bad swing is just an opportunity to make an amazing recovery. After all, we don't remember the vast majority of shots in a round. But we do remember that heroic shot, that sand save, whatever shot that came off better than we expected. Mistakes are a chance to learn, and taking a risk is a way to make a memory."

I left Grant trusting that my middle-aged swing could handle anything that Pacific Dunes threw my way. And I went to the course with a positive and even confident attitude, having hit some beautiful shots on the range, but also just excited to see what kinds of lies I could find out there.

Yet the confidence that I had felt in the van driving over from the range morphed quickly into a rapid heart rate. Although I couldn't see much in front of me due to the fog, I would discover later that the 1st hole as Pacific Dunes presents itself as a gentle-ish handshake. The hole is short, only 370 from the tips and we were playing up one tee: 304 from the green tees. Luis had learned this much about me: "No need to bring a sliced lost ball into play," as he pulled a 3-iron. When I swing true, this club carries about 205, which into the fog and up the gentle hill of the 1st tee would likely leave me with about a 115-yard wedge in. Of course, swinging true was not in the cards as my rapid heart rate was not quelled by several deep breaths and an overly quick transition resulted in a duck hook, the ball traveling about 150 yards into the trees to the left. Like many, I don't think well or perform well when nervous. My poor tempo continued for several holes, as I struggled through two bogeys and a double on the first four holes. And yet I found calm as I walked backward off the amazing 4th green, enjoying the stunning view of the Pacific.

For Tom Doak, the young architect who was trying to make his mark at Pacific Dunes, he must've known that following up the dramatic oceanside 4th hole would present an enormous design challenge. The hole would almost certainly have to be played away from the ocean, into the dunes. He settled on an all-carry, middle-distance par three. Standing on the tee, I forced my focus away from the ocean, and instead to the dunes and pin. Luis assured me that there was a green up there somewhere, but I couldn't see a blade of its grass. Instead, I saw the yellow pin, and tall fescue dune grass all around—and no doubt, some greenside bunkers.

On the card, the green tee sat 181 yards from the middle of the green. With the breeze at our backs (the fog had momentarily lifted), Luis pointed over the dune on the left side of the green. "Land it on the front of the green and to the left," he counseled, "and the ball will funnel to the pin. Play it about 175." We agreed on a 6-iron. I'd like to think my mental game had something to do with my performance on the 5th. Or maybe it was Luis's description of the hole and his club selection. Or maybe I had a deep trust in my caddie. Or maybe it was just dumb luck. Who knows? But what I do know is that when I stood over my ball, I was freer with my swing and focused on the target. I played a high cut, a bit too far right of Luis' suggested landing spot, but actually tracking to the middle of what I had imagined to be the green. My ball settled 15 feet from the pin.

One of the most fun things about Bandon, or probably any walking-only caddie-based course, is the feeling like you're doing something you've seen a thousand times on television. I eased my glove, finger by finger, off my right hand and slipped it into my back pocket. I handed my 6-iron to Luis while he, always prepared, handed over my putter. We walked the two-football fields, through the tall fescue, to the back of the green. He surveyed my putt from every direction while I did the same. My speed had been excellent all day so far, I just needed the line. We agreed on two balls out. I took a few deep breaths, put the first four holes out of my mind, and struck the putt exactly how I wanted. Birdie. Fist pumps abound.

My elation was followed with a great par on the short par-four 6th, but then a streak of poor play for the final three holes of the front nine. The combination of ups and downs left me with a 42 on the front, solid but not outstanding play. And then Doak struck again. The tee on the 10th hole presents another take-your-breath-away moment on the course. While I licked my wounds from the front nine, I arrived at the 10th tee and gasped at awe at the ocean, in hiding for the past five holes. In the foreground is a middle-distance par three; in the background the Pacific's vast expanse. Yet, while 175 yards may be a comfortable six on a windless day, today I faced a foggy shot playing a solid 225 yards. Luis pulled my 3-wood and gave his usual advice to swing smooth. It felt like too much club— *could it really be a 50-yard wind?*—so my swing was tentative and the ball sailed short and right into the dune. I had to put my trust in my guide. These dunes on the 10th hole are sparely grassed, so I was able to find my ball easily. I chipped on to the green and carded my fourth straight bogey.

But the intermittent fog, along with Grant's continuous reminder to savor the opportunities to hit great shots, kept my mind out of the doldrums. I had to stay positive and trust in the process. I was still smiling as I arrived at what would become my favorite short par three in the world. Facing due north (the opposite direction of the 4th hole to our backs), we could see the full beauty of the green complex. The fog lay inland, just to our right. The green was surrounded by pot bunkers, fescue, and the mighty Pacific on the left. It's a short hole—a wedge or maybe a 9-iron at most. But now the wind was brisk, left to right. I stepped back, took a deep breath. My best short iron swings have a nice baby draw. Luis puzzled:

"If you play a draw, you could hold it against the wind. Too much draw and your ball will career down the cliff onto the beach. Too little draw and the wind would push the ball far to the right, into the fescue or, at best, a pot bunker. You'd have to start a fade at the ocean and hope that it fades back to the green, and not too short or too long." "I think it should be a draw." Luis readily agreed. It was a good swing, one that felt much slower than it was. I caught the ball square on the face. But clearly my subconscious forced me to be a bit too conservative with my draw swing, and the ball started in the middle of the green, not enough right-to-left curve. The wind pushed it just to the right of the green, still puttable on the fringe. Not bad, all things considered. Two putts later and I had another par.

I hadn't really noticed how strange it was to have two consecutive par threes—I was too distracted by the scenery. Yet Doak's quirky layout was just beginning. In all, the back nine at Pacific Dunes has four (yes, *four*) par threes, three par fives, and only two par fours—for a tidy par of 35. The fog was thick for the remainder of the round, so I spent a lot of time faithfully following Luis' directions, lost in the foggy isolation. We'd have to find our way.

What makes Pacific Dunes such a golfer's paradise is that with every frustration on the course, its beauty changes your mindset. The 13th is a perfect example of that: almost a mirror image of the 4th hole, but with more upslope. I managed to hit my best drive of the round: a solid strike from the center of the face, the ball pierced the fog, leaving me about 140 yards to the pin from the middle of the fairway. Among the many amazing walks at Pacific Dunes, the one from the 13th tee to the fairway might be the most spectacular. With the waves crashing just to the left, and small, gorse-filled canyon juts into the rough between the tee and the fairway, the walk brings in all the majesty of the surroundings. Not that we could see much of it, as the fog continued to fill every square foot around us. When we reached my ball, perched among the button mushrooms, Luis handed me an 8-iron—he had come to know my clubs and distances. I struck it well, but didn't play for the wind enough and landed on the right side of the green—destined to end up in the right greenside bunker. My initial reaction was disappointment:

two good shots and my reward was a bunker shot?! But I had learned a vital lesson from a wizard.

Grant Rogers had said, "savor your bunker opportunities. What we carry into the toughest shots will do more to determine the outcome than any technical ability. If you're tense and worried, you won't swing smoothly. If you're eager and relaxed, your body will respond." I knew he was right, but could I pull it off? I decided to try on the 13th hole. I smiled as widely as I could muster.

"I'm excited," I told Luis. "I can't wait to get up there and see what kind of brilliant bunker shot I get to play." Luis looked at me, no doubt suppressing a laugh. I was embracing the risks and the challenge, rather than cringing at them. We hadn't talked about Grant, and we didn't know each other well enough for him to know what I was doing. But he played along. I was going to will a good attitude. And wouldn't you know it, I got the ball out. On the first shot. To 10 feet. It wasn't a pro shot … Grant surely would have done better. But it was great for me. Luis and I lined up the uphill putt, I took a deep breath of salty air, felt the ocean wind rattling my pants, and drained the putt. What a par.

I smiled all the way up the dune and around the bend to the 14th tee. I love short par threes, as I continue to pursue my 1st hole-in-one. So, the 14th at Pacific Dunes gave me that feeling of anticipation that something great was about to happen. Downhill and downwind, I hit a comfortable pitching wedge that drew from the right side toward the center of the green. For a moment, I thought it was perfectly drawn, but it wasn't, and the ball kept moving left and landed on the left side of the green and rolled about 10 feet down the embankment. With a linksy lie off the green, Luis' direction was clear and firm: "putter is your best and only option." I obeyed. My putt made it up the hill, but came up left and short of the hole by about four feet. I missed the remaining putt and settled for bogey.

As we walked down to the 15th tee, I was stunned by what I saw: what had been thick fog was now wool-blanket fog. I would have to trust Luis more than ever. We were standing on the green tees and looked around. We could see each other, but couldn't see the gold tees just 10 yards away. But the caddies knew, they always knew.

They pointed us in the right direction. Luis smiled at me: "just rip it; we'll find it." We had to keep trusting our guides as to where to go, what to do, and that everything would be alright. The ball sounded good off my driver, and the initial sight of my ball flying into the fog was a moment burned into my memory. We walked off the tee laughing that our balls are probably still up on the fog.

I spent the final four holes drunk on the thick fog of Bandon dreams. We had navigated all of the danger successfully, and I actually felt proud of how I handled it. My swings were easy, my putts were solid, and the scores didn't matter. As I walked up the 18th fairway, trusting that Luis would find my ball yet again, I posed the quintessential question to myself: *which Bandon course did I like better?* It was like being asked which son I loved more—I love them both equally. The true sign of how much I love both is that the minute I stepped off both courses, I was drawn back to the 1st tee, wanting to play again. They are immaculate, and I am hooked on Bandon.

Agony

(2016-17)

I imagine that every father experiences this: the first moment when he sees a glimpse of his child as an adult. Not that his child has *become* an adult, but that the child does something that demonstrates the kind of responsibility and maturity that had thus far been elusive. For me, this moment came when Aidan was 15, and I was stuck on a twin bed, inconveniently placed in our living room, writhing in pain. I have experienced tremendous pain, but nothing quite like this.

It started as I hobbled over to the bathroom in my crutches, started to use the toilet, and noticed a strange and heavy ache on the right side of my lower back. I had never felt this discomfort before—it felt vaguely like gas pain, but it was in a different place. But since I had experienced so much pain in the past two months, I didn't think much of it. Just another annoying ache.

I had experienced so much pain because in July, I suffered a major bicycling accident. I'm not a roadie by any strict definition—I don't race or ride in biking clubs. But I love going out on my road bike for a few hours, to contemplate life and keep my body in shape. On a hot day in July—it was over 90 degrees—I set off on my usual ride. I'm lucky to live in a city where there are ample, paved paths for cyclists. While the surface isn't smooth compared to a regular road, the safety away from cars makes it worthwhile. I was feeling quite comfortable as I reached the eight-mile mark, about 30 minutes into my ride. I came upon a detour; the Minnesota Department of Transportation had closed part of the bike path—I would later discover, ironically, for ADA compliance—and I was redirected onto the street.

The road was a major county route, with two lanes each way and a speed limit of 55 miles per hour. This is not the type of road I would typically ride on, so I crossed the street in search of a sidewalk. Although not ideal, my plan had been to ride on the sidewalk for about a quarter-mile until I could get to a different bike path. I never reached my destination.

I was waiting at a streetlight to cross a side street parallel to the major road. I was going against traffic, and I watched as some cars turned right in front of me onto the side street. Sweat was pouring down my face; I took a sip from my water bottle. The light turned green and I proceeded ahead, crossing the side street, with my eyes focused on the incoming cars, some of which might turn right in front of me. I had no thought to look down.

With no warning, my front tire dropped down two inches and immediately stuck. I had inadvertently ridden into a railroad track. A split second later, I was crashing to the ground in front of oncoming cars cruising at around 55 mph. With my shoe cleats locked into the pedals, and my hands gripping the handlebars, there was nothing to soften the blow on my right hip. The cars, to my good fortune not too close to me, came to an immediate halt, and the closest driver and his teenage son rushed out of their car and came to my aid.

"Are you okay?," the father asked, frantically. I didn't even really know what had happened, and assessing how I was—sweaty, breathless, and in shock—took a few seconds.

"Um ... yeah. I think I can get up," I replied. I tried. The pain was immediate and beyond intense. I lay back down on the road. "I can't move," I said.

"We'll carry you." They lifted me up and helped me to the sidewalk, and retrieved my bike from the road. "Do you need me to call an ambulance?" I have no idea how I responded. I don't think I said anything. The pain was unbearable. My right leg was severely dislocated to the right. I don't know how it looked, but it felt grotesque. I could barely breathe. I'm sure he called an ambulance, but I have no memory of what he said or how much time elapsed. I remember being in tremendous pain, being unbelievably hot, and starting to shake. I tried to find a less-than-unbearable position on the sidewalk, but nothing worked.

"Do you need me to call someone else?" He got my attention, this heroic man who carried me off the road and was sticking with me.

"Um ... yes, my wife." I handed him my phone and told him her number. He called Theresa. I would find out later that she received a call from a stranger telling her that I was on the ground after an accident, that I was alive, and that she should come right away. I don't remember any of it. I do remember a small crowd gathering, including an EMT on her day off. I have no idea what anyone else said or what they did, but I do remember the crowd. Mostly, I remember the pain and the heat.

I don't know how much time elapsed—it could have been a few minutes or an hour. A police officer arrived to control traffic. I looked at her, expectantly. She spoke slowly: "there's nothing I can do for you right now. I just have to make sure everyone is safe." She had to ensure that we were safe from the drivers who drove by gawking at the scene. I was now, apparently, a scene. Throughout my 15 years as a father, I had prided myself on being the caretaker. When Theresa had gone through the physical traumas of our sons' births, I took care of her. When our sons were sick, I did my part to take care of them. One time, at a family reunion, when Aidan was only two, he had eaten more than a few strawberries—we think that every relative thought it would be fun to give him one strawberry—he gave me *that look* and I snatched him up as he was returning all the strawberries in a different form onto my shirt. Theresa saw what looked like blood all over my shirt as I ran him to the bathroom. "We're fine, I told her. Just a little throw up." For many years I had helped to heal the wounds of our family. Now, it was me that needed to be cared for.

When the firefighters arrived, I was both surprised and relieved. I don't know why a firetruck was dispensed—maybe they send all emergency vehicles in the area to come as soon as possible. Maybe there was a fear that a car had been involved and there was a risk of fire. The firefighter said, "we have to move you off the sidewalk onto a portable stretcher. Then, when the ambulance comes, they can take you to the hospital right away."

With the initial shock wearing off, the only thing I felt was pain. "Okay," I somehow responded. Several men in firefighter uniforms bent down. My injury was on my right side, so they wanted to lift up my left side to slip the stretcher under me. That meant that they had to push me onto my right side. My right leg was at a 45-degree angle, creating the shape of a letter k. There were so many moments in this 24-hour period when the pain was excruciating that it's hard to say which one was the worst. But this moment with the firefighters was one of them. This was real. My leg was mangled. I screamed in pain.

Just a short while later, the ambulance arrived and the EMT took over. While before there was a lot of care and concern, I didn't have a sense that the people around me knew *exactly* what to do. The EMT did. I don't remember his name, if I ever knew it, but I'll never forget his face. He looked me in the eye and explained everything. He was serious, focused. He also looked very young, but I had to trust that he knew what he was doing. "I need to get an IV started to get some fluids into your body. Otherwise, you could go into shock." Although I didn't think of it at the moment, the IV was also the primary way that I would get pain meds.

Getting the IV was a good distraction from the focus on my leg. Although I didn't see it happen, I assume that during this distraction, most of the people who had gathered went on their way. There was nothing for them to do. The EMT got the gurney and set it up next to me. I don't remember who did it, but two men lifted me—still on the stretcher—onto the gurney. They needed the stretcher back, so they rolled me onto the gurney. The pain was excruciating. A few minutes later, I was in the ambulance.

We sat in the ambulance for what seemed like hours (though it was probably more like 15 minutes). The EMT asked me about insurance. I wanted to lash out: *What the fuck does it matter what type of insurance I have? My leg is mangled. Get me to the hospital, now!* But I didn't. I knew he was thinking about me. At this point, Theresa arrived. I found out later that she had been busy with her day across town and had to drop everything to drive 30 minutes to find me. I'll never forget the look on her face: sheer panic.

"Are you okay?" She said it, knowing that I most definitely wasn't. But it was so good to see her. I lied and said I was okay. I handed her my wallet, phone, and sunglasses. She still marvels that at this particular moment, I was thinking about not losing these things. My bike would ride with me in the ambulance. "I'll meet you at the hospital," she said. Without my sunglasses, and with my regular glasses at home, I was thrust into a blurry world. It's not that I needed to see anything. I was going where they took me. It's just that looking through those foggy eyes of mine without the aid of glasses was a fitting description of how I would feel for the next few months: in a fog.

The fog came not just from the lack of glasses, but from a fateful decision I made a few minutes later. Since the EMT had arrived and put the IV into the back of my hand, he had asked me several times if I wanted "something for the pain." I said no each time. Now, we were safely in the back of the ambulance and he had to ask me a few questions. I'm sure now that he was assessing my mental condition. But at the time, I didn't think of his job, just that I had to focus on his questions.

"What is your name?," he asked, holding an iPad. I told him, finding some calm and focus that had eluded me since the accident. He asked me a series of routine questions about my date of birth, address, occupation, insurance policy, and other questions I don't remember now. "We will be at the hospital soon. Are you sure you don't want something for the pain?" Again, I replied "no."

We started moving, slowly at first. A minute or two later, we hit our first bump. I can't repeat what I screamed. That made me speak up, "I'll take something for the pain, now." I didn't really think about it. I was quite familiar with the opioid crisis in the United States, but I wasn't thinking about that. I knew that the vast majority of opioid addictions, and later deaths, begin with an accident or injury in which opioids are given to control pain. But I wasn't thinking about that. All I could think about was stopping the agony. He told me, "in just a few seconds, you'll start to feel warm all over." It happened instantaneously. I don't know if the pain subsided, or my recognition was diminished, or that I was high, but it happened right away, and they would keep my high for the next 24 hours or so. I remember the drive to the hospital—wondering if it would ever end. I remember being wheeled into the emergency room, with some people seemingly paying attention while many others ignored me. I remember my wife, looking at me with incredible concern and worry. I remember being put in a waiting room, which felt like a small holding cell. But all of it is foggy, as if I were looking through a windshield with a thick layer of ice. I could see there were people and machines … so many machines. But everything was happening in a blur.

Sometime later, Theresa returned with Aidan and Elliott. I had been wheeled into a regular room, and I had seen at least one nurse. I guess she checked my vitals, but I don't remember. I do remember seeing my kids. Elliott looked very worried. Aidan had a look that I'd never seen before: he was worried, but also determined. He was going to help in a way that he never had before.

Over the next few hours, I was moved to get an x-ray and then into the room that would be mine for the night. While I was now somewhat comfortable when laying on the bed not moving, every time I was moved somewhere, lifted onto the x-ray table or onto another bed, the pain was excruciating. They kept me on a steady dose of Dilaudid, an opioid over 50x the potency of morphine. Although I was foggy throughout, somehow I had the presence of mind to take off my bike clothes—the nurse wanted to cut it off—and they helped me get into a gown. No shower, though, so the smells must have been something.

My sons were intrigued when the doctor came to give us a report. He showed us the x-ray. I had broken the femoral head—the "ball" of my femur—off the rest of the bone. This was a serious fracture. I would need emergency surgery, to be performed by one of the best surgeons in the region, the next morning.

My wife took our boys home, fed them, and returned later in the evening, alone. The entire night was a fog; the room seemed to be a hub of some sort. With nurses, doctors, orderlies, and others coming in and out, seemingly all night long. Because I was kept on a Dilaudid high, while I was aware of what was happening and didn't sleep in any real sense, I wasn't able to advocate for myself. Someone came in to help me, and dropped a pillow—yes, a pillow—directly on my mangled leg. I don't know how many curse words I used, but needless to say they can't be put in print. And throughout the night, foggy as I was, all I really could think of was that I had failed my boys. This wasn't just a skulled chip, four putt, water ball, or snowman 8. It wasn't golf, it was life, and it was a complete failure. Some pretty big questions came to mine: *Would I ever recover? How would I even walk? How would I care for my boys?*

Hours later, I was being wheeled into the pre-op room. Theresa had arrived early in the morning, put up an appropriate stink about why I was in a room where I couldn't sleep, and I was moved briefly to a private room—she has told me. I don't remember any of it. Just the pain, and the mental fog, and the pain. And then, the anesthesiologist was asking me if I was scared. *No, my leg is in agony and I want it fixed. I want you people to stop talking to me and start fixing my leg.* It was a good, intense thought. I don't know what I said, either nothing or a meek "no." I was so high and in pain, nothing seemed to make it through my brain to my mouth.

And then, the agony was over. Photo-like images of myself in the operating room remain. Many people, each with a specific job, were busy doing it. One person talking to me, trying to get my attention. Machines beeping, lights shining: a space of complexity, yet utter simplicity. Their job was to put my leg back together so that someday, hopefully, mercifully, I would walk again.

I woke up in what felt like the far end of a gym-sized room. No one was around me. I could see there were nurses in the room, but everyone was busy tending to someone else. I tried to speak—*I'm awake.* But nothing seemed to come out. I noticed something right away—no agony in my right leg. Was it still there? I couldn't tell. I tried to lift myself up to see. Nothing happened. *Were my eyes even open? Was I dreaming that I was awake?* I couldn't tell. It seemed to last for hours as I struggled to understand what was happening, where I was, whether I still had my right leg, whether I was awake or dreaming.

At some point, a nurse came over. "You're awake. How are you feeling?" I don't know if I said anything. I remember thinking: *I've been lying here alone for hours, trying to get your attention. Where have you been? Why were you ignoring me?* My brain was playing tricks on me. It was probably a few minutes of waking up. But as my mind tried to make sense of where I was and why, I remembered to check my leg. I couldn't move it, but I didn't feel that seething pain. I could move my hands and arms, and my left leg seemed to work fine. But no movement on my right side. I didn't know whether to be terrified that I had no feeling in my right leg, or to be thrilled that there was no pain.

The next few hours are a blur. I don't remember leaving the recovery room, being wheeled into what would become my home for several days. I don't remember waking up in that room. I don't remember who attended to me, probably regularly every hour. I do remember Theresa, Aidan and Elliott coming to the hospital. Theresa looked stressed and anxious. I would only find out later just how difficult those 24 hours had been. I had been a healthy and fit 48-year-old man, who loved to golf, who biked regularly, who was active with the boys. She worried that she was now married to a man with the physical capabilities of an 88-year-old. While the boys were easily old enough to understand the severity of what I was going through, they mostly remained deep in their own world. I tried to reassure Theresa that everything would be okay, but the fact was that I couldn't move my right leg, and no matter how much the pain had subsided, there were no guarantees. Amazingly, she kept her tears in check.

A tall, male nurse came in. "This is a patient-controlled analgesia machine. It will allow you to give yourself a small dose of narcotic." He said it calmly and professionally, and then stated words I would hear over, and over, and over again: "It's important that you stay ahead of the pain, so give yourself a dose at the first sign that the previous dose is wearing off," he instructed. There wasn't any conversation, no weighing of pros and cons. There was simply the mandate to stay ahead of the pain. I asked, "What are the risks of taking the narcotic?" My question was dismissed: "there are no risks."

It seemed that the entire focus of my post-surgery care was to make me pain-free. I listened to my caregivers, and pushed the PCA machine several times each day to maintain a small but consistent dose of Dilaudid in my system. After three days, the IV was removed and I was given Oxycodone, tiny pills that I took orally every three hours, again to stay ahead of the pain. Notably, the doctors prescribed 20 mg per dose, two tiny pills—I only took one. My favorite nurse—an older Somali woman who had surreptitiously found some pieces of metal that she somehow reorganized into a kind of monkey bars contraption that allowed me to lift myself up from a prone position—was very worried about me. "You need to take all of your pills. If you get behind your pain, you won't be able to recover." I didn't care. I hated the foggy feeling more than I worried about severe pain. Nothing could match the pain of the injury.

In preparation for my discharge from the hospital after five days, Theresa went to the pharmacy to pick up the narcotic I was prescribed. Theresa told me later: "the pharmacist literally had nothing to say about risks of the narcotic, any potential dangers of overdose or drug interaction. They just told me to make sure you stay ahead of the pain, and take all of your pills." The medical professionals were clearly well-trained.

When we arrived home, despite the pressure from the health care staff, Theresa and I decided together that I would immediately begin to taper off the opioid to make sure I didn't become addicted. I kept delaying and lessoning the dose, and on the 11th day I resolved to stop taking the narcotic.

What followed was three days of physical and emotional agony as I went through acute withdrawal. In 10 short days, my body had gone from narcotic-naïve to addict. While I took smaller-than-offered doses at every opportunity, and tapered off the narcotic as quickly as possible over five days, I was hooked. My body had become heavily dependent on the drug, and after only 12 hours after the last pill, I experienced horrendous withdrawal symptoms. My body shook with chills and fever, I experienced terrible headaches and dizziness, my stomach felt like it was churning through the worst food poisoning, and my brain felt cloudy and vacant. It's difficult to articulate this fact: that opioid withdrawal is not about "wanting the drug." I didn't feel the need to get high. Rather, I felt excruciatingly sick and knew that the only way to stop feeling so awful was to take the drug. But I couldn't do it. I wouldn't allow myself to become a failed, drug-addicted father. I never took another opioid.

Over the next few weeks, we got into a routine of sorts. Every evening, I called Aidan to my side. There are 17 stairs in our home from the first floor to the second—I know, because I counted them every day. In order to climb them on crutches, I had to put my right hand on the handrail, and push hard with my left hand on the left crutch and hold all my weight on my left leg. Due to my injured leg and the general haziness of my opioid withdrawal, finding the right balance was extremely difficult. Aidan regularly had to hold me from behind to prevent me from toppling back down the stairs. He used all of his newly found 15-year-old muscles and guided me up the stairs every night.

In the morning, we did the same process in reverse. Because gravity made the process easier on my leg—and the danger of falling backward was replaced with the danger of falling forward—Aidan walked right in front of me, at the pace of an 80-something. As an aside: the physical therapists whom I saw during these weeks were congratulatory: "you're doing so well! You're far ahead of the average time recovery for this injury."

I was pretty excited, until I asked, "What is the average age for this particular injury and recovery."

"Ahem," they cleared their collective throats, "80." *So I'm recovering faster than an 80-year-old: something to celebrate for sure.*

Anyway, every morning after I made it down the arduous path to our main floor, I found my place on a twin bed that Theresa had temporarily set up in our living room. It would be my primary resting place for the daytime during the rest of the summer. But despite a clear mandate from my doctor, a strong mandate from my physical and occupational therapists, and a plea from my wife, and *every other person I knew*, I had made a commitment to do something that next weekend that I just would not miss: I had agreed to coach Elliott's August Classic team.

Elliott had just finished a terrific baseball season and was voted one of the most valuable players on his team. There's a special reward for the top three players on each league team: they get to play in the August Classic. After competing against all the other Metro teams for the season, the top three players on each team are joined into eight or so *super-teams* that compete for an all-star trophy. For the first time in his short baseball career, Elliott had earned that chance.

But he needed a coach. The other dads from the team were either non-coaches, or they had made other plans. I had volunteered—before the accident—and I wasn't going to force Elliott to miss this opportunity simply because of a stupid accident. So, just days after my brutal injury in which my leg had been saved by emergency surgery, and amid the worst opiate withdrawal that I could imagine, I got a ride from another parent to coach Elliott in the August Classic.

There were some things I just couldn't do. While I had planned to be the third base coach during games, I couldn't possibly do that. In fact, I only got to the game using the kind of walker usually reserved for octogenarians. I also couldn't stand up for more than a few minutes. So, I had to plant myself in the corner of the dugout, ask the team to gather around me, and coach from the bench. My main contributions were creating the batting orders before the games and talking to players from the bench. These were minor contributions, and when an errant throw flew past the first base-man and straight into the dugout, hitting me but fortunately not my leg, I really wondered whether it was worth it. But being able to give Elliott a high-five after watching him bat in a run with a double—well, that was worth every ounce of pain.

Later that fall—the day when I first saw Aidan act as a man—began as most days had begun the previous few months. I slowly made my way down the stairs with his help. I had progressed enough in physical therapy, opioid recovery, and crutch mastery that I could get around competently on the first floor without help. I could get to the bathroom, make myself a meal, and even drive. Nothing was easy, but I had learned how to live a relatively normal life on crutches. Late that morning, I went to the bathroom and as I was using the toilet, I noticed a strange tinge in my back. It wasn't the normal golf-induced lower back pain, or even the upper back pain that I sometimes felt from sitting too long at the computer. This was different. I was more of a dull ache, and more on the side of my back. And at the time, I just felt like gas pain. I didn't think much of it.

Elliott had fall ball baseball practice, and while I couldn't help coach his team, I could drive enough to drop him off at practice. It was a short 20-minute drive down one of our main city streets. From the time we got in the car until we arrived at practice, the dull ache had grown to a nearly intolerable pain deep inside and to the side in my lower back. This was no gas pain. I told Elliott that I wouldn't be able to stay for practice, and I texted his coach to ask for him to find a ride home for my son. Once he was out of the car, I started letting out moans of pain as the agony in the side of my back kept growing. It wasn't the sharp pain of a broken leg, but it was every bit as awful. I had to pull over numerous times as I tried to drive myself home. I parked in the garage, managed to get out of the car on my crutches, and made my way into the house. I went straight to the bed, doubled over in pain. I spent the next hour moaning in pain, with only our dog and cat to hear me.

About an hour later, Theresa came home from work. Hearing the moans, she knew immediately that something was seriously wrong. She assumed it was my leg. "What happened? Are you okay?," she asked urgently. I couldn't get any words out between moans of pain. "Is it your leg? Where does it hurt?"

"It's not my leg," I managed to get out. Something else was wrong, and I didn't know what to do.

"Should I call an ambulance?," she asked.

"No," I said firmly, but unpersuasively. She didn't know what to do, or how to help me. She saw that I was doubled over in pain, and now knew that it was not my broken leg. I don't know how I looked exactly, but I know that I couldn't lay in most positions due to my broken leg (I couldn't, for example, get on all fours and try to relieve this pain). It felt like my right side in the back was being crushed by some invisible force.

Aidan came home from school soon after. Theresa was unsure what to do—she thought she should call an ambulance, but I had said no. "What should I do? Should I call an ambulance?," she asked him. I heard her and meekly responded, "no." But with the kind of decisiveness that only an adult can demonstrate, Aidan told his mother that she had to call an ambulance.

"Do it, right now," he ordered. She called immediately. I continued to moan in pain on the makeshift bed in our living room, Theresa having no idea how best to help me, Aidan becoming the decision-maker. Only later would I marvel at how calm he apparently was in that moment of crisis. Only later would I come to realize that the fact that he was able to make such a decision was, in fact, the first real sign of his maturity. He was becoming a man.

The ambulance came within 10 minutes. They came into our house and quickly assessed the situation—male with broken leg, moaning in pain with some unknown problem. They asked me some questions, took my blood pressure, and offered me narcotics. I was still in the long road of recovery from my opioid addiction, so the last thing I would be doing was taking more opioids—that much I knew. Whether the opioids had anything to do with my condition I'll probably never know. But I wasn't going to make that problem any worse.

"Can you walk?," they asked. I didn't think I could, given that walking meant using crutches, and the pain was so intense that I couldn't stay still for more than a few seconds. So, they got their mini wheelchair, put me on it, and wheeled me out to the ambulance. As our neighbors gawked, and I couldn't help but moan in pain, I was put in the ambulance and taken back to the hospital where I had been just two months before. I was learning to hate that place.

At the hospital, I spent several hours unable to get comfortable on the bed. I couldn't really move without leg pain, and the pain in my back continued unabated. They repeatedly offered opioids, and I repeatedly said no. The doctor came in: "I don't yet know for sure, but I'm pretty convinced that you have a kidney stone. Here is some medicine that will help you to use the bathroom. Drink as much water as you can."

Thirty minutes later, the nurse came in. "Take this to the bathroom and pee in it." She was all business. I did what I was told. Under the power of crutches, I managed to make it down the hall to the bathroom, took a deep breath, and dropped my pants. Relief. I filled the cup, and lo and behold there was a tiny stone in the cup.

I couldn't leave the hospital until they tested the stone. Sure enough, it was a calcium stone, formed in my kidney. It was one of the most painful things I have experienced, rivaling the pain of a broken leg. I laid in the hospital bed, taking slow breaths and feeling like I was aging by the minute. Breaking my leg had been agonizing for me. But my injury, and the subsequent kidney stone, had also created the space for Aidan to step up and show the man he was becoming. I was so proud to see my boys rise to the occasion, be decisive when we needed it most, and to care for me as I had spent so long caring for them. My tears of pain quickly transformed—I was one proud dad.

Bandon Trails (Bandon, OR)

It's amazing how an injury will show you how much you take common activities for granted, and that's a lesson I had learned many times over. Almost every day before the accident, and for years since, Theresa and I have frequently taken long walks. It started before

Aidan was born. She had read in one of her pregnancy books that long walks were particularly helpful. But while the physical benefits abound, the relationship benefits are more important. Almost every day, the walk gives us a chance to talk. So often, life with children becomes a minute-by-minute effort to keep them safe, content, and well-fed. It can be all-encompassing. The walk gives us time away from them, and time when we can just be together. Of course, walking without them wasn't always possible. For years, it was walking with them: in strollers, trailers, scooters, and eventually bicycles. As soon as they could be home alone together, or they were off doing whatever with friends and teammates, we'd take advantage of the time together.

Some days are filled with energetic conversation—about the boys, of course, but also about work, our parents, finances, and the state of the world. Other days, we barely speak, content to just be together. Through it all, the daily walk sustains us. When my orthopedic surgeon said that I might not ever walk again, it wasn't just my leg that was in so much pain.

And that may be why the walk on Bandon Trails—perhaps the least famous of Mike Keiser's Oregon coast courses—stays with me like no other round of my life. When I was in Bandon, I played more visually stunning courses than Trails, as the locals call it. I had more wow moments on other courses. But on no other course was the full experience of the walk more profound. I've read that this was Coore and Crenshaw's intent—to take the golfer on a walk through the woods. And what a walk it is.

Bandon Trails sits on the southern end of the property, just south and inland from Bandon Preserve, which sits just south of the 16th and 17th holes on Bandon Dunes. Unlike all of the other courses, there isn't much sense of the landscape when you arrive, usually by the resort's van at the roundabout near the clubhouse. From there, the 1st hole of Bandon Preserve is visible, and much of Bandon Dunes spans in sight below and north up the coast. As you begin the walk toward the clubhouse, the practice green appears, and the first sighting of the course: the 18th green. It's as if Coore and Crenshaw want to show you how you'll feel at the end before they take you through the mysterious walk through the woods. They will only show you the walk, one hole at a time.

For me, the round at the Trails was my fourth round at Bandon. My days' earlier jitters at *simply being* at Bandon Dunes had passed, replaced by a renewed focus on my game. I had been swinging well, learning some of the nuances of American links golf. I had learned that, as they say, "putter is always an option." I had learned to keep my lob wedge in the room and instead play a variety of shots on the ground. I wasn't very good at them, but I was committed to trying all them. As a special treat, I had a chance to play with a staff professional, Michael Chupka, who had a bag of persimmons, hickories, and old irons on his back. Michael is the kind of golfer I love to play a round of golf with. He's incredibly talented—he played the antique clubs with ease—warm and welcoming, and willing to offer tips without being overbearing. The perfect person to walk the trails with.

We set off to the 1st tee walking on—yes—a trail. The tee is not visible from the clubhouse, but the opening hole was familiar after playing the other courses on the property—the fairway sat below an elevated tee, with large dunes creating a runway of sorts. Not visually intimidating, the 1st hole felt welcoming, as if the architects were beckoning us to join them on the trail. From the one-forward green tees that had been my staple that week, the hole measured just over 350 yards. I confidently pulled my 3-wood, hoping to put it straight down the middle with a baby draw to follow the contours of the hole. It was one of the few times that I've stood on the 1st tee on a one-of-the-best-in-the-world course and not felt shaken with nerves. I was thinking about how far I had come from the injury. Although not the most solid strike, I did find the fairway comfortably. And the walk began.

Or more like a stroll. I don't know what it is about Bandon Trails, but as I stepped off the tee and began down the fairway, white button mushrooms all over, I felt this enormous sense of being enveloped by the course. Like Charlie's first step into Wonka's Chocolate Factory, it felt like a treat would come at every turn. And I just wanted to walk farther and farther into it.

After an opening bogey on my card, I gazed back at the hole we had just played: the dramatic vista behind the dunes, with parts of Bandon Preserve and Bandon Dunes visible and the vastness of the Pacific Ocean. And yet while the view behind us was stunning, the magnetic force that Coore and Crenshaw had created was pulling me in. It's hard to compare holes across the Bandon courses, but it's quite possible that the best collection of par threes is at Bandon Trails. The par-three 2nd features an elevated tee looking down on the transition from dunes to trees, with several dunes in the foreground, and a particularly massive dune to the right of the green. The dune blocks some of the view of the bunker that sits at green level to the right. To the left and long is the woods, with trees overhanging the green from the back. The result is a mini amphi- theater, with a green sitting diagonally to the right, surrounded by sand and then trees and dunes. It's not a long hole—about 165 yards—but gauging the wind at our backs, and the downhill, proved challenging. I pulled an 8-iron, figuring that it would be better to be short than long, and determined not to hit a weak slice. I didn't. Instead, my iron contacted the ball with controlled ferocity, and I put a terrific draw on the ball. Unfortunately, the designers knew that a well struck draw, played to guard against the dunes and sand on the right, would produce a ball flight that turned away from the rightward angled green, as my ball did. Plop. I could almost hear the ball land in the deepest part of the pot bunker over the green to the left, and ominously, I didn't see it move. Grant Rogers' words rang in my ears: "Get excited. Every bunker shot is an opportunity for a heroic shot." It was a solid swing, resulting in a ball flight that would produce many good results if I could repeat it.

Arriving at the green, I walked over to the pot bunker well to the left. I don't know its exact dimensions, but it felt like it was just a few feet in diameter. And the sand was deep, especially close to the lip where my ball landed and had not moved. Somehow, I would have to get my ball out of the bunker, with enough height to clear the lip, and enough pace to get to the green. No small feat, I would soon discover. I looked at the buried lie, and I didn't see how I could simultaneously get enough under the ball to clear the lip, but with enough of the ball to carry to the green. Michael was more confident: "just take a good swipe at it," he told me, "I'm confident it'll get there." I had my doubts, but I had to try. I had to smile. This was my chance. I got my sand wedge, dug my feet into the sand, and took a whack. I was relatively sure that one of three things would happen: 1) The ball wouldn't move and I'd have to do the same thing again, wanting to bury my head in the sand; 2) The ball would come out low, hit the lip, and trundle back down to my feet; or 3) I would get too little sand, the ball would just clear the lip and fly powerfully over the green into the dunes in the distance. Miraculously—*did I even have my eyes open?*—the ball came out clean, with enough height to clear the lip, and enough power to make it to the front of the green. The shot left me with a 30-foot putt, which I knew I wouldn't make, but I didn't care. I was so happy—ecstatic really—that I faced what felt like an impossible shot and made a respectable swing. Two putts later, I was in again with bogey. But it felt like a victory as we walked, at long last, into the woods.

For the next few hours, I would follow the trails that Coore and Crenshaw laid for us. Up and down, to the left and right, through the woods, along the fairways. The course was meant to feel like the holes were found on a walk through the woods, much like a complex spiderweb or a stunning vista. And it does. Hole after hole, we arrived at the tee to find the next hole. Very few holes are visible while playing the previous ones, and each hole presents a new visual challenge. I traded par and bogey over the 3rd and 4th holes, with decent but not great shots.

Then I arrived at one of the most amazing holes in golf. The 5th hole at Bandon Trails doesn't get much press. It's not oceanside and not particularly noteworthy for its length, or for the size and shape of the dunes. Yet it's one of the most dynamically designed par threes I've ever played. The center of the green sits 125 yards from the green tees. Today, the pin was set five yards closer to the front, leaving me with a perplexing decision. The dangers are clear: any short shot will be swallowed up by one of the three front-facing bunkers. These bunkers, cut into the ridge in front of the green, were impossibly deep. "Don't leave it short!," my coach-for-the-day implored. To the left of the green was probably the safest miss, with some fairway and playable rough. To the right flirted with disaster, with trees, and a false-right, where any ball to the right would fall down to the large mouth bunker. Long was also safe, but it would have to be long straight, because the green was surrounded by a variety of dunes plants of unusual shapes and sizes. With pitching wedge in hand, I committed to a solid swing that would not go right. I pulled it off, although just barely. My ball landed on the front of the green, just 10 feet from the pin. But the back to front slope of the front half of the green meant my ball would trickle back to the front fringe, leaving a tough 18-foot putt up the hill. I let out a breath … I made it onto the green. Two putts later, a well-earned par.

I traded two bogeys and two pars over the next four holes, meandering between native plants, fairway, sand, and trees, mentally soaking in the vegetation of southwest Oregon. One of my favorite walks at the resort is the one between the 9th and 10th holes at Bandon Trails. It may seem innocuous, with no ocean view or obvious vistas. It's just a walk through the woods, with a pit stop at the snack shack. It's not a long walk by any means, and there's nothing particularly memorable. But that's the charm—just a stroll through the woods. There's something about it that relaxes the mind, a kind of reset in between nines.

During the walk, I asked Michael a few get-to-know-you questions. "How did you end up at Bandon?" Michael shared some of his background, mostly centered around golf. "Do you have any kids?," I ventured. I wanted to know what kind of father he would be: a man who played hickories better than most of us play modern clubs. No such luck.

He replied, "I have not yet made that kind of commitment." It's an interesting perspective: having kids as a commitment. I hadn't really thought of it that way. I had thought a lot about getting married as a commitment, but having kids was just what we wanted to do.

Michael asked me, "What's it like to be a father?"

I thought about it for a moment as we strolled. "It's the most amazing, nerve-wracking, thrilling, centering, rewarding, maddening thing I could imagine." What else do you say during a five-minute stroll through the woods? But Michael was clearly someone who was interested in more than just the oversimplified clichés that are normally repeated on a golf course. "I love my sons so much, and they have taught me so much about how to be a man."

"What's the most important thing they have taught you?," he asked.

"To stay in the moment," I responded quickly and with certainty.

"Really. What do you mean?," he followed up.

"I mean that everything about being a father is so challenging, and I never know if I'm doing the right thing. I just have to do the best I can in each and every moment, to try to be the best father I can be. No two moments are the same. I just have to try to do my best."

"Hmm, sounds like how I play golf."

"Exactly."

This brief conversation would stick with me and help to revive my appreciation for Michael, the course, and the life I was living. Yet despite my reinvigorated mood—and stomach—the back nine would not start well. With the left/right misses close at hand, I pulled driver and faced a slight-right dogleg on a sub-400-yard hole. In retrospect, I probably should have played a 3-wood, with a wide fairway even my weakest shot would have been fine. But in that moment I didn't, and the generous fairway was not enough, as my ball flew high and far to the right. On this occasion, there was no hope in finding my latest donation, so I re-teed a provisional and took another whack at it.

One never knows what "clicks" when things change, but whether it was the second double bogey that put to rest all hopes of a special round, or whether it was the swing with the 8-iron that just "felt right," for some reason, I played the rest of the round in 2-over-par. Eight holes: four pars, three bogeys, and one of the best birdies of my life on the famous 14th hole. The quick cart ride up the hill to the 14th tee was instituted in response to a golfer collapsing while attempting that hill by foot, not to mention how much a cart ride up this hill had sped up play. Michael pointed out the sign—from the high point just north of the 14th tee, Mike Keiser had his "aha" moment, when he knew that he had found it. We all took in the view, and more importantly the moment. Everything that he had created emanated from that moment.

There are challenging holes that test every bit of the golfers' imagination. There are picturesque holes in which golfers are presented with stunning visuals that catch their breath. There are short par fours that entice the golfer to rip driver and try to earn a birdie putt. And then there is the 14th hole at Bandon Trails. It's one of those holes that bores into the center of your consciousness and, like the most intense dream of your life, will never let go. It's short, and challenging, and picturesque. It's almost straight downhill, less than 300 yards, with a fairway that slants significantly from left to right, with an impossibly narrow green perched some 30 feet above the bottom of the fairway. The best drives will go left and stay left, rolling down the hill to the green. Every other drive, even very good ones, will fall off to the right, leaving an impossible pitch up the hill, over the bunker, with only a vain hope to hold on the green. Otherwise, the other golfers in your group will be like tennis fans watching your ball go back and forth across the green.

My drive joined the throngs of other golfers who hit down the hill to the right side of the fairway. Needing a wedge to clear the bunker, I got very little advice from my caddie—just hit it to the flat part. Some things are best not detailed or explained. He didn't tell me that my ball would almost certainly roll over the back. He didn't tell me just how narrow the green was. He didn't tell me that this was one of the more impossible shots on the course. Luis just instructed me to "clear the bunker." And, miraculously, I did. I hit just about a perfect wedge shot—the ball landed at the very top of the hill, just left of the sand trap, and it had enough momentum to bounce up and over the lip of the green, and yet the top of the hill blunted its speed just enough for my ball to hold the green. I could have tried that shot 100 times and not done any better. Somehow, Luis knew that less was more, keeping my mind free by not warning me of the dangers lurking. I practically skipped up the hill to find my ball, sitting just six feet from the pin. With Luis giving me his most careful read of a left edge, I jammed my putt into the hole. Birdie! What a thrill.

After trading a par and a bogey on the 15th and 16th holes, I was in a kind of hiker's high as we walked to the next tee. Of my many favorite spots at Bandon Dunes, one of them is surely the tee shot on the 17th, which pitches northwest and away from a great view of the 5th green. I love that spot, and it put me in such a great mood (as if I needed anything else!) to hit my 6-iron 160 yards to the green. While the yardage called for a 7, Luis suggested: "there's more wind than we can feel coming off the ocean. Use another club." I did, and hit it beautifully, with a high draw that landed on the back of the green, a little over 20 feet above the hole. With a gentle putt down the hill, and a short tap in, I was in with another par—my fifth par (plus a birdie) on the back nine.

After a short walk through the trees, we reemerged among the increasingly familiar dunescape to the 18th hole. Although the Pacific is not in view, the final hole feels much more similar to the 1st, and all of the holes at Bandon Dunes and Pacific Dunes, than the rest of Trails. It's a wonderful link to the rest of the resort. With a slight dogleg right and bunkers framing both sides of the fairway, I was ready to hit a solid closing drive. The ball came off my club without the hoped-for gusto, however, but was still safely on the right side of the wide fairway. From about 150 yards, I played an equally wipey fade with my 7-iron and missed the green, short-sided, to the right. There was just enough rough on the right side to require a chip, which I executed without the needed precision, and watched as my ball rolled past the cup by seven feet. Unable to make the par putt, I wrote in the bogey on my card, shook hands with Michael and Luis, and walked into the bar to share a round of needed IPAs.

As we waited for our beers, I couldn't help but reflect on the walk on the trails of Bandon—and the remarkable fact that I was walking at all. My life had been turned upside down with that terrible fall, and somehow, the people I love most had been there to catch me. Aidan had been fully present, stayed in the moment, and took charge when my kidney was revolting. While it was a risk, having the chance to see the joy on Elliott's face playing baseball was a fantastic moment. These events—really the past 15 years—came together as I shared with Michael my thoughts about fatherhood:

it's about staying present, every day, as much as possible. And it's the way to play this game we love. My ball had come to rest in some terrible lies in my walk around the Trails, but I had stayed in the present and I loved every moment of it.

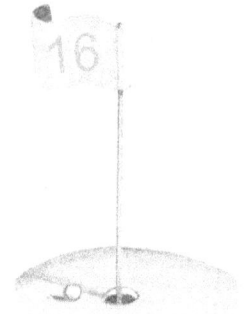

Consequences

(2016-17)

Theresa and I had read and talked about it repeatedly—the teenage years. We knew that teens took risks, made bad decisions, didn't recognize the consequences of their actions. The attributes of the stereotypical teenager were well known to me, not to mention the staggering car insurance payments that I would soon have to make. Yet when Theresa woke me up at 2:00 in the morning, I was hardly prepared. "Aidan's in the hospital," she told me. She had just received a call from the emergency room. I was a sprinter in high school track and soccer player in college and abroad, but I never moved so fast as I did that early morning. I knew something was seriously wrong, of course there was—he was in the hospital. It's 2am! This is very bad.

The last time I drove to this particular hospital, in the heart of our downtown, very early in the morning, Theresa was in labor with Elliott. During this trip to get to Aidan, I don't remember saying anything in the car. We both knew what we didn't know. We both knew that it could be very bad. But we also knew that he was alive, and at that moment, nothing else mattered. We parked in the downtown ramp, not realizing the serpentine walk we would have to take through the skyways, asking each security guard to point us to the emergency room. When we finally arrived—about 30 minutes after we woke up—there was a long line in the emergency room. We waited at least an hour, standing and watching the serious emergency staff deal with severe injuries urgently, minor injuries with patience, and (mostly) angry family members who couldn't see their loved ones. The waiting room was full, and all of us were full of anxiety. "Can we see our son?," I asked numerous times.

"Not yet," we were told, with an amazing amount of calm grace. I'm sure the staff were thinking, *Who do you think you are? Don't you see the line?* But they didn't say it. They just smiled and said we would have to wait.

We looked at each other often, both terrified at what we would see when we could finally see him. We didn't have any details other than that he was alive. We had no idea whether it was an accident, or an overdose, or a fight, or something else. When your son is 15, anything bad is possible.

He finally emerged, walking under his own power, but clearly not fully himself. There was only one thing to do—a long hug. There were no words to say—he was alive. It took my breath away. And all we could do was hold him. The three of us held on to each other, until we noticed that the doctor was standing there to give us a report. "Your son was unconscious when the ambulance arrived—apparently, another teen called 911 when your son was unresponsive. We had to keep him here for several hours for observation. All of his vital signs were normal, so we didn't run any additional tests, pump his stomach, or anything else. We're pretty sure it's alcohol poisoning." Aidan had just spent several hours in a hospital, drunk to the point of unconsciousness, slowly waking up, terrified and coming to understand what he had done to himself.

"Thank you, doctor." I hugged Aidan again.

We don't know whether he had passed out asleep, or something far more dangerous. We may never know. But at the moment when he walked out alive, there was nothing else to do but hold him. It was one of those moments when what's really important becomes crystal clear. I didn't care about the car he had driven the previous night. I didn't care about the clothes that were in terrible shape. I didn't care about what laws or family rules he might have broken. The only thing that mattered was that he was alive.

These are the moments of fatherhood that put everything in perspective. Aidan had a problem, one severe enough to put him in the hospital in the middle of the night. And no matter what I might have thought he needed the day before, I now knew clearly that we had to face the problem. These are conversations that you never want to have with your child, especially not a child that you have held since he was born. But we had to talk. I waited until late in the morning when he had slept off whatever poison he had put in his body to go up to his room. I knocked gently on his door. He was clearly up, and likely ready for this conversation.

"Aidan, we have to talk." He knew the words before they came out of my mouth.

"Dad, I know what you're going to say," as if he had been practicing his response for hours.

"What happened?," I asked.

"I don't remember," he responded. I don't know if it was the look of disbelief on my face, or that he was prepared for this response, or what. But he quickly followed with "really, I don't remember."

I have to admit that I didn't believe him. I've been drunk before, and I figured how much could be remembered. I hadn't done exactly this: I didn't pass out and end up in the emergency room, so I recognized that I didn't *really* know. But I chose not to believe him.

"What do you remember?"

"I remember hanging out with my friends, and the next thing I knew I was in the hospital." *Oh, really.*

"What were you doing with your friends that you do remember?" I wasn't going to let him get away with it.

"We were just hanging out." *Sure ...*

"What were you doing when you were hanging out?"

"You know, just hanging out." These are the cases where general questions gets a father nowhere. I needed to be specific.

"Who was there?"

"I don't remember. Friends."

"Which friends?"

"You wouldn't know them." Well, either he was lying, or they were generally people I didn't know—which almost certainly meant that they were older.

"Was anyone drinking?"

"I don't remember."

"We're you drinking?" He swallowed hard. That was it. I was piecing it together. He was with a group of older kids who were drinking, and he wanted to fit in. He wanted to be included. But he had too much, much too much. When he passed out, one of the other (drinking) kids panicked—thinking that he was injured or dead—and called an ambulance. Or at least that's the story I was putting together in my mind.

"Do you have anything else you want to say?"

"Dad, you don't have to consequence me." He was turning the conversation to his planned money moment.

"Oh, really. Why is that?"

"I've consequenced myself. Whatever you do to me won't be as bad as how I feel about myself right now."

Sometimes, your child says something that makes you simultaneously enraged at its ignorance and enthralled by its brilliance. This was such a moment. *You have no fucking idea*, I thought to myself.

"You're grounded until further notice," I said. But secretly, I loved my son even more for having the temerity to take responsibility for his own punishment.

*   *   *

While Aidan was pushing his body to its physical limits, and our minds were reaching their breaking points, Elliott was thinking about whether he would be able to go to Cooperstown the next year. Never one to share his excitements or fears, it was difficult to tell how Elliott felt about baseball, but he sure did put in full effort. Elliott had been an excellent player when he played 10U baseball—clearly one of the best on his AA team. When we did the post-season review, the head of the program told me that he would have made the AAA team the next year, had we not gone to Japan. Like most youth teams, getting on a team is much more difficult than staying on a team. Once a kid makes the top AAA team, they likely stay unless they have a truly terrible season. As a result, the 12AAA team—the "Cooperstown Team"—is made up almost entirely of returning players. That means making the team the year before is a likely guarantee of making it the next year—in fact, the club promises every kid who makes the 11AAA team the opportunity to go to Cooperstown, even if they don't make the 12AAA team.

Elliott knew all of this as he prepared for tryouts. Although the kids are generally kind to each other, the tension was high as the 11-year-olds (the next summer's 12-year-old players) went through the fielding, throwing, hitting, and catching drills that constituted their tryout. We dads sat in the stands watching. Some dads got really involved taking their sons aside to give them pointers—some dads even yelled from the sideline. I was not one of those dads. While I wanted to be there to bear witness, so Elliott could talk about it with me when he finished, I wanted to be a silent witness. This was his hill that he had to climb, and my talking to him (or yelling at him) would only distract him from what he had to do.

He came off the field disappointed. Although he had played baseball in Japan, he played for a terrible team (of non-Japanese players; the Japanese teams were outstanding), and he definitely felt like other kids were passing him. As well, while his growth spurt was years away, some of the oldest kids in the group had already started puberty. He felt small, and slow, and just not up for it. I tried to remind him that any team would be great fun, that there was nothing so special about the Cooperstown team, but since he had gone with his brother, he really wanted it. I, on the other hand, wasn't disappointed to miss the walking-ATM feeling that the Dreams Park trip was designed to induce.

It wasn't meant to be. While Elliott played better than he thought at the tryouts, he wasn't selected among the top 12. He wasn't going to Cooperstown. He didn't say much about his disappointment. It's hard as a father to really know what's going on in the pre-teens' mind. But my assumption was that he was pretty bummed. It was one of the first times he had to face that inevitable life situation where you really want something that others don't think you deserve. I knew what a valuable life lesson this would be, and I also knew that he would have a blast playing baseball the next year with his new team (which he did!). But I also felt his pain, the kind of pain that fathers wish they could take away from their sons, but know—with absolute certainty—that they cannot. He would have to take on this disappointment on his own.

Old Macdonald (Bandon, OR)

My round at Old Macdonald had a similar feel—alone, with only my own wits to get me through the journey. I had played that morning meandering the southern trails at Bandon, and had an afternoon tee time further up the coast at Old Mac. We finished our lunches and said our goodbyes, and off I went on the shuttle. Old Mac was (at least in 2019) at the north end of the property, the longest shuttle ride. Of course, 10 minutes is hardly long, but it did give me a chance to take half a breath. After a morning round, I was to play 36 this day at Bandon, in glorious, if appropriately windy, weather.

When I was a teenager myself, I had a chance to play the Old White Course at the Greenbrier. I don't remember anything about it but knew that it was one of C.B. MacDonald's great courses. I also knew that he had designed Chicago Golf Club, the National Golf Links of America, and the ill-fated Lido Course, which Mike Keiser had initially asked Tom Doak to recreate at Bandon. The story goes that Doak and Keiser agreed that recreating the Lido course was impossible on the land north of Pacific Dunes, so Doak would instead create a course that pays homage to one of the great golf course designers in the classical era. According to all reports, Old Mac delivered, in spades.

But I was in a strange mood. Playing golf on a late afternoon in July at one of the great golfing destinations of the world, I was alone. It was so quiet at the 1st tee box that I wondered if I were in a dream. The starter was my only point of contact, and he handed me a GPS tracking device. Apparently, some poor soul years before had gone out late afternoon alone and collapsed of a massive heart attack. No one else was on the course, and it took several hours before anyone noticed he was missing. Now, the policy is if you go out alone, they track you to be sure you keep moving through the course. I was happy to oblige, as I was fit enough to walk my second 18 of the day, and eager to discover some of the secrets of Old Mac.

I came to regret being alone, if nothing else to know where to hit the ball. I spent so much time trying to figure out the line, usually getting it wrong. The fact that I shot 83 that afternoon, in heavy wind and no guide, is a testament to how well I played. On holes 6, 7, 15 and 17, I hit some of the best drives of my life, certainly of the trip. But with no guide and not a clue about where to aim—especially on approach shots—I was lucky to escape with only 35 putts.

The first four holes I was in a state of awe. I was thrilled to be playing Old Mac, taking in the course, with dunes both more massive and more serene than either Bandon Dunes or Pacific Dunes. And yet while the first two holes are tame and relatively straightforward—with strong wind and little course knowledge—the greens and surrounding bunkers become a treacherous endeavor. I struggled my way to 6-over after the first four holes. I was in the sand three times, teed off too far to the right of the ghost tree on the stunning but quirky 3rd hole, and spent an extra 30 minutes trying to get the hang of the long putts that I butchered the first time.

Even though they're iconic, the first four holes really didn't make much of an impression on me. Of course, I won't easily forget the ghost tree, and the second shot on the 3rd hole into that punchbowl green is so much fun. But it wasn't until the 5th hole that Doak's brilliance was revealed to me. The 5th hole sports one of the largest greens in the world. It's truly massive. But its size isn't what makes the hole: it's the visuals that the hole creates, almost like looking up a giant set of steps into heaven. At the bottom of the flight of steps is a huge waste area, filled with mounds of fescue and sand everywhere. But the mess down below is easy to ignore as the enormous green appears ahead. And just a slight tilt of the head up and the expanse of the Pacific is once again apparent. While it'll be a few more holes before the Pacific becomes a true part of the course, the taste of the Pacific on the 5th is undeniable. My eyes were pulled down to the waste area, and up toward the ocean. My mind was everywhere except focused on the shot ahead. I looked back to the 4th hole—no one in sight. In fact, from the 5th tee there's a decent view of much of the course. I could only see a few groups on the entire course, all in front of me. And I still had to play the shot. So, I did my best to focus my mind. This is the shot I had to play. *It doesn't matter if the ocean is there; what matters in this moment is to focus on the shot at hand.*

And so, I talked myself into turning my attention away from the ocean, and instead toward the expansive green. It's easy to misunderstand this green, because while it is huge, its flats are also tiny—each step of the green is just a few dozen feet. This day, the pin was located on the second step on the left side. That meant that I had to find a way both to get my ball on the left side of the green and on the correct step. A step or two too low, and my ball would trundle back into the fescue or sand. A step or two too high, and I would be putting down a treacherous, multi-tiered green with nothing to stop the ball. I decided to err on the side of being too low and risk not clearing the bunker. I just made it, with a 30-foot uphill putt that I managed to get down in two. My first par at Old Mac. I savored it as I walked all around the green, hitting a few treacherous putts from locations I hope I never have to face. And it was brilliant. Whatever imagination had failed to ignite in the first four holes was lit on #5.

With only three pars and two doubles, it was a front nine largely to forget—or, maybe better said, I will gladly only remember the three-hole stretch from 5 to 7, which began on a massive and thrilling green and ended in the throes of the Pacific. I needed to turn things around on the back—not easy when the 10th hole presents a long and challenging par four. With fairway bunkers in and around the landing area, there's no aiming for a golfer of my stature—I simply gripped and ripped. The remnants of the swing feelings from the failed 9th drive were still very much at play, and I sliced a second drive in a row. *Weight too far forward? Clubface too open? Swing path too steep?* These are not the thoughts one should have entering the back nine of Old Mac. I resolved to stop thinking about score and start taking in fully what I was experiencing.

I've never been to Scotland, and therefore have never seen St. Andrews in person. Of course, like any obsessive golfer, the phrase Road Hole conjures images of an impossible drive over a hotel to an impossibly narrow Y-shaped fairway. From there, the long second shot can only be described as terrifying, with a dungeon-like bunker in the stomach of a kidney-shaped green. As if to add insult to injury, the false front repels any shots short of the green, and the road (and wall) gobbles up any shot long. If I ever have a chance to play it, I may very well choose to hit two 6-irons and a wedge and hope for a par putt. If ever a hole had "triple-or-worse" stamped on it, it would be the Road Hole. So, needless to say, I wasn't eager to face Doak's version of the road hole on the Oregon coast. Although there is no road to speak of, the shot is a bit blind from the tee with a large, gorse-covered dune ("hotel") in front, the right side is lined with thick fescue and more gorse ("road"), the fairway is narrower than most on the course, and the elevated, kidney-shaped green seems to caress the most foreboding of bunkers in its concave curve.

After two straight slices, I redoubled my concentration on keeping my weight back and closing the clubface through impact. I succeeded, a bit too well, as my long drive rolled through the fairway into the left rough. I was very pleased with the driver transformation, however, and it was a positive omen of things to come. From the left rough, I faced an 8-iron to the green, knowing that anything short would be repelled by the false front or swallowed by the bunker, and anything long would easily fall over the back. Somewhat miraculously, I produced a wonderful iron swing, with a high ball flight—it just needed to clear the bunker. It did, by a few feet, and then started rolling on the hard green surface. Of course,

I couldn't see exactly where it landed, or whether it stopped. But I crossed my fingers and continued my walk.

The ball had landed over the bunker and had managed to stop. It was an all-time great shot, and I didn't care so much about the birdie putt. My putt proved my indifference, as I barely made it to within three feet, but somehow managed to get the par putt into the cup. Did that achievement match a par on the Old Course's Road Hole? Hardly. But parring a replica still felt good, really good.

The 12th hole looks truly impossible from the tee box. Doak's "Redan" is as fortified as they come. Although there's no bunker in front—Doak placed the deep bunker left of the green to catch any balls hit too far left—its elevated stature and 45-degree right-to-left angle suggests that it's impossible to hold the green. As I've learned, a curving ball still bounces straight, so even if I were able to hit that needed draw, a ball that landed on the green would almost certainly roll off the back. From over 200 yards, moreover, I wouldn't be able to play a club with enough height to hold the green. I decided then and there that I'd play this as a par four, assuming that any shot short would come back down the hill, and anything that looked good would roll off the back. I pulled a hybrid, figuring that it gave me the best chance to get to the back part of the green, and swung away. It wasn't a good swing, more like a swipe really. But I got the ball in play, about 10 yards right of the green. I hit my pitch with great trepidation, knowing that I had to hold the green or I was looking at double. It came up just short on the fringe, which allowed me to breathe again. Two downhill putts later, and I was in with that predicted four. And somehow, letting out that big breath turned my round.

To this point, I was 10-over after 12 holes. I would play the final six holes at 1-over. I hit every fairway and only missed one green: the 18th. I finished with an excellent 3-over for the back nine. I had walked to the 18th tee imagining telling the story of The Streak to my golfing buddies: *Yes, I wasn't playing well until some kind of switch went off and I parred the final six holes.* I was saying these words to myself as I walked to the tee, somehow managed to tee up my ball, and hit the ball without a single thought about what I was doing. In retrospect, I was lucky that I caught most of the ball on the center of the clubface, and while it was an ugly looking drive, the hard fairway gave it a good surface to roll toward the bunker on the right side. Fortunately, the ball stayed short of the bunker. Unfortunately, my ball came to rest in a bit of a hollow, where I couldn't get a full clubface on the ball with my 4-iron. As a result, I hit a knuckleball that came up about 20 yards short of the green. With the pin tucked to the right of the punchbowl green, I'd have to get the ball up fast, and hopefully stop it quickly. I don't have that kind of spin in my bag, but I did get it up and the bowl effect did keep my ball in puttable range. Two putts later and I was in with a 40 on the back nine. Doak's tribute to the great C.B. Macdonald had now seeped thoroughly, and unmistakably, into my bones. It helped put into perspective what's important in golf.

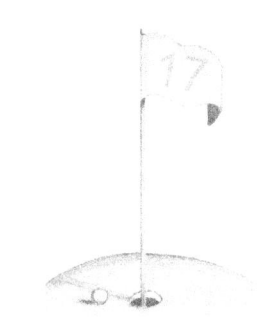

Driven

(2018-19)

I stood on the 1st tee when the starter asked, "Have you played Sand Valley before?"

In fact, this would be my first foray on this particular Coore and Crenshaw course. I'd read about Sand Valley since its opening the previous year, and I was eager to play it.

"No, this is my first time."

"You're going to love it!" I believed him, although what I was experiencing was a cross between the euphoria of teeing off momentarily at Michael Keiser's (the son of Bandon Dunes founder Mike Keiser) stunning and somewhat perplexing Wisconsin creation, and the foggy feeling of highway hypnosis resulting from over 900 miles of driving. How I ended up at Sand Valley, driving a used car given to me the day before, revolves around four central facts about my oldest son, Aidan: 1) he was 16; 2) puberty had given him a new, adultish body; 3) he was hormone crazy for the girls, as we called them; and 4) he had access to our car. Those of you who have parented teens may already know where this story is going.

There's been a study of teen drivers, and its findings go something like this: there are two basic factors that dictate how successful a driver will be: skills and experience. Over the first few months of driving, teens gain skills rapidly as they learn simple tasks, like how to turn the steering wheel, how hard to press the accelerator, when and how to use the brake, and how to use the mirrors. As they develop those skills, their confidence grows more or less on par with their skills. At the same time, teen drivers have only a tiny fraction of the experiences they need to be a fully mature driver. Even the best driving lessons can only put teen drivers in a small number of situations, and therefore their experience lags significantly behind their basic skills.

On top of that, while experience tends to grow on a relatively even slope—it takes a year to get a year of driving experience—skills tend to build along steps. Drivers will learn a large number of skills very quickly, then reach a plateau for a year or two, then will develop another set of skills, then reach another plateau, and so on. Teen drivers tend to reach the first plateau right around 4-6 months of driving, where their skill level plateaus as they slowly build more experience.

Confidence, on the other hand, tends to follow skill-building but without the plateaus. Teen drivers gain confidence rapidly as their skills build rapidly. When their skills plateau, however, their confidence grows as if they were still becoming markedly more skillful. So if you imagine a scale of 1-100, where 100 is a fully mature driver, a teen driver may build skills from 1 to 10 in the first few months, and then stay there for a few months. But their confidence quickly grows to 20 or 30, without much more experience and virtually the same skills they had months before.

Well, Aidan was exactly at this stage—the skills of a four-month driver, the confidence of a two-year driver—when he asked to take out our 10-year-old Toyota Prius. Generally speaking, we liked it when he drove the Prius. While it's more or less a tin can on wheels—with very little protection if there were an accident—it also can't be driven fast. So, while he wasn't as protected from another driver as he might have been in a bigger car, he was much more protected from himself when he drove a small hybrid.

As a father, I tend not to interrogate my teen sons. While my questions certainly might feel to them like a cross-examination, I really only ask a few basic questions: "Where are you going?" "With whom are you going?" "When will you be home?" Just the facts. Usually, the answers are brief: "to my friends," "with my friends," "late." Whether it's a failing of mine or not, that's enough for me.

"Have fun!" I usually respond.

After he took the car, I didn't think much of it. Whatever I was doing that day I did, without any concern for Aidan. He was 16, and as much as I might have wanted to protect him for his own safety, I was very good at letting that worry go. I didn't fret every time he got behind the wheel, I didn't stay up late just to be sure that he got home safely—although he did have a midnight curfew, and he did have to knock on our door to let us know he was home—and I generally didn't worry about him behind the wheel.

But maybe I should have—although I still don't know that worry would have changed the outcome. Sometime in the early afternoon, I got *the call*. Thankfully it wasn't the *nightmare call*, where a police officer calls parents to tell them the most unimaginatively awful news. No, this was Aidan calling.

"Dad, I got in an accident." His voice tremored.

"Are you okay?"

"Yes, I'm okay?" Thankfully.

"Is anyone hurt?"

"No, everyone is fine." *Deep sigh of relief.*

"But the car is bad." *Okay. Just take it in.*

"Where are you?"

"I'm on the street across from a cemetery." Despite the ambiguity of his internal GPS, I knew exactly where he was, less than two miles away.

"Stay on the phone, I'll be right there." I threw on my shoes and dashed out the door. "Are you still there?"

"Yes, I'm here."

"Okay, I'm driving there. Tell me what happened."

"I was driving with Daisy and Lydia, heading toward Daisy's house. I was turning left, waiting for the light to turn green. Then, I had a green light. I didn't see the car coming from the opposite direction." Apparently, without an arrow to stop opposing traffic, Aidan began his turn without seeing or judging oncoming traffic and was smashed by a minivan in the front end. Everyone was shaken up, but no one was hurt. The other driver was there, waiting for me.

When I arrived at the accident scene, I could see that Aidan's hands were shaking. The two girls were standing off to the side, talking on their cells. The other driver was calm, but clearly annoyed. I double-checked to make sure everyone was okay. First, Aidan. We were about the same height by now, although it wasn't long before he passed me. I looked him in the eyes. "Are you okay?" He said yes—physically, he was fine. But I could tell that he was a combination of terrified and mortified, scared, and embarrassed.

"It happened so fast," he said.

I turned to the girls. "Are you both okay? Did either of you hit your head?"

"We're fine," they said in unison.

"Sometimes pain comes later. Please let me know if you get a headache or something hurts."

"Okay," they said, again in remarkable unison. Had they practiced?

Then, the other driver. "Are you alright?"

"Yes, I'm fine," she assured me. We took photos of our respective insurance cards. Then, to the cars. Her minivan had a clear dent in the front bumper. It would have to be replaced. But otherwise, the minivan looked fine.

On to our car. In my mind, I knew that the Prius was fragile. I knew that it was built to be fuel efficient, not to be a super safe vehicle. But when I saw it, hit by a minivan probably going no more than 30 miles an hour, my throat was stuck in my chest. The entire engine had moved several inches closer to the driver's seat. The front end had collapsed like a giant accordion. The front tires were bent grotesquely to the right, as if preparing to park on a hill in San Francisco. It was a stunning sight to see the metal box—which had moments before carried three teens including my son—transformed into a crumpled mess. OMG.

But thankfully, Aidan had dodged this particular bullet, and his friends were fine. We called the police, who told us that they'd only come if there was an injury—tax dollars well spent—then pushed the car off the road, tried to sweep up the mess, and walked to my car. Once inside, I asked them to explain exactly what happened. I asked some more pointed questions.

"Were you watching the road?"

"Yes!"

"Are you sure you weren't looking at your phone that very second?"

"Yes, I'm sure."

The girls corroborated. "Aidan never uses his phone while driving."

"Was there music on? How loud was it?" I knew what they'd say.

"Yes, it was on. No, it wasn't too loud." *By whose standards?* A few minutes later, I dropped off the girls, who again assured me that they were fine. It was now just me with Aidan; I know he feared the worst.

I'm sure some fathers would blow up at their son at this moment. *What the hell were you thinking? Do you know how close you were to being seriously injured or worse? You put their lives at stake! Do you realize that the car is probably totaled?* Maybe because I had that type of father—or maybe because I had learned over the years that blowing up never worked—I swallowed those thoughts. I didn't blow up. I walked him through what would happen next.

"You may have some whiplash, which is a neck injury. You need to tell me right away if your neck starts to hurt."

"Okay," he replied.

"Your friends' parents may want to talk to me about what happened. Please let them know that their parents can call me at any time."

Again, just "okay." I wasn't reaching him.

"I have to call our insurance company. You will have to talk to them to answer all of their questions." This got his attention. He looked at me as if to say: *can't you handle if for me?* He tightened up. Maybe it was just too much truth, or maybe he was afraid to lie to someone as official as an insurance agent. Whatever the reason, we walked through what we had to do later that day.

And so we did. There was never any yelling or screaming. Never any major confrontation. Just workmanlike, as I took care of the details and required him to be a part of it. I wanted him to know all the consequences of a car accident, and how it would affect our family. My mother had recently purchased a new car and had planned to give Aidan her old Toyota Camry. He was supposed to be a lucky teenager with his own car. Not anymore.

Within days, the insurance company declared the Prius a total loss, and they came to tow it away. We were down to one car, with three drivers (Elliott was a few years away from driving). Theresa and I would share the other car, if we could get grandma's Camry. Coincidentally, I had to go to Washington, DC for work in April. I was doing research and needed to spend a day at the National Archives. Conveniently, my mother lived about 45 minutes from the Archives, and I had planned to see her and borrow her car to drive to the Archives. *If I fly to DC, I could drive the car back—a 1,100 mile drive.* It was decided.

Some people love to drive. I've had those moments, and with a nice car I'm generally up for a drive. But driving my mother's Toyota for two full days is not my idea of a great road trip. I would have to do something to make the trip *tolerable*. As I looked at the map, I started to realize that I could do much better than tolerable. I could make a short pit stop at Sand Valley, which was just about 40 miles out of the way. I could make this happen, if only the weather would cooperate. The end of April in Wisconsin can be tricky. It could be cold. There could be snow. Or it could be sunny and warm-ish. There was no way to know in advance, but I was going to try.

As luck would have it, in the days leading up to the drive, it became clear that it would be warm enough to play, and it had been warm enough for a month that there was no chance of course closure due to snow. The course would be open. So, I just needed to worry about April showers, Chicago traffic, and two grueling days of driving. I confidently called the course and made a 1:00pm tee time. It was happening. So, on the day of the round, I was on the road at 6:00am, coffee in hand, with a five-hour drive in front of me, imagining the central Wisconsin sand dunes.

Sand Valley (Nekoosa, WI)

At times, in golf and in life, things work out better than planned. It doesn't happen often, but I've learned to embrace these days when it does happen. I couldn't believe it, but Chicago traffic wasn't its normal beast, and I was able to make it to Sand Valley in under five hours. I was in the parking lot before 11am. As absurd as it sounds when arriving at a place called *sand valley*, I was surprised by the amount of sand in the parking lot. I gathered up my clubs (yes, I had flown to DC with my clubs with the hope that I could play Sand Valley—crazy? Of course!), put on my golf shoes, and walked up the hill to the pro shop. There was sand everywhere, a middle-of-Wisconsin beach. Michael Keiser is a genius.

"I have a tee time for 1pm, but I'm here early and was hoping I could play early," I told the assistant pro.

He gave me a warm smile. "Let me see what I can do." He checked his computer.

"I have a tee time in 10 minutes, but you'd have to tee off on the 10th tee—today is our caddie training day and they are teeing off now on the 1st hole." A short van ride later, and I was walking up to Craig's Porch to be greeted by the warm and eager starter. He had spoken to the pro and was ready for me.

So, without so much as a practice swing, we walked down the steps to the 10th tee. After exchanging our pleasantries, I took in the stunning view. Most of the holes are obscured by dunes, but you can get a clear sense of the topography of grass and sand and very, very few trees. Without the benefit of a warmup, and hours of driving under my belt, had only one swing thought: *slow transition*. I managed to make decent-but-wipey contact as the ball faded to the right side of the fairway. I wasn't getting home in two with that drive, but the ball was sitting nicely on the fairway and a solid 3-iron should put me in a good position to wedge to the green. I thought of all these scenarios as I walked down the hill into the massive expanse of Sand Valley. It's a monster of a course, in all the best senses of the word. Coore and Crenshaw have done a brilliant job designing a sand-based links in the middle of the Midwest. While it doesn't *feel* like a links in any real sense, it plays like one. Trees are sparse and the sand dunes are massive. As well, the fescue forms hard fairways where only the gravity of a naturally-formed sand mound stops the ball from rolling. I found that out the hard way on several drives and approach shots which, though hit well, just rolled through the fairway or through the green. It's truly a course that has to be played along the ground.

After a strong 3-iron put me just 125 yards from the pin, my wedge to the green on this par five was true, although 30-feet short and left of the pin. I'll never know whether a proper warmup on the putting green would have shown me a better line as my putt traversed the 10 feet of break. What I do know is that my putt raced past the hole at least eight feet. Missing the comebacker left me with an opening bogey. Frustrating? Yes. But the magic of Sand Valley, I would soon discover, is how quickly the course reminds the golfer to forget. Like Aidan totaling our car, Sand Valley helped me to catch and release. Each hole presents a new feast for the eyes, created by a brilliant combination of Coore and Crenshaw's imagination and the sand dunes formed in central Wisconsin thousands of years ago. As my smile widened as I encountered each new hole, I actually played the next eight holes (remember, for me it was the back nine) in only 2-over par. I hit all but two fairways, and only missed two greens in regulation. My favorite hole was the punchbowl 17th (my eighth), a long par three in which the green is hidden from the tee. You can play a draw or cut, and either way, you're likely to get your ball rolling down to the green. Just be sure to clear the top of the dune and hope for a solid landing spot. With a great hybrid from the tee, I ended up on the lower left part of the green, with a long uphill putt. I managed to cozy my ball up to three feet and secured a solid par. Overall, a very solid first nine.

My back nine (actually, the front), was much more perplexing than the first nine I played. The 1st hole is a visual puzzle, at least for those of us who can get a case of the rights from time to time. The fairway is much below the tee, and it's difficult to gauge how far left to hit to clear the waste area. But too far right creates a much longer second shot, and more of a slope to the fairway. The best drive is probably a 3-wood draw, up the left side. But on this day, I hit another wipey fade. It worked out okay, as I remained on the fairway and had a 9-iron in, which I managed to hit pin high just 15 feet to the left. Although I was getting used to the rock-hard greens, I didn't sink a putt all day. Solid par.

As is often the case for me when I am playing well, I start to imagine what it will take to break par. *Just a few birdies over the next eight holes*, I told myself. I was six out of eight fairways, and eight out of ten greens in regulation. I was hitting the ball as solidly as I ever have. Did I have three birdies in the bag? *Nope*. Not this day.

The next two holes punished me for getting my mind out of touch with my body. I missed the fairway left on the 2nd hole, only to overshoot the green. This was an inauspicious miss, because Coore and Crenshaw had placed their most sloping back-to-front green on the 2nd hole. I was faced with an impossible chip from the back of the green to a pin just five feet from the back fringe. Needless to say, after my chip I watched the ball roll ... and roll ... and roll down the hill to the front of the green. Another two putts later and I had added to my bogeys for the day.

I would add another one immediately, but then only two more bogeys for the rest of the round. When I take stock, I remember the brilliance of the 5th hole more than any other. From the high point on the course, overlooking much of the front nine with views over this vast expanse of glacier-induced sandscape, the 5th hole presents a unique challenge. The hole plays at least 50 feet downhill, and thus I was tempted to play less club. Yet the severe false front leading to more sand or a very difficult chip from below the green suggested that I should err on the long side. I did, playing the number and hitting the ball just past pin high. It was one of my most satisfying pars. Walking down the slope from the high perch of the 5th tee, I couldn't help but reflect on my journey to get to the course. I had been problem solving for weeks, helping Aidan to make sense of his accident, dealing with the insurance company, arranging to pick up my mother's car, and driving it from the east coast through Chicago into Wisconsin. It seemed that only as I walked down to the green could I take a breath and appreciate how lucky I was.

I still had more holes to play, though, and had to find the mental fortitude to finish the round as solidly as I began it. The 7th hole is probably one of the signature holes on the course. The truly massive sand dune on the right dominates the view, despite the generous fairway. I hit my worst drive of the day, my only true slice that flew high and *plop*—right into the sand. From there, I had to choke down on a 5-iron, but I managed to find some stability with my feet and hit an excellent shot back to the fairway. Trying to ignore the huge bunkers to my left and to the right of the green, I hit a strong 6-iron and left myself with a 17-foot uphill putt. I didn't have enough juice on the putt, however, and left it short. Fortunately, I drained the four-footer for another par.

The final two holes were perplexing for their brevity. The 8th hole plays 135 from the tips, almost straight uphill. The green is largely hidden by the hill, and the massive bunker in the front swallows any balls that don't quite make it over crest of the hill. I struck my pitching wedge very solidly, but even from the orange tees, I played too much for the short pin position and rolled back down into the aforementioned bunker. Another two putts after a heart-stopping blind shot from the bottom of the sand, and I was off to the final hole with another bogey.

When I'm presented with a 300-yard par four, I know that I *should* consider not laying up. While I don't have the distance to make it to the hole, I've learned from Bryson and others that the analytics suggest that I'll score better the closer I am to the hole off the tee. But near the hole, I could see the one row of trees (to the left of the green) and bunkers all around. I wasn't going for this green—no way. *But how mortified will I be if I choose to lay up and don't hit the ball solidly.* The "safe" play—say a 5-iron off the tee—only is safe if it's struck well. And one of the more embarrassing shots in golf is laying up poorly. *If you were going hit such a wayward shot, why not hit driver?*

So, as stood on the tee, I had two thoughts: *I'm going to lay up ... so, don't screw this up!* I chose my hybrid and came close to doing just that, hitting more of a draw than I wanted and barely managing to stay right of the long stand of coniferous trees. I was left with a 100-yard wedge to the back of the green, which I struck beautifully. A seven-footer for a closing birdie. I was thinking more about the elation I would feel than actually reading the putt, and ... yep, missed it on the low side. Still a closing par on a gorgeous April day in Wisconsin, a great way to prepare for the final 200 miles to bring home to Aidan a sandy, used car.

Complete

(2019-20)

I'm awfully lucky to be able to tag team with Theresa. We love our sons, and both of us need breaks. Early on as parents, we learned the look. It's the look you give your partner when you've been with the kids for a while, or you have just had a very hard moment, and you need a break. There are no words exchanged, just the look. And Theresa and I know the look so well that no words are ever needed. We just do a quick handoff, and that's it. We had done it hundreds of times by the time Theresa ventured for a six-week adventure to India. *How many golf trips does that buy me?* Yes, that's right. I would be single parenting for six weeks, having to handle everything she normally handles. The boys didn't eat as well; they probably didn't sleep as well. And they missed her momentously—as did I. But generally speaking, we made it through. We put our heads down every morning, got through breakfast, school drop-offs, dog walks, and then school and work. We had minor scuffles, and lots of exhaustion. But we made it through ... or so I thought. One Saturday night just a few days from the end of my time as a temporary single-parent, Aidan (now a 17-year-old) was out late with friends. We had a rule—he could stay out later than my bedtime, as long as he checked in when he got home. I don't know exactly what time it was, but my guess is around midnight. I asked him if everything was okay, and he cheerfully replied, "Yes. Goodnight." Soon after, I had fallen into a deep sleep.

The next morning, I woke up early with the dogs as usual, fed them and let them out to do their thing. Sometime around 8am, Aidan came down.

"Dad," he asked, "do we have any Band-Aids?"

"Sure," I replied, heading over to the first-aid box. "What size do you need?"

"Pretty big." Okay. I went into the first-aid kit and pulled out what Band-Aid brands euphemistically calls their large size. I handed it to him.

"That's not big enough," he intoned.

"What do you mean?"

"Well," he sheepishly told me, "it's not really a cut."

"What do you mean?" My voice was betraying the calm I was doing my best to uphold.

"It's kind of a ... I don't know ... gash?"

"A gash?" I was no longer trying to uphold any calmness in my voice. "Let me see it."

You know those moments as a parent when all the things you thought about your child—good judgment, self-awareness, street smarts—vanish in the blink of an eye? You know those moments when what you thought would be an *obvious* response simply doesn't happen? Like when the child drops their glass and spills milk all over the floor, and they just stare at it? Or when they watch the dog peeing on the carpet and they casually say "the dog is peeing?" Or when they feel sick and they don't tell you until *after* they have thrown up all over your suit at an important event? Yes, that's the moment that was unfolding right before my eyes. The gash was about four inches long, about two inches wide, and, grotesquely, about an inch deep. I couldn't quite see to the bone—it was in a fleshy part of his upper leg—but I imagined it was right there. It was, indeed, a major gash. *Did he get stabbed!?*

"We have to go to the hospital, immediately."

"What? Dad, you're overreacting. It's fine. It's just a small cut."

"No, this will not heal without stitches. We are going right now. Get dressed."

I dropped everything. I woke up Elliott to tell him he would have to be with the dogs. "We are going to the hospital—your brother needs stitches." Elliott woke up with a combination of annoyance, worry, and intrigue.

"Aidan is going to be fine. He just has a bad ... um, gash on his leg. I need you to wake up and be with the dogs. And no, you can't see the gash." I tried to answer all of his questions and simultaneously let him know that there was no choice, and we were leaving immediately.

We were in the car in two minutes. On the drive to our local children's hospital, I asked him what happened. He was vague in a way only teenagers can be. He said a lot of words—about friends, about running, about bleeding—but he wouldn't tell me what happened. Or did he? It's a conversation style that I've learned about over the past few years. I know he's telling me what happened, I just need to be a codebreaker. So, what was the code?

"Where were you last night?," I asked.

"We were in the woods."

"Where?"

"Near Hidden Beach." Ah, the key to the code. Hidden Beach is a lakefront woodland area nearby where teenagers go to drink. He probably doesn't remember exactly what happened.

"Did someone attack you?"

"No, absolutely not!" *He remembers some things.*

"Did you fall?"

"Yeah, I think so." Okay, the pieces are starting to fall into place. *He was drunk, and for whatever reason that only a teenager would understand, he and his friends were running. And he fell.* Teens love that Hidden Beach is off the beaten path. Kids love the seclusion. And they also treat the place like their communal trash can. There are broken bottles, pieces of metal, and all kinds of other garbage. *He fell and landed on something sharp, which cut him severely. And it was dark, so he didn't know how bad it was. And in the middle of the night, when he came home, he didn't want to tell me what happened.* All of these thoughts raced through my head as we arrived at the emergency room.

I told him sternly, "it's very important that you tell the doctor the entire truth. If you want me to leave the room so you can tell them exactly what happened, I will. But you can't lie to the doctor. They need to know everything because you may be at risk of tetanus, or another type of infection."

"Okay." But his look clearly said *oh shit.*

We sat in the waiting room for about 30 minutes. The nurse came to get us and asked the usual questions. I offered to leave the room; Aidan asked me to stay. Apparently, his fear about what was happening—and wanting me in the room to comfort him—overwhelmed his worry about me hearing what he was telling the nurse. He told the story again: he was with his friends in the woods, they decided to run, he fell and somehow cut his leg. That's it.

The nurse saw the cut. Alarmed, she blurted, "When did you do this? When?" She was shocked when he said "last night." And she gave me a death look: *And you let this happen?* I wanted to explain to her that it was his fault. I wanted to explain that he came home late, and I don't usually give him a head-to-toe examination to make sure there are no gashes in his leg. I wanted to tell her that *he didn't say anything.* Instead, I said nothing and took the fall. I gave her a look of resignation: *Yes, it was my fault.* That's what fatherhood is all about.

When the doctor came in, Aidan got a long lecture about the dangers of leaving a serious gash open and the possibility that he might get an infection. She told him all of this while she was irrigating the gash for at least 20 minutes. That was after they had given him an anesthetic to dull the pain. A dozen or so stitches later, and with his pride well-swallowed, we left the hospital. We didn't say much on the ride home. He was exhausted, and the dad in me was torn: *do I comfort him and allow him to rest all afternoon, or do I sit him down to give him yet another long lecture about personal responsibility?*

I looked over and his eyes were closed. He wouldn't listen to what I had to say in this moment anyway. After all, he was just a boy, although increasingly in a man's body. I let him go back to sleep. I was left with nothing at the moment but my own thoughts.

Mammoth Dunes (Nekoosa, WI)

My alarm was set for 5:30am. I planned a three-hour drive, a one hour warm up, and then a round at Mammoth Dunes. This was the only way I could squeeze in my round on a drive to Chicago. But my fear of sleeping through the alarm and therefore missing my precious tee time forced me awake at 4:30. *Should I get up an hour earlier? Should I go back to sleep?* I laid in bed, thinking about whether I should get up for the better part of an hour. How many of us spend time thinking about what we should do, and thereby guaranteeing an outcome?

When I finally woke up with the alarm, I had to hustle. Feed and take out the dogs, pack the final items in my car, eat something for the ride, and then get on the road. It was 6:10am, and I was on the road for Nekoosa, Wisconsin. I had plenty of time to think about David McLay Kidd's links creation, this time in central Wisconsin. Of course, Kidd would not be linking the farmland to the sea, but unlike most of the Midwest, these inland sand dunes provided a remarkable plot on which to create a course. These massive dunes, created during the last Ice Age as the glaciers pushed sand from ancient seas inland, would provide a canvas for Kidd's creativity. I had heard about the course, seen it from a distance when I first played Sand Valley, but today I would be experiencing it for myself.

But first, I had to get there. I was going on a long journey, from my home in Minneapolis to my alma mater, Oberlin College, near Cleveland. The drive was 12 hours, which I didn't want to do in one day. So, what does a golfer do when faced with a long drive that would require a stop along the way? Find a golf course! And the Sand Valley Resort just happened to be right along the way. My plan was to leave home early, drive to Sand Valley, play Mammoth

Dunes in the late morning, teach my class online, go to bed, wake up in the morning to play their namesake course, and then continue my journey to Ohio.

Although the trip was exceedingly complex, I wasn't going to miss it. I was to be inducted into the Oberlin Athletic Hall of Fame—in a few days, I would become a member of the famed Heisman Club. Yes, the same John Heisman whose name dons the trophy for the best college football player every year. Heisman was the head football coach at Oberlin in 1892, and the school's athletic hall of fame was named after him. I had first been nominated shortly after I had graduated as the most prolific points scorer in the history of the men's soccer team: 46 goals and 24 assists for 116 total points in just 67 games. In the 30 years since I graduated, the closest any player has come was 88 points. I wasn't getting inducted into a professional hall of fame, but for me—a D-III athlete—this was a tremendous honor. I wasn't going to miss it. But I wasn't going to miss the chance to play Mammoth Dunes, either.

I arrived at 9:30am, in preparation for my 10:35am tee time. After getting situated at the resort, a took the brief shuttle to the practice facility. "Looks like rain will be holding off until 4 or so," our driver announced. *Thankfully.* I had brought my umbrella but left it in the car. My rain jacket and pants were in my bag, but I always found playing in rain gear incredibly suffocating, not to mention the difficulty of keeping gloves, towels, and scorecards dry. While the clouds looked unsettled, I took my driver's weather intel as gospel and set myself up on the range next to the box of balls, honing my swing. I listened to several 20-somethings ribbing each other, preparing for what was clearly a high stakes buddy trip. I heard references to $300 and lots of intergroup wagers. Little did I know that I'd be in the thick of it.

As I finished my warm-up on the range, I wandered over to the practice chipping and putting green. I hit a few chips and pitches, a few long practice putts, and walked over to the shuttle. As I was walking over, I noticed something falling from the sky: something heavy, something wet. At first, just a few scattered drops—nothing to worry about. By the time I was back at the practice green adjacent to the 1st tee of Mammoth Dunes, the scattered drops had become a steady mist. I had to make some changes: on went the rain jacket and the rain cover for my bag; away went the towel and my regular glove; out came the rain gloves.

By the time we teed off a few minutes later, the steady mist had strengthened to a light rain. We would play the 1st hole in that steady light rain. From the tee box, the fairway is stunningly wide. I was introduced to my playing partners for the day: three of the six 20-somethings from the practice facility. These guys were best friends, out for a not-so-friendly competition. The other group told me: "Watch out! These guys will try to teach you a lesson." *What the hell does that mean?* I laughed. "After I birdie the first, they'll want a lesson from me!" I retorted, trying my best to show that I could rib them back. After all, I was returning to my alma mater in a few days where I'd be reunited with my teammates—the best ribbers I had ever known. They laughed, ooh'ed and aah'ed, and announced that they were playing from the orange tees, stretching out to 6,587 yards. When I heard myself agreeing to join them, I had a sense of what the other group meant.

As a man in my fifties, with not much hair on top and a grey beard, playing the almost 6,600-yard tees on a golf course that I was encountering for the first time, in heavy wind and rain, was—how to put it mildly—*unwise?* I spent the entire day chasing their tee shots, hitting hybrids and 4-irons when they were hitting 9-irons and wedges. The poor decision became clearer and clearer as the day progressed.

Yet while the first drives of my playing partners all sailed far left on the 1st hole as their draws became hooks, my drive was impressively straight (although not impressively long). The other guys chirped. "You're slow playing them," they howled. I smiled. *I'm going to show them how to play golf!*

The length of my shots seemed to increase with the heaviness of the rain. My drive had left me about 180 yards from the pin, and I hit a nice draw with my 6-iron, which landed just short and left of the green. Unfortunately, to get my ball from just off the green to the pin, required maneuvering around a massive hump on the left side of the green. If I hit the hump too soon, my ball would fall sharply to the right before the hole, likely leaving me with a 15-footer at best. If I carried the ball too far on the hump, I would run the ball past the hole, leaving about a 15-footer. I tried to catch it just right, deciding to err on the long side rather than leaving it short. And that's what happened, as my chip bounded over the hump and rolled to the back side of the green. I missed the 15-foot comebacker, opening with a solid but disappointing bogey.

By the time we had made our way to the 2nd tee, the light rain had become a heavier rain, and everything was getting soaked. I had long since ditched my regular glove for my rain gloves, but I hadn't donned my rain pants. I would resist that wardrobe change, as my scorecard rapidly disintegrated into something resembling oatmeal. The score would have to go on my phone.

I traded pars and bogeys for the first five holes, leaving me 3-over after five holes.

From what the guys told me, the 6th is one of their favorites on the course. At only 308 yards, some golfers choose to go for the green. All three of them tried, and they sailed their drives way left of the fairway. I wasn't going to go there and hit a weak fade into the rough on the right. While they searched for their balls, I found mine in light rough and measured my second shot—with a back pin, and tough conditions, I felt like I would need all of my 6-iron. I took a mighty lash and saw my ball flying high, drawing to what looked like a perfect part of the green. With the mounding in front, I couldn't tell what fate awaited my ball, but I was happy with the swing. The ear-shaped green—with the middle facing the hole, as if the green is listening for balls to arrive—is one of the most curious greens I've ever seen. With high mounds on both sides, any ball that hits to one side or the other of the green will funnel to the middle. If the pin is cut on one side of the ear, the only way to putt to it from the other side is to putt off the green, into the hill, and watch the ball come tumbling down. I have no idea how my ball got to its resting place, but there it was, eight feet below the hole, in perfect position. After the guys made it to the green and took their long putts, I lined up for mine. As I was reading it, one of them asked: "Is this for par?"

I replied, somewhat curtly, "no, birdie."

"Ooohh," they chorused. The banter began as they tried both to encourage and rattle me. My focus was true, though, as I buried the right to left putt for a thrilling birdie.

Riding high from my birdie, we arrived at the 7th tee as the rain began to subside a bit. While the guys started pulling off rain gear, I wasn't so sure. The tee shot is blind, but they gave me a good aiming point in the distance. While they hit long draws, apparently too far left, I hit a short fade to the right side of the fairway. I was able to find my ball without a problem, as they searched for theirs. While I was waiting, I noticed a marshal parked off to the right. I made conversation with him for a few minutes, and then asked him for a distance to the inlet bunker—it kind of looks like a thumb coming off the sand "hand" from the left side. He said he had no idea, and I didn't have my scope. I guessed it was 230 yards, so even though it was downhill I thought a 4-iron would be a safe choice. I hit a fantastic shot, high and far and straight—straight into the bunker. Thank you, Mr. Kidd. When I arrived, I realized that it was more than just a bunker, it was a deep chasm filled with sand. I took the steps down into the depths and played an 8-iron, struck well up the hill to the hidden green, but clearly too far right. I found my ball just off the green on the right side, but with the firm fescue, it was indistinguishable from the green. I treated it like a left-to-right 30-foot putt, and hit it nicely to two feet. A comfy par.

Things took a turn for the worse, however, as I bogeyed five out of the next six holes. At least in part, this was due to a scream-worthy moment on the 11th tee. I wish I could say that I remember much about the 11th hole. I remember it's a par five, and the hole is so wide it fills much of the full horizon. Anything left is liable to find sand. Anything right is safe, but far from the green on this sharp dogleg left hole. But I don't know this because I remember it, I know this because I went back and looked at the course map. What I remember is pain. Intense pain. As the guys were banter-ing with their friends who were now approaching the 10th green,

I was squaring up to hit my drive on the 11th tee. As I pulled my club to begin the backswing, I felt an intense pain emanating from my left ankle. It was coming from the bony protrusion of the tibia, the larger of the two bones below the knee. As I was beginning my swing, with my left ankle facing almost perfectly toward the 10th green, one of the guys skulled his chip and it flew, yes, straight into my ankle bone. A perfect hit. And the pain was immense. Yes, it's only a golf ball, and it's only an ankle. But for someone who had a lifetime of taking ankle abuse, that ball stung. And somehow, I had to put my ball in play just seconds later, attempting to downplay the pain that was throbbing up from my ankle. After I hit a lazy fade down the right side, I walked—no, limped—down the hill toward my ball. By the time I found it in the right rough, far from the green, I was starting to wonder whether my ankle was broken. I gritted my teeth. *Carry on.* For reasons only the golf gods can understand, I hit my best shot of the day: a solid 4-iron back to the fairway on the left side. From there, going straight back up the hill, I hit an excellent sand wedge just 12 feet left of the hole. While the putt was tricky—a hole cut right on a ledge—I was able to two-putt for another par.

I'm not sure if I parred the 11th despite or because of the pain, but I certainly wasn't walking well through at least the next two bogeys. But all that was just prelude, for the crescendo of Mammoth Dunes is clearly the drivable par-four 14th. Measuring only 297 yards, with a speed slot on the right side that will bring just about any solid drive down and to the left to the green, my playing partners were licking their chops. I watched as two of the three hit high fades which caught the speed slot and rolled down the hill, in both cases rolling well past the green into the sand beyond. I didn't have that problem, as my drive—although solid—did not have the distance to reach the speed slot and instead rolled straight down the hill to the fairway on the left. From there, I played a comfortable lob wedge to 10 feet. While I didn't make the birdie putt, I was fun to see them play the hole, while also watching the group behind send balls our way.

With my ankle still throbbing, but not sharply, I traded a par on the long par-five 15th, and a bogey on the short par-three 16th.

As we walked out of the protection of the dunes, the wind picked up even more and was now howling, straight into our faces. A long hole at 427 yards from the green tees: *just play it as a par five*. I hit a very good drive, straight to the middle of the fairway. Yet the 215 remaining yards seemed impossible. I pulled 3-wood, assessed the sand all around—including two small bunkers short and right of the green—and hit one of the best 3-woods of my life. The ball seemed magnetically pulled toward the pin. With the rolling fairway and distance, I couldn't see the ball, but I knew from the ball flight that it was a great shot. When I found it on the green, just about 15 feet from the pin, I gave myself a hidden fist pump. I would have to wait a while for my guys to get their balls to the green, as they were thrown asunder by the wind. After they reached the green, I sized up the putt, which I really thought I was going to make. No such luck, however, as I committed the cardinal sin of leaving it short. No matter—I walked off with the feeling of birdie on a tough hole in this wind.

We turned for home, facing the clubhouse in the distance with the wind at our backs. At only 511 yards, I had visions of reaching the par five in two. Of course, I had no idea yet what lay ahead, but with the ultrawide fairway and wind-aided distance, I felt confident. Big mistake, as my swing was profoundly off-kilter, and I hit a terrible duck hook right into the sand. I watched jealously as my partners hit excellent drives, putting themselves in position for that elusive eagle. From the sand, the best I could do was hit a 7-iron over the lip to get back to the fairway. I was happy with a well-struck hybrid, but I still had 200 yards to the green (to add salt to my wound, my ball came to rest right next to the drive of one of my guys). Anyway, with the wind howling, I hit an excellent 4-iron straight at the green. I waited in anticipation for my ball to land on the green until I saw it, tragically, hit at the very top of the sand and roll ten feet back down into the trap. I was there in four. After a decent sand shot up and onto the green, I had to suffer through two more putts to card a double, while I watched two birdie putts hit the bottom of the cup. While the ending was anti-climactic to say the least, I had had a blast at Mammoth Dunes. If you can't have fun on this wild ride of a golf course, you can't have fun playing golf.

Wild

(2020-21)

For most of his pre-teen and teenage years, Aidan declared that he wanted a motorcycle. At first, we sort of smiled at him, patted him on the head, and encouraged his dreams. "What do you like about motorcycles?," we'd ask. Over time, his desire hasn't waned, yet our alarm about the seriousness of this desire for a donor-cycle has reached a fever pitch. After he turned 18, he announced: "I'm an adult, and I'm going to get a motorcycle someday." He's right.

It's a stunning, and humbling realization that your child is going to make whatever decisions they want to make when they are an adult. No matter what you think, no matter how hard you have tried to instill a set of values, ultimately they are going to make their own choices. Of course, we hope that the choices our children make are good ones—that they pursue a successful path in life, however they define such a path. We hope that they don't make choices that get themselves severely injured or worse, but you can't protect them much anymore. Ultimately, it's up to them.

As a result, sometimes I have a terrible feeling that Aidan might make a choice that could lead to serious harm or his own death. And this feeling is so much worse than the fears I carried as a father of a young child. It's even worse than the feeling of him driving a car, which although it's potentially very dangerous, my strong feeling is that the safety measures—seat belts, airbags, *four wheels!*—are going to mitigate the harm of his accidents. A motorcycle, by contrast, puts him at great physical risk. And there's nothing I can do about it. Luckily, I have come to know my sons as young adults, and the values they have learned, the values that I'm proud to say that we have taught, are strong. They value their own lives as much as I do, and I look forward to seeing them live these values during the next stage of fatherhood.

Nevertheless, the feeling of helplessness as a father has been growing steadily over 18 years. During my first days as a father, I felt like our actions would have a direct and immediate consequence on the health and well-being of our sons. Now, there's very little we can do short of providing money, food, shelter, and so on. If they use these necessities well, it'll help them. But beyond that, there's little we can do to shape our sons' lives. We can provide advice, but they may ignore it. And of course, we can try to model the kinds of behaviors that we hope to see, but whether they choose to follow those models is entirely up to them.

And that, maybe, is the entire point of being a parent. Our children are not *ours*. They're human beings, and as their father I have had an outsized role in their lives compared to most of the seven billion people on the planet. But that outsized role shrinks every day, and by the time they're 18, I've become a deeply interested observer and occasional advisor, but can't be much more.

We tend to think that major life accomplishments come with pomp and circumstance. The graduation ceremony, weddings and funerals, the birth of our children. So, when something major happens without any ceremony or celebration, it's a bit disconcerting. So many of our most important memories in raising our children come in those everyday moments that were assumed to be forgotten. I didn't wake up the morning in which our sons took their first steps expecting to remember that day forever. I didn't take Elliott to taekwondo practice assuming we'd spend the next few hours in the hospital.

And I didn't wake up on a spring day expecting to realize that I had completely failed. But that's what happened on the day I stuck around at Elliott's baseball practice to watch him run.

The Covid-19 pandemic struck just before baseball season of Elliott's freshman year, and baseball was cancelled. He had really been looking forward to it, albeit nervous about the transition to high school baseball. He had played for so many years, and playing in high school was the obvious next step. Tryouts would begin as soon as the weather broke for the spring. Or so we thought. As March arrived with snow still on the ground, the whispers of a new disease spreading from a wet market in China had hit a fever pitch in the New York area. The World Health Organization declared a pandemic, and governors across the country were declaring a shutdown. Among so many other things, the baseball season was cancelled. Elliott spent so much time sitting at his desk, taking classes remotely, and likely playing video games. I think we were all in shock and trying to get through this historic disruption. That first year of the pandemic was a blur as we focused on not getting that deadly disease.

A year later—and two days into tryouts—Elliott announced one day, "my shins hurt." I didn't think much of it. After all, he was just playing baseball again after a long layoff, his body would hurt.

"I'll get you some ice." I figured he would feel better in a day or two. Then, after a week of tryouts, I got an email from his coach: "Elliott says he can't run. Has he seen a doctor?" I questioned him.

"Elliott, what's going on with your legs?"

"I told you, my shins hurt."

"Okay, get some ice. I'll call the doctor and make an appointment." We took a quick visit to the doctor who ordered an x-ray. Nothing broken.

"Keep icing every day," the doctor ordered. As far as I was concerned, that was all he needed. I expected that Elliott's body would recover, once he started running again.

But I was wrong, so wrong. About a week later, I decided to stick around at Elliott's practice and watch, inconspicuously, from a distance. What I saw shocked me beyond belief: Elliott literally couldn't run. I watch from my car and he clearly tried to keep up with his teammates, but his legs just didn't seem able to move in a normal gait. *How could I have been so ignorant about Elliott? Was I so focused on getting Aidan to the finish line of graduation? Was I letting my own memories of wanting to escape from the social nightmare of early high school betray me? Had Elliott really spent most of 9th grade sitting?* After practice, I made a concerted effort to look at the muscles in his legs. They had atrophied so much that they looked like toothpicks. It would be a slow, long recovery. I sat him down: "Elliott, your legs have lost most of their muscle strength. You have been sitting so much this past year, and your legs can't support you right now. We have to build up your muscles." He looked at me with a fear and anger I hadn't seen from him before. We had been so close, and I had let him down. We would start weight training at the gym as soon as possible.

It was many weeks before Elliott started to get his leg strength back, but he did. He was able to run better and had a tremendous season at the plate. He was named Most Valuable Offensive Player. While I sat at the awards ceremony at the end of the season, listening to the coach laud Elliott for his prowess as a hitter, I could only think of my failure. I applauded Elliott and smiled at him. But inside, I felt like a failure.

Over the years of fatherhood, I had spent so much time trying to figure out what my sons needed and then doing my best to provide it. I try to read their moods—not an easy task for shape-shifting teenagers. I want to be the father that they love and trust and confide in. When I see evidence that I haven't quite achieved those things, it feels like a weight, like I played it pretty well but made too many bogeys, and a double bogey or two. I try to tell myself that there's no perfect round, that being a father is not about being error-free.

I'm human, and sometimes I'm distracted with work, or I fail to read the signs my sons are showing me, or I'm a bit too selfish, or not selfish enough, or a one-in-a-century pandemic hits and our lives are turned upside down. But all of that is okay. What's important is how you bounce back from mistakes, try to learn from them, and then put them behind you. *Catch and release.* If you're thinking about your mistakes, you're living in the past, not focused on the present.

Maybe there are professional fathers who know how to make it through error-free, but I'm not one of them. I'm just a dad, who didn't have a good model of how to be a dad, trying to be the best dad I can be for my sons. And being the best I can be means staying in the present, and accepting my own mistakes as well as my sons', as an inherent part of life. It means, in short, that the ball lands where it lands, the grass grows the way it grows, the wind blows and changes in a split second, the imperfections of the turf are what they are, and all I can do is to do my best with the circumstances I'm faced with. All I can do is play it as it lies. And for a lifetime of that, I am truly, remarkably, profoundly grateful.

Epilogue

This book is organized according to my life as a father. In reading the book, it might have been shocking to many golfing fathers that I had been able to play all of these courses at those particular times in my life. Did I really play Torrey Pines with a newborn at home? Could I really have snuck out to Bethpage Black while my wife had to deal with our terrible two-year-old? I played the Straits course with a six- and three-year-old at home? Did I really get to travel to Bandon Dunes four times over eight years? The answer to all of these questions, of course, is no.

In order to tell one golf story at a major course each chapter, I had to organize the rounds by themes, rather than by year. As of this writing, I've only taken two trips to Bandon Dunes, and all the rounds described here were played on the first trip. I've had the good fortune to play two rounds each at Torrey Pines, but they didn't occur when my children were very young. Like many new fathers, I spent most of my non-work hours with my family, and had little time for golf. It was only after my grandfather died in 2007, when I decided that my children were old enough—Elliott was two years old—for me to start to venture out on a golf course from time to time. In the first few years after starting to play more seriously, I mostly played nine-hole rounds at Columbia Golf Course, a muni in my hometown of Minneapolis. I would play these rounds after work, or sometimes would wake up early on a weekend to sneak out for two hours before the kids began their days. With all the parenting I did, I didn't have a lot of time for golf.

It wasn't until 2011, when Elliott had begun school and my job opened up much more available time, that I began to play in earnest. For four and a half years, I played more than 40 rounds a year, breaking 80 about 10 times per year. That pattern continued until we moved to Japan at the end of the summer 2015. During the remainder of 2015, and the first half of 2016, I didn't play a single round of golf. I did bring a few clubs to Japan—anything for golf!—and put those clubs on my back a half dozen times and went to experience a Japanese driving range. Although it was a challenge to figure out how to purchase balls—in this small part of Yokohama, near where we lived, the local driving range didn't see much *gaijin* play, so no English was spoken there. That was it for golf during that year abroad.

When we returned to the states in August 2016, I played a number of rounds to try to get my swing back. I never really did. Then, in 2017, I decided to try to get back to the level I had been at in 2015. I practiced all winter, and while a very late spring start—my first round of the year was mid-May—delayed my rounds, I began 2017 with some of the best golf of my life. I played 10 rounds, and broke 80 six times, with a best of 74. I seemed to be headed toward a renewed excellence, with par in sight. Then, tragedy struck as I broke my leg in a terrible fall described in Chapter 16. I wouldn't play golf for the rest of 2017 and wasn't able to return to golf until September 2018: fully 57 weeks after the accident. After a second time committing to winter practice, I returned to golf in 2019 with a desire to play at previous levels. Since then, I have been playing the best golf of my life, for the first time twice shooting a round at par.

Generally speaking, I have placed these rounds in the book in the order in which I played them. But even that order is subject to artistic license. If I played a course more than once over these 18 years, I generally wrote about my first round, unless I had no record (or memory) of the specific shots on each hole. In those few cases, I replayed a course to ensure that I could remember it, took copious notes, and wrote about that round instead. I hope my readers will forgive me for this fictional element in an otherwise non-fiction memoir about the parallels between fatherhood and golf, and the lessons that we learn from one and can apply to the other. Those lessons have been the guiding light for my story, and my life.

Acknowledgements

In October 1998, in a small music club once owned by Prince, I met the love of my life, Theresa Hutchison. What followed has been a dreamy love affair, and a lifelong partnership. This book, both literally and figuratively, would not be possible without her. We loved the years we spent raising our two sons, and we now move on to that underestimated time that some people call the "empty nest." I couldn't imagine sharing that nest with anyone else.

To the many women who were especially vital in bringing our boys safely through the birth process, thank you! Of special mention are Linda French and Marjorie Crenshaw. Their timeless wisdom about labor and delivery ensured that our boys were in good hands.

Over the course of the years living the stories, and then writing about them, I have incurred a number of emotional debts that can never be repaid. I hope these words are a small token of my thanks. My friend and golf buddy, Vic Rosenthal, sadly died before being able to read these words. More than any other person, Vic showed me how to be the kind of father I have always hoped to be. He was a constant inspiration, both on and off the course. I loved being able to share the tee box with him for so many years. When I walk across the Swilcan bridge, I will think of Vic.

My good friend Nick Tampio helped me through one of the most difficult phases of my life, and helped me get back on track. We are now living the lives that we envisioned while lifting weights some thirty years ago. My college teammates helped me find my inner prestidigitator, among them Andrei Straumanis, Jason Chicoine, Steve Friedman, Miles Pufall, Shannon Sims, Mark Herron, and James Willie.

To my golf teachers—Grant Rogers, Mike Hinton, and Aaron Shafranski—I have learned so much about the game, my swing, and what it means to shoot par. Together, they brought this thirty-handicap golfer down to the low single digits. Grant's words are a constant reminder to enjoy every minute: "The best golfer is the one who is having the most fun!"

Special thanks to my mentor, Jeffrey Isaac. While this book is far afield from our formal expertise, Jeff taught me how to write in the full sense of the term. I will always be indebted for the almost thirty years of one of the most meaningful relationships I've ever had.

To my golfing family members (Uncle Kenny, Uncle Nelson and my mother, Judy) and the rest of my extended family (my sister Katy, my wonderful aunts and uncles and my cousins), we have done our best to uphold Elmer's golfing traditions. Our relationships and their guidance over the years has been most meaningful.

I have met many wonderful golfers on the course—some dads, some not. Men like Blake Brinker, Mike Matthews, Peter Gordon, and Dick Helde, and so many others, have been great to golf with and even better men. Together, we share a love of this perplexing game. But golf is always more about the relationships, and I treasure the time on the course that we've shared.

I was very fortunate to serve as Board President of the First Tee of Minneapolis for over a decade. Through that work, I met hundreds of kids, and many adults, who love the game as much as I do. Teaching kids the timeless values of integrity, hard work, and respect, among many others, is truly yeoman's work. I have been so lucky to spend so much of my time on this journey to teach kids the right values.

Another stroke of great fortune has been the opportunity to travel to the amazing golf courses described in this book. From my unannounced arrival at Torrey Pines, to the years-in-the-making trips to Bandon Dunes, to the fortuitous rounds at Sand Valley and Erin Hills, to the break-from-parenting celebratory rounds at the Classic, the Wilderness at Fortune Bay, the Quarry at Giants Ridge, to my magical round at Bethpage Black, I've had circuitous paths to get on these courses. But these rounds have given me some of my best golfing memories, and to the staff at all of these courses, I am so grateful for their foresight, creativity, and commitment to great golf experiences.

Several people took time out of their busy schedules to give me concrete advice on this book. Of note is Wayne Coffey, an accomplished author, who provided sage advice about getting this book published. Nash Pater and I had a great round at Mammoth Dunes, bonded quickly, and he was instrumental in connecting me to Jim Sitar. Jim, who has guided these stories from original manuscript to final book, is a brilliant editor and a visionary in the golf world. This book is vastly better because of Jim's keen insights, and the mistakes are all mine.

Most importantly for this book, though, are Aidan and Elliott. It has been the greatest joy of my life to bear witness to our two boys, growing up over the years. From the day they first let out screams announcing their presence in the world, I have been head-over-heels in love. Although like any father/son relationships we've had our share of arguments and tough times, I hope this book conveys the magnitude of my love for both of them. While they are now venturing on their own journeys in college, I have treasured the years described herein. These two boys, once just a figment of our imagination, have grown into truly outstanding men. This book is an ode to them.

ABOUT THE AUTHOR

Matthew F. Filner grew up in Washington, DC and earned degrees from Oberlin College and Indiana University. He is a professor of Political Science at Metropolitan State University. Matthew is a former board president of The First Tee of Minneapolis. He lives in Minneapolis with his wife, with his two sons in college.

Printed in the USA
CPSIA information can be obtained
at www.ICGtesting.com
JSHW051352140923
48130JS00007B/4/J

9 781956 237108